Useful Work

Useful Work

PHOTOGRAPHS OF HICKORY NUT GAP FARM

Ken Abbott

Essays by Rob Neufeld

GOOSEPEN STUDIO & PRESS Conover, North Carolina

Designed by, set in Quadraat by,
and published for Ken Abbott
by Nathan W. Moehlmann,
Goosepen Studio & Press,
Conover, North Carolina.
WWW.GOOSEPENPRESS.COM

Image file preparation by
Rocky Kenworthy, Dot Editions,
Asheville, North Carolina.
WWW.DOTEDITIONS.COM

Printed on GardaMatt and bound
by Conti Tipocolor, Florence, Italy,
in an edition of 1,500.

ISBN 978-0-9898125-6-6
LCCN 2015940519

This project was supported by
the North Carolina Arts Council,
a division of the Department
of Cultural Resources.

www.ncarts.org

Contents

It has been ... because of its commanding position, a genuine landmark. It is 45 minutes from Asheville on a fine motor road & just two miles & a half from a little village called Fairview. It has an altitude of 2,700 feet so you can imagine how fine the air is & it is just at the crest of one of the Blue Ridge ranges with a most superb view across the valley at the mountains in the distance & at the little town lying far below. There are 50 acres of bearing apple trees — 2,500 trees so the present owner tells us, & superb old oak & chestnut trees on the grounds, wide porches, the finest spring you can imagine flowing so freely that it can be piped to the house by gravity & the loveliest little cement lined "springhouse" for keeping milk & butter etc. cool. Then there is a big farm & a dairy & a huge vegetable garden. Of course the house is just the simplest kind of an old southern wooden farmhouse unpainted, but it has a great deal of atmosphere & is by far the most distinguished place around Asheville....

— ELIZABETH MCCLURE to MARTHA CLARKE, July 7, 1916

Preface: A Legacy of Beauty
at Hickory Nut Gap Farm

I REMEMBER THE FIRST TIME I WENT to the Big House to photograph. I'd chaperoned my daughter's preschool class visit to the farm a couple of weeks earlier and was enchanted by the old inn, surrounded by hundred-year-old gardens and rows of august boxwoods, near the top of the winding road up Hickory Nut Gap. The place had a time-capsule quality, suited to its early history and well-preserved architectural detailing and style, but it was clearly no museum — there were signs of a busy contemporary life, with a story of its own to tell. Our host, Annie Ager, introduced us to the farm, telling of her family, the McClures and Clarkes; the Farmers' Federation they started back in the early 1900s; and the beginnings of the old inn's contemporary life as her family's home. It was a beautiful setting, rich in lore, and I looked forward to coming back with my camera.

So on a fall morning, camera and tripod on my shoulder, I walked up onto the porch of the grand old house and knocked on the hand-hewn door, which was ajar. The antique hardware didn't seem to be working too well. I could hear voices inside, but no one responded to my knock. I tried again, a little louder, and then again. Finally, I heard someone clomping toward the door, and a moment later a big, bearded fellow swung the door open and said in an exasperated but not unfriendly way, "Why are you *knocking*? Just come in!" I hadn't met John Ager, Annie's husband, before, but he invited me to make myself at home. And then undistracted by me, he went back to his work while I wandered around photographing for several hours, till all the film I'd brought was gone. Over the next four years I visited many times, being careful *not* to knock of course. I photographed the fine portraits on the walls, the library's old books and memorabilia, and Elizabeth McClure's historical murals, and exhibiting a degree of nosiness that did not endear me to Grace, Annie's housekeeper at the time, I even photographed such things as the unmade beds and a kitchen sink full of dishes. I photographed the springhouse and other outbuildings, the view from the porch, Elizabeth's gardens, and the boxwoods.

Over the years, I learned more of the history, and my imagination was captured by the sweep of this family's heritage: from the Mayflower and the Waldorf Astoria, to barn dances and Farmers' Federation picnics, including stories of travelers along the old road welcomed and made at home over the years by this generous family. As essayist Rob Neufeld relates in the following chapters, it's a great story. The characters are lively, engaging, and colorful; the setting is lovely; and the story with its ties to important contemporary issues of agriculture, land preservation, and community is inspiring and relevant. Like a good photograph, all the pieces fit together and suggest the shape and order of a larger truth.

IN 2004, THE YEAR I BEGAN photographing at Hickory Nut Gap Farm, I suffered a serious illness that shook me up considerably. Added to that, the war in Iraq was being launched, and while driving from my house to the farm, I would listen to reports about it on the radio, which left me feeling hopeless and low about the world. So I came to the farm needing to recuperate, as Jim McClure, Annie's grandfather, had almost ninety years before. I was looking for a place to work that was restorative and would allow me to focus and create something. I suppose it's a truism that during trying times we seek connection, connection with community and place and to something larger than ourselves — some sort of spiritual connection. Though Jim and Elizabeth McClure had a strong Christian faith and tradition, a faith that remains a foundation for the family at Hickory Nut Gap Farm today, what I responded to at the "Big House," as the community calls it, was its embodiment of Elizabeth's faith in beauty.

Elizabeth once wrote in a letter to Jim, "Everybody wants beauty — it seems always to quicken your sense of being alive and that means happiness and peace and a blessed conviction that you are really necessary in the scheme of things." As Neufeld notes in his essay "Welcome to the Big House," Elizabeth's faith led her to create a house that would express "through itself, law and order and proportion and repose and aliveness." In this way, Elizabeth was reaching out to claim what all artists, it seems to me, hope in some way for their work — that it be true and complete enough that "through itself" it opens people's eyes and creates the connection we seek. It's a lot to ask of art, and a lot to claim for an artist, but it's a hope and a goal I identified with in Elizabeth as I framed her life's work filtered through ninety years of busy family life.

A PICTURE SOMETIMES ARRIVES like a gift, received in a glance — a locus of possibilities. I was teaching a photography class at Western Carolina University in 2006, and one day I brought my students to Hickory Nut Gap Farm. We were photographing in the house, and as I walked through the kitchen, I noticed a silver pitcher next to the sink. Initially it reminded me of a pitcher that was part of the silver service my family had when I was growing up, an item that in our house sat mostly unused on a sideboard in the dining room, but that I understood nonetheless was of value and ceremonial importance. I also remembered it as being the object of a familiar chore, the pre-dinner party polishing that showed me the simple optical beauty of my surroundings reflected in silver. Seeing the pitcher that day in the kitchen brought those memories back to me. I also noted the shape of the handle, which for me linked the object aesthetically to the family matriarch, Elizabeth McClure. So, I stopped to take a look with my camera.

I noticed that the pitcher was dinged up and bent so that it stood just a bit skewed on the counter. Instead of presenting itself on a silver platter, as ours had, this one waited beside a jelly jar of salad dressing and dirty dishes. I loved the color of the worn blue countertop and the burnish of the aluminum trim tacked to the counter and how those things worked with the still beautiful luster of the old silver. I also noted the way the other vessels on the counter, in their varieties of clarity and translucence, paid homage to the subtleties of the reflected light from the silver.

As I made the picture that day, I recognized that these formal qualities were gifts in themselves, but the larger gift came later, when I learned that this pitcher, despite its daily utility, was also an important part of the family's heritage. After showing Annie the photograph I'd made, she told me they used the pitcher to bring water from the springhouse for the table and that was all they ever used it for — every day. And so the silver pitcher had served for ninety years as an aesthetic connection for the family to Elizabeth, but also as a connection to the place and the spring water she had cherished.

For me, one of the great lessons of the Big House and the family at Hickory Nut Gap Farm is that we should honor beauty and our past and reach toward intimacy with our given place. Like a camera lens the pitcher focuses the family story. Yet in the photograph of it, we are also reminded that there are dishes to wash and work to do. As I mentioned earlier, Grace, Annie's housekeeper, didn't have much use for me and my attentions. Both she and her son Clarence never hesitated to ask me if there wasn't some aspect of actual work I might like to help them with around the house or farm — if I was willing to put the camera down for a bit. In this way they, too, took part in tradition. Elizabeth's daughter, Elspeth, liked to say, "If I don't share this beautiful place with others, God might think it wise for someone else to have it," but she was also notorious for putting idle family members and even casual visitors to work, imploring them to "Be useful." Though credit for this impulse may lie partly with nervousness about idle hands and the devil's work, it seems to me that the bulk of the inspiration came from her conviction, like her mother's, that people want to be part of something larger and that by participating in the useful work of such a place and community people are inspired and uplifted. Elizabeth Bahnson, Elspeth's granddaughter, sharing what she had learned from her grandmother, wrote, "It is through work that we come to love a place. Work gives us the opportunity to participate in a place, to make our life part of its life. Work is an expression of love." It's been a great honor and pleasure to work in this place, amid this family and community.

— KEN ABBOTT, July 2015

Welcome to the Big House

WHEN, IN 1916, HONEYMOONERS Elizabeth and Jim McClure hit the road in their Hudson, which they nicknamed "donkey," to ascend into the southern mountains and live "like gypsies," as Elizabeth wrote in one of her many letters to her cousin Martha Clarke, it was their intention to find a farm where he could recuperate from ministerial overwork. Jim had moved mountains of attitude in Iron River, Michigan, where he used the power of his beliefs to transform a profit-minded mining town into a community-minded one. Then his health collapsed. He checked in at the Jackson Health Resort in the Finger Lakes region of New York and came under the care of a doctor who advised Elizabeth to have Jim "refuse to feel responsible about anything or anybody." Responsibility was his reason for living, but living was a prerequisite for taking responsibility.

In their correspondence, Elizabeth had anticipated their marriage as a "union of heart & soul & body through mutual longing to be more nearly one with God in order to further His purposes." God's purposes, Jim had felt, were not to be fulfilled in churches, but in the lives of men and women working to make a healthy and compassionate society. The McClures were wanderers, but they were not lost. They would know it when they found a place that could be host to their dreams. "One day," as their daughter, Elspeth McClure Clarke, recounted in an unpublished 1999 memoir, they "drove out past the little town of Fairview [North Carolina] and started up the steep, winding road towards the Hickory Nut Gap. As they rounded a curve they saw an old grey house right below a mountain, at the top of a long sloping pasture. As one, they both exclaimed, 'That's the place for us!'"

The road, at that time, followed a different path than today's Route 74A. It passed close by the east side of the house, which had, for several decades, welcomed drovers and vacationers for a night or a fortnight in what had been called Sherrill's Inn. At first, Elizabeth and Jim renamed the house "Old Tavern" to honor the history. They later created a new identity — "Hickory Nut Gap Farm" — and continued to cherish the old by retaining the house's main features. They installed a steam heating system, painted the weathered siding white, and paneled the dining and living room. Yet they left the oldest parts — including a circa 1800 log cabin and what became the study — as is. They preserved, as revelations of beauty, the hardware, assorted doors, and windows that held panes of rainbow-colored blown glass.

THE NATIONAL REGISTER OF HISTORIC PLACES states that John Ashworth built the log cabin in 1806. Ashworth died in 1805, so it's probably older. John's wife, Nancy "Ann" Ashworth, as Fairview historian Bruce Whitaker notes in the August 8, 2012, edition of *The Fairview Town Crier*, "was a doctor or a witch depending upon whom you asked. Either way she tended the sick, made potions, and cast spells. People were a little afraid of Ann Ashworth since she was known to put a spell on anyone who made her mad."

Fearing Cherokee raids, either the Ashworths or their predecessors built a blockhouse around 1791 that was subsequently used as a smokehouse, and a springhouse was constructed to receive water coming down from Ferguson Peak. Elizabeth McClure, describing the canvas of her new homeplace to Martha Clarke, her chaperone when she studied art in France, not only noted the house's panoramic porch and the farm's apple orchard, but also "the loveliest purest water … that you ever tasted."

ELIZABETH'S ARTISTIC BACKGROUND has greatly influenced Hickory Nut Gap. In her earliest letters to James "Jim" McClure, she told him how the people who ran the daycare in Chicago where she worked failed to appreciate her aesthetic. "The old wheezes," she wrote, "have said to me that they think it is practically a waste of time [to put paintings] up in a place 'where they won't really be appreciated.'... I am convinced that the masses always respond to beauty when it reflects or interprets what they can understand."

The value of beautiful things was one of the few tensions between the McClures when they set up home, for Jim was frugal and Elizabeth wanted fine objects, such as a silver tea service, to connect people with the spirit of perfection. "We can create a house," she wrote Jim two months before their wedding, "that will express, through itself, law and order and proportion and repose and aliveness — all those things that you will be constantly opening people's eyes to in what you *say*. I want equally to open people's eyes to it in what they *see*."

The first people to see what she was about were the workers the McClures engaged to implement their plans — John and Esther Shorter, African American farmers who moved from their home five miles away to a tenant house at Hickory Nut Gap; Jim Davidson, a N.C. State agriculture school graduate; several farmhands; and, later, Will Boone, a Daniel Boone descendant, and his young family.

In 1918, Shorter, Davidson, and Fin Sinclair, who was from nearby Gerton, gathered in Jim's study to discuss the formation of a farmers' cooperative that would later become the famed Farmers' Federation. The study had been where the previous owner, Judge Phillips, had stored hams in ashes. "Jim and Elizabeth had to wheelbarrow out nine loads of dirt and debris to even find the floor," John Ager notes in *We Plow God's Fields: The Life of James G. K. McClure*, a biography of James "Jim" McClure, Jr.

America had entered World War I, and Jim organized Red Cross drives. He was getting to know his neighbors. Around this time, as well, two children were born to the McClures — Jamie, in 1919, and Elspeth, in 1923. Elizabeth began implementing her landscape design, which included the boxwoods that now create elfin passages to the front door and the badminton court, and while Elspeth was in her crib, Elizabeth started work on her mural of life at the time of Sherrill's Inn (*see page 143*).

"The work of supervising the household often stopped her," Elspeth writes, "but she did manage, with my father's eager encouragement, to finish the first five [of eight] panels before I was old enough to notice what she was doing. But I do remember her painting the last two. I would come into the room, and she would ask me what I thought and sketch a figure as I watched." Elizabeth included many children in her portrayal of life at Sherrill's Inn, built by Bedford

Sherrill on land he bought from John Ashworth in 1834. In one scene, a boy chases a chicken while well-dressed vacationers arrive on "Sherrill's Flying Cloud," an Albany-made stagecoach known for its lightness, speed, and width, as well as for its jolting discomfort. Sherrill's father-in-law, Dr. John Harris, who owned the property that is now Lake Lure, had procured money from the state to improve the road through the gap to Asheville, and twenty-three-year-old Bedford jumped on the entrepreneurial opportunity, making his place a trading center as well as a resort.

On another mural panel, two passengers, dressed in top hats, tailcoats, and white trousers, work at dislodging the stagecoach from a muddy rut, not an uncommon event. The gentlefolk generally came in the late spring and summer, whereas drovers, pictured in separate panels, came with their turkeys, pigs, sheep, and cattle at harvest time. As the stagecoach approached the inn, the driver would blow his horn to inform the Sherrills how many guests were arriving, so they each could be greeted with a glass of applejack or peach brandy made on the premises. The inn had seven bedrooms. The downstairs four were quite small. The upstairs three were accessed only from the porch's double staircase. Many famous guests stayed, signing a register that is now housed in UNC Asheville's Ramsey Library.

PERHAPS THE BUSTLING ATMOSPHERE was not too different from what the McClures, Clarkes, and Agers have experienced — a flow of guests who enjoy good food, the charming setting, easy hospitality, and a flirtation with rural lifeways. Doug Clarke, one of Jim and Elizabeth's grandsons and now the primary caretaker of the Big House, says, "When I was growing up, my parents [Elspeth and Jamie Clarke], who had an apple stand here, let people wander around all over the house and grounds because they had very gracious personalities and wanted people to come to their home — and the more the merrier."

Life at Hickory Nut Gap for its residents was work, but for awed visitors it was a lost Eden, especially when they were introduced to the charms of hoe and spade. During Jamie Clarke's tenures as a U.S. Congressman, political aspirants seeking his influence bought into the farm ethic. Jamie's wife, Elspeth, John Ager recalls, "would come out, and she'd drag them down to the garden. And she'd say, 'Well, you can weed while we talk.'" Doug Clarke says that one day Chuck Robb, the Governor of Virginia, came to help raise funds for his father's congressional campaign, and Governor Robb found himself waiting at the house for an arranged ride after Elspeth and Jamie had gone to church. "So, I was in charge of Chuck Robb," Doug says. "And his ride didn't come and didn't come. And, finally, I had to go somewhere, and I said, 'Mr. Robb, you know, if somebody comes to buy eggs, just tell them the can is over there.' He was fine. He said, "Okay!'"

Today, hard work and idealism have combined with business pragmatism not only to make a living off the land for the fourth generation of the Hickory Nut Gap Farm family, but also to help lead the way in the region with healthy and ethical community progress.

What Time Tells

PAPERS CONGREGATE IN CUBBYHOLES, you notice. Pictures appropriate walls. Fussiness is not next to godliness. In any case, for those who wish to understand the wonder of family legacies, the evidence stacks up here like cairns on the moors. The framed print in the library depicting the Covenanters — Scots who had vowed by God to oppose an Anglican takeover in 1638 — hangs on a low hook behind a soup tureen. The rebels in the illustration had needed to meet secretly at night in a mountain pass for fear of brutal persecution. This conventicle also served as a rally for survival, just as the Hickory Nut Gap family's core beliefs have been a touchstone in trying times. The ancestral homeland of the McClures and fellow Highland Scots nurtured personal traits, such as high-mindedness, self-sufficiency, and anti-elitism that ultimately found their geographic match in the mountains of North Carolina. Abbott's photograph of the kitchen sink in the Ager household looks out, through a window, to the local mountains — a kind of hands-in-the-dishwater reverence.

According to family lore, the McClures fled Scotland and took refuge in Ireland at about the same time that Alexander Peden, the legendary Presbyterian minister, became a wandering prophet and outlaw. This was after 1660 when the restored King Charles II succumbed to the Cavalier Parliament and a second wave of repression began tyrannizing Presbyterians. The McClures came from Dumfries, on the Irish Sea, about sixty miles southeast of Peden's hometown and on the other side of the Southern Uplands. Yet the family and the minister may have been acquainted. Peden's wanderings took him to Dumfries, which was a Covenanter hot spot. Robert McClellan, leader of the Pentland Uprising of 1666, which began when Covenanters disarmed soldiers who were beating a non-conforming Scotsman, marched his rebels to Dumfries where they captured the local commander in his nightshirt. Following McClellan's ultimate defeat, Dumfries became the site of many hangings. Memorial gravesites dot the landscape. Presbyterianism had been a response to the Catholic Church first and then to the English Protestant version of hierarchical church power. A millennium before John Knox founded the denomination in Scotland, the people there had resisted papal influence.

IN 1638, ARCHIBALD M'CLAUIE SIGNED the Covenant of Cardoness, thirty miles west of Dumfries, identifying himself as one of the ministers who joined the Edinburgh group of Covenanters at the risk of losing land and position. He is most likely an ancestor of the Archibald McClure who emigrated to Ireland and then America.

Covenanters had affirmed the populist nature of the Presbyterian resistance by taking the National Covenant to churches throughout the country in order to gain a consensus. In *We Plow God's Fields*, John Ager quotes historian G. M. Trevelyan regarding the Scots' sense of conviction: "The Covenant with God embraced all ranks from the highest to the lowest. In every parish men signed it, weeping and lifting their right hands to heaven. When the Scots display emotion, something real is astir with them."

The movement had been sparked, the previous year, by an Edinburgh market woman, Jennie Geddes, who, when she heard the English mass spoken in the High Kirk of Edinburgh, shouted at the minister, "Wha daur say Mass in ma lug (who dares says Mass in my ear)? Ah hope ye get piles, ye auld fart!" The alternative version has her saying, "De'il gie you colic, the wame o' ye, fause thief," meaning "Devil cause you colic in your stomach, false thief." Then she started a chair-throwing riot.

Okay — it's a legend. But legends carry legacies, such as tales of miracles that make one believe in predestination and a purpose larger than oneself. In 1685 when preacher Peden returned to Scotland, it was the Killing Time, and his band escaped murder by dragoons when he asked God to "cast the lap of thy cloak over auld Sandy [his nickname]," whereupon "a dark cloud of mist came betwixt" the hunters and hunted. Not long before that a mother and daughter of the McClure clan, escaping to Ireland in bales of hay, managed to preserve their family line when bayonets, thrust by soldiers, missed their flesh.

ACROSS TWO CENTURIES AND AN OCEAN, in 1847, Archibald McClure — age forty-one and father of four — took a business trip from New York to the old country of Ireland from where his family had immigrated. A hurricane wracked the ship on his return, and he became gravely ill. James Gore King, a fellow merchant, nursed him back to health and thus earned the honor of having his name given to the McClures' next child, James Gore King McClure, Sr., whose portrait now looks out from a shelf on the desk in the Hickory Nut Gap study (*see page 31*).

Like the McClures before him, James G. K. McClure, Sr., carried within himself a religious intensity evidenced still today by his notes, sermons, and stories that fill the desk. He moved from New York to Lake Forest, Illinois, to serve as the minister of a landmark Presbyterian community. His son, James McClure, Jr. (the "Jim" married to Elizabeth), grew up with a dual legacy. From his mother's side, he inherited a romantic, wild streak and lived the life of a cowboy while working on a Texas ranch at age sixteen. Roped back to Illinois, he attended Yale and headed in a new direction with the help of patrons who, like his father, wanted him to become a minister. "I commit you to God," his father said to him before young Jim left to study at the New College of Edinburgh, in Scotland, a theological school. Jim's mentor there, Rev. Marcus Dods, filled him with the idea that "in a time of transition, such as this, when every old belief was called into question ... the hand that could form the mould had the control of the new world."

UPON HIS RETURN TO AMERICA, Jim went as a minister to Iron River, Michigan, a mining town. He had already come to feel that organized religion was out of touch with the true calling of the Social Gospel, which he delivered to his congregation with surprising results until he had to step away because of a physical breakdown. After a long recovery and a move with his newly wed wife, Elizabeth Cramer, to Hickory Nut Gap, he found himself at a ministerial crossroads: take one of the two jobs offered him to lead churches in the north or devote himself away from the pulpit to his community of Southern mountaineers. Joined by his brother-in-law, Rev. Dumont Clarke, he chose the latter path, establishing a cooperative called the Farmers' Federation and a church-based outreach program called The Lord's Acre. Dumont shared Jim's faith and populism. He installed a lectern under the steering wheel of his car, so he could read Bible verses while driving. At stops, Dumont entertained families with tricks and jokes. Jim, too, was sociable, and he was a great leader, possessing unspoken animation inherited from his Covenanter forebears. The family's faith has always been expressed in their commitment to community, the McClures, Clarkes, and Agers welcoming and including many visitors and workers over the years in their family life at the farm.

48

Kicking Back the Covers

"WHAT ARE THE FAMILY STORIES that you all keep hearing?" I asked a gathering of McClure-Clarke descendants and in-laws gathered around the big table in the old house. "There's the story of this woman right here who rode off with the Indian," Doug Clarke spoke first, aided by a nod to the portrait of Elizabeth Williams Skinner on the wall above the fireplace. With this association, we traced the family's maternal line back from the current elders' late mother, Elspeth McClure Clarke, to her mother, Elizabeth Cramer McClure, to her mother, Susie Skinner Cramer, and finally to Susie Skinner's mother, the portrait sitter, Elizabeth Williams Skinner.

As Elspeth writes about her collection of Elizabeth McClure's letters, "My mother told me stories about Elizabeth Williams" that had been passed down the line. Williams, orphaned at an early age, had gone to live, in the 1850s, with a guardian at Fort Dearborn (whose site is now a Chicago landmark) where "Indians would come to the fort to sell fur. When she grew older, she galloped over the prairie with a young Indian brave. He gave her a horse hair ring and called her 'Oqua Neequa Boqua,' which meant 'Wild Rose of the Prairie.' When I was little and my mother told me this story, I used to wish she had married the Indian. But she married the young lawyer, Mark Skinner, and in 1870 he took her to Europe and Mr. G. P. A. Healy painted her portrait in Rome."

Family portraits in their settings, turned-down beds, lived-in rooms, people, pets, and horses — the irrepressible spirit of family unites the many elements of Hickory Nut Gap carried through the generations. In her portrait Williams doesn't seem to indulge in being painted by a master. With similar unceremoniousness, the dog bed to the right of her portrait in Abbott's photograph (*see page 23*) doesn't apologize for hanging out with the heirloom table, which Elspeth's father's father's father, Archibald McClure, commissioned in Albany, New York. "It may seem very presumptuous for me … to write an autobiography," the table itself had ahemmed in a 1906 publication, after having moved to Lake Forest with Rev. James G. K. McClure, Sr., its second owner. Given voice by his son Jim McClure, its ghost-writer, the table makes note of guests who had broken bread on its mahogany surface — including state governors, future presidents, intellectuals, and a lot of ministers.

"One day the Rev. Dr. William Swan Plummer of South Carolina came to dinner" in Albany, the table relates. Plummer had a long white beard that made him look like Michelangelo's Moses. When he said grace, an oracular voice issued from his beard, asking that "the blessing that abode upon the house of Obed-Edom while the ark tarried in it might abide with this house." Upon hearing the name, "Obed-Edom," the boy at the table — Jim McClure, who had been nudging his sisters — could not suppress his laughter, though it caused Rev. Plummer confusion and distress.

A WILD STREAK RUNS THROUGH the family, but more often than not, the vitality channels into a resolute sense of responsibility, something for which the horse may be a symbol. The horse galloping across a framed drawing on a wall in the library illustrates a story about responsibility that Jim McClure liked to tell. In his book, *The Horse that Won the Race*, dedicated to his grandchildren, Jim writes of a young minister who took up a racing challenge from another horseman and forgot to give a promised ride home to an elderly woman stranded at a church gathering one winter night. "Yes, I had won the race," the minister reflects in his shame, "but what about poor Aunt Margaret whom I had entirely forgotten?"

In 1881, Rev. James G. K. McClure, Sr., moved with his wife, Annie, to Lake Forest, Illinois, to serve as the pastor of the Presbyterian Church. When his second child, and first son, Jim McClure, reached adolescence, Jim chauffeured his father in a horse-drawn buggy to parishioners' homes, observing how his father made people feel at ease.

The family's sense of service to others has been embraced by Jim McClure's granddaughters. Susie Clarke Hamilton, among other duties, leads Hickory Nut Gap Farm Summer Camp with her sister, Annie Clarke Ager. Annie herself initiates girls and boys at the farm into the wonder of horsemanship. One of these students is Susie and Annie's brother Jim Clarke's granddaughter, Hallie Cox, who, Jim says, "dreams of a utopian world of people and horses."

COMMUNITY — AND PARTICULARLY the community of the McClure-Clarke family — embraces its members through its stability, non-judgmental support, and teaching by example. "I loved my grandfather," says Susie Clarke Hamilton about Jim McClure. "He would take us lots of places. They were having the Farmers' Federation picnics then. I went from the time I was four years old until I was ten. He would also bring us down to the little bridge across [Ashworth Creek] for the sunset special. We'd watch the sunset and stay at the bridge and play." This distraction "got us out of the house and let everybody else get on with doing what they had to do. My mother was very busy. She had a lot of other children to take care of."

Susie's daughter, Annie Louise Perkinson, had a similar relationship with her grandfather, Jamie Clarke, as well as with her grandmother, Elspeth McClure Clarke. Annie Louise accompanied her grandfather to Washington, D.C., when he was a U.S. Congressman and noted how he walked to Capitol Hill through a poor, African American neighborhood, saying hello to everyone. The residents knew him as "Mr. Granny," for Elspeth had taken her neighbors under her wing with openness and humility and had established herself as "Granny."

This kind of openness has directed Annie Louise's mother's life. After "surviving" the Age of Aquarius, Susie testifies, and the "craziness" at the art school she attended in Atlanta, where "everybody was throwing paint and dropping acid," she made her way to the L'Abri Fellowship in Switzerland and then the associated church in London where she met her husband, Dr. William Hamilton. After Susie gave birth in England to Annie Louise and William, her second child, she moved back home, and the L'Abri concept took hold. It affirmed what her mother, Elspeth, already practiced.

"We shared rooms with lots of different people," Annie Louise says. "We had pregnant women living with us who wanted to keep their babies; gay people whose families had rejected them; an exchange student who was Muslim and whose exchange family wouldn't keep him." Susie Clarke Hamilton's younger brother Billy, an environmental lawyer, says, "You always felt like you were sharing your house with a lot of people. We didn't always like that growing up. You'd come down in the morning for breakfast, and there'd be someone sitting there and you didn't know who it was."

It had been Billy's job, at times, to engage the new guest in useful work. "What that meant," he says, "is that a ten- or eleven-year-old boy was in charge of a college student who had lost his way and was trying to find himself in the country or in charge of some man from England whom Susie had sent over here who was in drug rehab and was in his early thirties."

Being the eldest child of the next generation, Annie Louise's job in the family had been to serve as personal assistant to her grandmother, Elspeth. She helped her grandmother write her book about Elizabeth McClure; she cut her hair; and she arranged the flowers in the guest rooms. Though Annie Louise went on to establish, with her husband, Isaiah Perkinson, a flower, vegetable, and berry business called Flying Cloud Farm on the property where Jim McClure had held his "sunset specials," her road there had not been direct.

"I didn't know I could be a farmer when I was growing up," Annie Louise reflects. "I went to UNC Chapel Hill for two years, left home to get away from dirt, children, animals, and any sort of connection to my name. I dyed my hair pink and pierced my nose." Actually, she had pierced her nose in Berlin, arriving there after having picked strawberries in Schleswig-Holstein. She had just turned twenty-one, the Berlin Wall had recently come down, and Berlin was full of squatters occupying unclaimed buildings. She then traveled to France to join some of her father's relatives at a campsite and showed up with only a book on Gandhi and a drum, having been pickpocketed on an overnight train. At the campsite, she met a man whose uncle ran an organic farm in Devon, England, and with a monetary boost from her relatives, she headed there for a self-arranged internship. The Devon couple, Annie Louise relates, "were direct-marketing their produce in Totnes. I was inspired. I saw it as an opportunity and realized — Asheville, local food. It was 1994, just pre-local-food-movement, and I kind of went, 'Oh.'"

Annie Louise enrolled at Warren Wilson College when she returned home

and met Isaiah there. They established their direct-marketing business of produce and flowers on fourteen acres that belong to the entire family. The business model incorporates Annie Louise's great grandmother Elizabeth McClure's aesthetic sensibility, that beauty be a part of workaday life. Along with bountiful produce, the couple grows flowers for weddings and for holders of shares in their CSA, a community supported agriculture program. "Sometimes when I'm making a bride's bouquet," Annie Louise says, "I actually go out in the field and make it in the field just because I want to think about that bride."

Of the two-dozen-plus living, adult descendants of Jim and Elizabeth McClure, eleven are actively involved, as of 2013, in the local family's land stewardship and farm businesses. Many others have developed environment-, arts-, and travel-related careers. In 2009, the family put nearly four hundred of their acres into a conservation easement for agricultural uses, guided by Susie's son, William, who works for the Southern Appalachian Highlands Conservancy. It was a major turning point.

JAMIE AGER AND HIS WIFE, AMY, had by that time established their business, Hickory Nut Gap Meats, on land leased from the family. The network that Jamie set up to sell grass-fed beef to grocery stores and restaurants throughout the region is their security, he says, for it will survive the loss of specific farmland. When the family affirmed their commitment to Jamie and Amy's business, the couple expanded their operation, planting four varieties of berry bushes, ramping up agritourism, and stepping up their role in establishing a model for profitable, organic, local food growing.

It was at Warren Wilson College that Jamie met Amy, the brainy student who felt she had to leave Kentucky to see the world. He took her horseback riding, and on her first trip she fell and gashed her head, a kind of initiation, she thought, as she was transported back to the Big House in a pickup truck with hay blowing around her. A business and environmental studies graduate, Amy now handles the accounts while Jamie puts into effect a combination of what might be called idealism and farmer's sense.

Grass-fed beef was his first project and cause. "You've got this triple whammy" with the current feed-lot-based beef industry, he says. "Beef is seen as bad to eat, [the industry] is bad for the environment, and the cows aren't treated well. With grass-fed beef, you have a whole paradigm shift. That's what makes me excited. Grass-fed beef works, and I'm inspired about the scalability of it." The scalability involves engaging other small farmers in the process. This network is complemented by agricultural, ecological, and spiritual philosophies. Jamie grows his grass thick and deep into the winter, so when his pregnant cows reach their third trimester their diet is organic. He manages his fields and forests through the activities of his livestock and implements biodiversity and staggered timing of crops. He and Amy make sure that every person and animal is happy, not only for the sake of these beings, but also for the benefit of the business and the consumers. "I like to have fun," Jamie says, "and I like it to work, to have systems in place that people can enjoy."

PHILANTHROPY IS A PRESIDING THEME in the family story, from the ministry, to politics, to land stewardship. Though John Ager was elected to the North Carolina House of Representatives in 2014, Jamie Clarke, John's father-in-law, served numerous terms as a U.S. Congressman, which probably moved his children away from such a career because of the demands they saw it make on him. "My father was like a strong work horse," says Doug Clarke, youngest child of that generation. "He just kept going…. My mother thought that being a congressman's wife would be an awful job, but once he did it, she threw herself into it. She adored my father. People thought of my father as not being ambitious," Doug reflects, "but he was, though he didn't appear to be. I remember helping him when he was running for his second term in Congress. He was about to go on for a television interview on election night, and they'd just told him he had lost Rutherford County. Oh, I could see his face. They said, 'We're going to interview you now.' He said, 'I'll just go in the restroom.' I had never seen my father comb his hair before. I saw him combing his hair and trying to look his best, and I realized he really cared." John Ager adds, "He was a very competitive man, but he was self-effacing."

Doug Clarke's son Mark has taken yet another path that nonetheless circles back to the family. After earning a degree in creative writing from UNC Chapel Hill, he came home to work with his cousins Jamie and Amy. His poetry makes an aesthetic out of useful work, such as this unblinking description in his poem "Dinner" of his mother, Betsy, slaughtering and plucking chickens:

She dips and lifts the sopping bird,

like steeping a teabag, till the wings hang heavy with water.

Then she parts the soft fluff from the breast and pulls

dripping pinfeathers from the wings and tail.

The skin is sallow underneath, covered in pock marks

and wispy hairs. When the carcass is picked clean,

she lays it in the snow.

        Soon the patch of white

around us is laced in bloody lines and scattered plumage.

Six plump hens, like muffin tops in the snow.

Intent upon engaging her employees in the best use of their talents, Amy Ager has asked Mark to create an exhibit of images and text to document the progression of the family's farms. Tradition and change are major themes. Sitting around the big table at the Clarke-McClure gathering mentioned at the beginning of this essay, Billy Clarke asserted, "Place is very important here. A lot of what you do, as with this old house, is fix it. When you fix it, you learn not to suggest that things should be changed." William Hamilton's wife, Molly, added that a family friend said to Elspeth when her mother, Elizabeth McClure, died, "Don't ever change anything in this house. Your mother did a perfect job of decorating everything." Yet, Elspeth had told her granddaughter, Annie Louise, that "the only constant is change."

"I also remember," Annie Louise recalls, "asking her about the future of the land and the house and what she wanted. And she said she had no idea, it was up to the next generation."

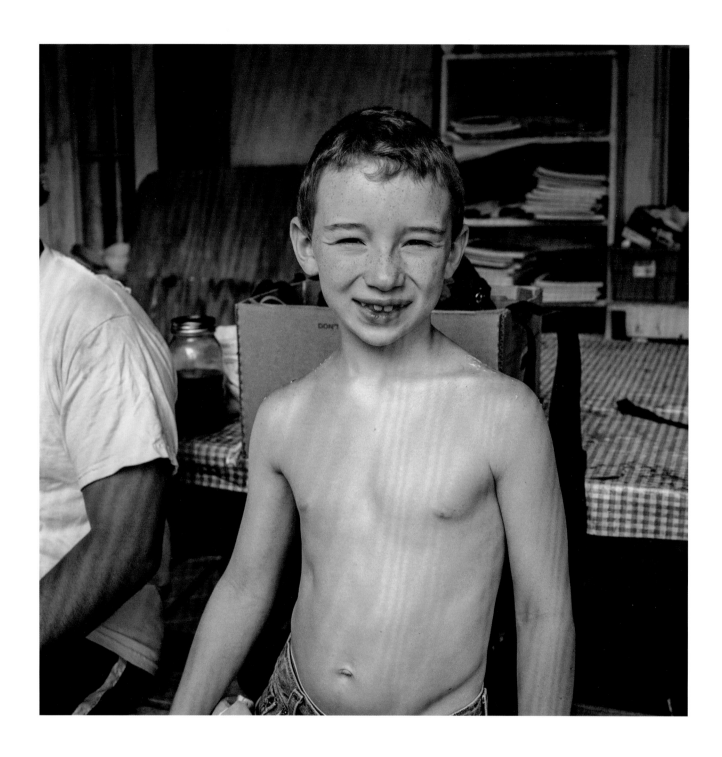

ACKNOWLEDGEMENTS

MY WIFE AND DAUGHTER AND I MOVED to Asheville from Colorado in 2002, and in those early days when I stepped out onto the porch in the morning, into the damp, fragrant air of Western North Carolina, I felt like I was standing inside of a giant terrarium. The filtered light and the surroundings were so lush compared to the dry and brilliant place I had come from. Our new home has been generous in these and many other ways, and I'm thankful for the community we have found here and the work I've felt supported in doing.

Photographing at Hickory Nut Gap Farm gave me an excuse to hang out with a really inspiring group of people, in a beautiful place. Getting to know Annie and John Ager and the members of the extended Clarke family has been a gift in my life, and I can't imagine a better way to learn about and build connection with my new home. I'm very grateful for the generosity and support they have given me and this project.

Many people helped me select and sequence the photographs for this book and reviewed my writing for the preface. It was a process that I wasn't sure would ever end. (More accurately, it did end a few times, but then started up again.) Mimi Fenton, Diana Stoll, Jeff Kinzel, Mark Johnstone, Deb Gelet, Eric Baden, and Helen Robinson all gave generously of their time and attention during this process. I'm grateful to Martin Dewitt, former director of the Fine Art Museum at Western Carolina University; Alex Harris, of the Center for Documentary Studies at Duke University; Chan Gordon, of The Captain's Bookshelf, in Asheville; and to all those who have assisted and encouraged me along the way.

Several institutions provided support for my project. In 2006, while driving home from a day of photographing the Big House, I received a call informing me I had won an Artists

Fellowship from the North Carolina Arts Council. They are a very important resource for North Carolina, and I have benefited from their support in many ways. Western Carolina University Fine Arts Gallery, the TSK Foundation, the Mary Duke Biddle Foundation, and the McClure Fund also provided important support, which allowed me to keep the work moving forward. The Southern Appalachian Highlands Conservancy, which administers conservation easements in the region, served as my fiscal sponsor for a period, and I appreciate their help given how busy they are with preserving places like Hickory Nut Gap Farm. Asheville's Media Arts Project became my fiscal sponsor for the publication fundraising, and I'm grateful to them. I received support for the publication from several individuals, including my mother, Lois Abbott, and my brother and sister-in-law, Curtis and Maryvonne Abbott. The Clarke family provided support through the McClure Fund, as did Tom Kenan's TSK Foundation.

I invited Asheville historian and book reviewer Rob Neufeld to write the essays for this book, and I think it's accurate to say that he fell for the place and the family, as I did. I know readers will appreciate Rob's gem mining in his interviews and research and his affectionate and personal approach. I feel very fortunate to have found Nathan Moehlmann of Goosepen Studio & Press to help edit and to design and produce the book. He did a beautiful and thoroughly professional job, and I enjoyed learning about the process from him. Rocky Kenworthy of Dot Editions swooped in at the end to provide mad skillz in preparing my scans for printing, and I can't really imagine now that I ever thought they looked good enough before he worked them over.

My wife's work as a physician brought us to Asheville, and I'm grateful to Jennifer for encouraging me in my work and for sharing the building of our community here with me. My daughter, Helen, and I did a lot of learning about our new home together. It was her preschool class's field trip on which we met Annie Ager and discovered Hickory Nut Gap Farm. My son, Yohanes, who joined our family in 2009, has been a good sport about the trips he's had to take with me to the farm on photography and book business, though I think the primary attraction for him all along has been the trampoline at the Big House.

My late father, Frank Abbott, instilled in me an appreciation for history and human achievement. I know he'd like this book. I dedicate it to him.

NOTES ON THE PHOTOGRAPHS

Page 2   While on her honeymoon, in June 1916, Elizabeth McClure wrote to her cousin Martha Clarke, "We are just having the time of our lives.... Tuesday night we slept at a farm and were royally entertained. There were box hedges growing in the front yard that the farmer's mother had planted 60 years ago and some quaint old furniture within...." The boxwoods must have made an impression, as she planted many at Hickory Nut Gap Farm, forming hedges now almost one hundred years old. *June 2006.*

Page 3   Light filters through wisteria vine, projecting shadows onto the unusual double-stairway on the porch of the house. Below the stairs is the wood box, a frequent winter destination for those who have fed the house's many fireplaces over the years. *November 2008.*

Page 9   In the mural room, paintings by Elizabeth McClure illustrate the history of Sherrill's Inn. On the west-facing wall, the main panel depicts the arrival of the Flying Cloud Stagecoach, perhaps delivering lunchtime guests up from Asheville for the day. The panel to the left depicts the drover's road crossing the gap on its way to coastal markets. *November 2005.*

Page 10   "Our place here is just a dream, darling, and some day we will be sitting [you] ... down on a wide porch with a whole stretch of superb mountains out in front," wrote Elizabeth Cramer McClure to Martha Clarke, on August 20, 1916. "Then dear, you'll be set down to a table full of country food & after that tucked into bed (perhaps a four poster) with a fire in the grate & a warm comforter over your toes & you'll sleep as you haven't slept in years.... In no time

John Shorter was an African American man who grew up in Fairview. He and his wife, Esther, were Hickory Nut Gap Farm's first employees and the "heart and soul of the farm," according to John Ager. On their first visit to the house after purchasing it, Jim and Elizabeth's Hudson got stuck in the mud on the drive up, so John pulled the car up the hill with his ox-team. He is shown here walking to the barn to milk the cows.

you'll be just as fat as butter again & you'll forget all about this cruel war...." The porch at the Big House provides a celebrated and memorable view of the Swannanoa Mountains. *November 2004.*

Page 15   In this detail of the mural on the west wall of Big House's mural room, we see Mr. Sherrill standing by the stagecoach wheel, offering a tray of welcoming libations to guests just arriving. Perhaps it is Mrs. Sherrill's famous peach brandy. Note the quilt airing on the roof over the porch. *March 2008.*

Page 16   The McClures added on to the western end of the house, enlarging the kitchen and the master bedroom above it, creating this hallway from the dining area into the kitchen. On the right is Elizabeth McClure's painting of her daughter, Elspeth. *December 2004.*

Page 22   The dining room table, made in the late 1800s and brought from Albany, New York, wrote its own "autobiography." (See the essay "Kicking Back the Covers.") The painting over the

LEFT: *"The house under Elizabeth's transforming genius is a gem in its rare setting. I wonder at all that has been accomplished," wrote Phebe Ann Dixon McClure, on October 9, 1918. Elizabeth McClure is raking leaves near a large locust tree that still stands in this spot.*

RIGHT: *A view of blossoming trees, probably apple trees, in the spring of 1918.*

fireplace is of Elizabeth Skinner, Elizabeth McClure's grandmother and namesake. It was painted in 1869 by George Peter Alexander Healy (1813–1894), also portraitist to several American presidents, including Abraham Lincoln. Elizabeth Skinner's father, Mark Skinner, was a member of the Illinois statehouse and an important leader in early Chicago. Healy was a family friend. Family lore holds that Skinner had been an early supporter of Lincoln's political career. *January 2005.*

Page 23 The many fireplaces of Sherrill's Inn had most likely been tended by a servant, probably a slave in antebellum days. The warm glow of the fire and the smell of woodsmoke are cherished sensations of the house today. To the right of the fireplace, the metal cabinet on legs is a plate-warmer. Murphy, a family dog, makes his bed in the corner under the floor lamp. *December 2004.*

Page 25 Creating what Rob Neufeld characterizes as "a kind of hands-in-the-dishwater reverence," the window in the kitchen looks out over the Swannanoa Mountains to the north. *June 2007.*

A view from what is now the pasture just below the house. The road in the middle foreground is the old stagecoach road, which passed just in front of the house. The fence encloses the vegetable garden, and on the right is the smokehouse, the oldest extant building in Buncombe County today. May 1918.

Page 26　　The old clock's mechanism has run out of time, despite the attentions of fifth-generation grandchildren. The photographs flanking it date from Jamie Clarke's Washington, D.C., tenure. Clarke was a U.S. Congressman from North Carolina's 11th Congressional District for three terms. *December 2004.*

Page 31　　The desk sits in the study adjacent to the library, which was Jim McClure's office. The photograph is of his father, James G. K. McClure, Sr., who had been pastor of the First Presbyterian Church of Lake Forest, Illinois, and became president of Lake Forest College in the same town and of McCormack Seminary in Chicago. He was also an accomplished baseball player for the Albany Nines. His sermons were an important inspiration for Jamie Clarke, his grandson, and are stored in this office. *June 2006.*

Page 32　　The library occupies the ground floor of the oldest part of the Big House, a two-story log cabin built by John and Nancy Ashworth in the 1800s. In the 1870s, the Sherrills built the rest of the original structure around the Ashworth cabin. The McClure library contains Elizabeth's art books, titles pertaining to Presbyterian religious theory and Appalachian natural history, and family memorabilia. *January 2005.*

Elizabeth and Jim McClure with their dog,
Bowser, in the dairy courtyard. May 1918.

Page 33   *The Covenanters*, made from an engraving by George Harvey, hangs over the fireplace in the library and depicts a crucial episode in the family's Scottish history. *January 2005.*

Page 35   The old kitchen, now the "egg room," had been part of the original structure of the house built by the Ashworths in the early 1800s. Today it is where the eggs are washed, and it also serves as a place for displaying many keepsakes, including wooden clogs from a visit to Holland. The food dish on the table is for the house cats. *March 2009.*

Page 36   Annie Ager, Jim and Elizabeth McClure's granddaughter, sits at the kitchen table in front of a wall of artwork and photos. The paintings on the wall are of, from left to right, Matilda Shorter, John Ager, and Nanny Suttles and were painted by Annie's sister, Susie Hamilton. Matilda "Mamie" Shorter and Nanny helped raise the Clarkes' eight children. *January 2005.*

Page 37   John Ager works in his office in the Big House master bedroom. His original office had been in one of the farm buildings that burned to the ground in 2008. John is an author, a land preservation activist, and as of 2014 a District 115 N.C. House Representative. Married to Annie Clarke Ager, he wrote a biography of her grandparents, *We Plow God's Fields* (Appalachian Consortium Press, 1991). *June 2007.*

John Shorter plowing the vegetable garden below the house with his ox-team. May 1918.

Page 38   Murphy the dog sleeps on an old hooked rug in the entry hall. The rug is a product of one of the industries fostered by the Farmers' Federation, a cooperative started by Jim McClure to improve and develop markets for Western North Carolina's economy. *August 2005.*

Page 39   Grace and Clarence McAbee work in the egg room, the old kitchen. *December 2004.*

Page 40   Clarence McAbee carries eggs to the house for washing. Annie Ager keeps about five hundred chickens. The eggs are washed and boxed in the old kitchen of the Big House and then stored in the springhouse before distribution to numerous natural food stores in the Asheville area. Clarence has worked for Annie for many years and is Grace McAbee's son. The McAbees live just down the road in a cabin built for the family in the early 1900s. For a fascinating discussion of the McAbees' homeplace cabin, see *Cabins and Castles* by Douglas Swaim, with essays by John Ager and Talmage Powell (Historic Resources Commission of Asheville and Buncombe County, 1981). *March 2006.*

Left to right, Aunt Hetty (Harriet Stuart), Grace Meeker, and Elizabeth McClure. This photo, from May 1918, is captioned in the McClure family album "Canning for Hoover." This refers to U.S. Food Administration head and future president Herbert Hoover's efforts to promote volunteerism in food and humanitarian aid to Belgium during WWI.

Page 41   Grace McAbee, shown standing at the back porch of the Big House, worked for Annie Ager for many years, caring for the house and cooking. She passed away in 2012. Grace was cherished for her moral strength and character and had little use for anyone who poked about with a camera. She frequently offered to put the photographer to work doing something more useful. *September 2006.*

Page 43   The silver pitcher on the kitchen counter is from Elizabeth McClure's wedding silver and is used daily to serve water from the spring at mealtime. "The source of the spring is about 300 feet above the house on the side of the mountain & the loveliest purest water will come running down to the house that you ever tasted," wrote Elizabeth Cramer McClure to Martha Clarke, November 10, 1916. *July 2006.*

Page 45   The wood-fired stove in the kitchen serves as the democratic center of activity. Cats and dogs frequently gather in this corner, snoozing by the warmth of the stove, as those tending to the many chores of the day step over and around them. *December 2005.*

*A view of the springhouse and
the dairy courtyard, April 1918.*

Page 46   The window above the kitchen sink looks out on a large vegetable garden. The photographer wishes it known that the blue countertops should never be replaced. *December 2004.*

Page 47   The kitchen counter at lunchtime. Duke's Mayonnaise, a regional favorite, enjoys a central position. *January 2005.*

Page 48   The bookcase in the living room leaves space above it for two photos. At top, Jim McClure and Miles Parker getting ready for a hunting trip. At bottom, the road through the gap, shortly after its construction. Below the photographs is a ship in a bottle, a keepsake from travels perhaps. *August 2005.*

Page 49   Murphy the dog hangs out in the living room. One of Elizabeth McClure's paintings, from her student days in France, hangs over the fireplace. Titled *The Autumn Garden*, it shows the influence of her studies in Giverny, France, where she had observed Claude Monet painting haystacks in the fields next to her school. *December 2004.*

In the early 1920s a new road was built. This photograph shows a nice view of the curves just below where the driveway now meets the road. Trees now obscure this view of the valley.

The caption on the photograph border reads, "This was the way the old tavern looked when we moved in, but a little paint and some vines worked wonders." A view from 1916.

*This view of the house from the driveway, made in
1919, is now mostly blocked by the large boxwoods
Elizabeth loved and that today stand ten feet tall.*

147

AMERICAN PAINTED FURNITURE

AMERICAN PAINTED FURNITURE

1790–1880

CYNTHIA V. A. SCHAFFNER AND SUSAN KLEIN

PRINCIPAL PHOTOGRAPHY BY SCHECTER M. LEE

Clarkson Potter / Publishers
New York

FRONTISPIECE *Detail of a chest, late nineteenth century, Cortland, New York; maker unknown; constructed from mustard crates and decorated with sponging and faux graining with scenes of Cortland, New York; 53 x 34 x 14 inches.*
COLLECTION OF GAEL MENDELSOHN.
ABOVE *Detail of Figure 5.35.*
PAGE v *Detail of Figure 4.21.*
PAGE vi *Box, circa 1820, Baltimore, Maryland; maker unknown; wood originally painted "robin's egg blue" with freehand decoration, with the interior retaining the original wallpaper lining; 8 x 11 x 6¹/₂ inches.*
COLLECTION OF STILES TUTTLE COLWILL. PHOTOGRAPH COURTESY OF ERIC KVALSVIK.
PAGE vii *Chair, one of a set of six, 1820–1830, New York; maker unknown; stenciled and freehand decoration with gilding on wood; dimensions unknown.*
COURTESY OF ROBERT E. KINNAMAN & BRIAN A. RAMAEKERS, INC.
PAGE viii *Corner cupboard, 1830–1850, Schoharie County, New York; maker unknown; the pine with vinegar graining on the front panels of this corner cupboard was created by combining the top coat of paint with vinegar; dimensions unknown. The artist has painted a faux keyhole on the front with the initials "M.S./W.S."*
COURTESY OF ROBERT E. KINNAMAN & BRIAN A. RAMAEKERS, INC., AND KELTER-MALCE ANTIQUES.
PAGES ix, xii *Detail of painted and decorated panels from a sample box containing ten panels, 1800–1830, Dablic, New Hampshire; Moses Eaton; painted and decorated pine and brass; box: 8³/₄ x 15¹/₁₆ x 2⁵/₈ inches; panels: 6⁷/₈ x 14 x ¹/₈ inches.*
COLLECTION OF THE MUSEUM OF AMERICAN FOLK ART, NEW YORK CITY, 1980.28.1A–K, GIFT OF THE RICHARD COYLE LILLY FOUNDATION.

Text copyright © 1997 by Cynthia V. A. Schaffner and Susan Klein
Photographs copyright © 1997 by Schecter M. Lee

Published by Clarkson N. Potter, Inc., 201 East 50th Street, New York, New York 10022. Member of the Crown Publishing Group.

Random House, Inc., New York, Toronto, London, Sydney, Auckland

http://www.randomhouse.com/

CLARKSON N. POTTER, POTTER, and colophon are trademarks of Clarkson N. Potter, Inc.

Printed in China

Design by Donna Agajanian

Library of Congress Cataloging-in-Publication Data is available upon request.

ISBN 0-517-70083-2

10   9   8   7   6   5   4   3   2   1

First Edition

For James A. and Abigail Halsey Van Allen,
my father and mother.
—*Cynthia*

For my parents, Rhoda and Alfred Tananbaum,
who taught me to appreciate antiques. Special recognition is
due to my husband, Bob, whose enthusiasm has
been an important stimulus in keeping this project alive.
—*Susan*

CONTENTS

II. COUNTRY FURNITURE 101

ACKNOWLEDGMENTS

WE ARE GRATEFUL FOR A group of scholars, art institutions, and dealers who provided assistance and valuable information in the research of painted and gilded furniture:

CURATORS AND MUSEUM PEOPLE

Donna Baron, Old Sturbridge Village
Edwin A. Churchill, Maine State Museum
David Conradsen, St. Louis Art Museum
Wendy A. Cooper, Winterthur Museum, Gardens & Library
Burt Danker, Winterthur Museum, Gardens & Library
Donald L. Fennimore, Winterthur Museum, Gardens & Library
Janie Fire, Museum of American Folk Art
Alice Cooney Frelinghuysen, The Metropolitan Museum of Art
Cathy Grofils, Colonial Williamsburg Foundation
Martha C. Halpern, Philadelphia Museum of Art
Medill Higgins Harvey, The Metropolitan Museum of Art
Barry Harwood, The Brooklyn Museum
Lynne Dakin Hastings, Hampton National Historic Site
Susan Hendricks, Lyman Allyn Art Museum
Darrell D. Henning, Vesterheim: The Norwegian-American Museum
Stacy C. Hollander, Museum of American Folk Art
F. Carey Howlett, Colonial Williamsburg Foundation
Julian Hudson, Prestwould Foundation
Ronald Hurst, Colonial Williamsburg Foundation
Peter M. Kenny, The Metropolitan Museum of Art
Jennifer Lawrence, Abigail Adams Smith House
Jack L. Lindsey, Philadelphia Museum of Art

Barbara Luck, Abby Aldrich Rockefeller Folk Art Center
Jennie Munson, Winterthur Museum, Gardens & Library
Richard Oman, Museum of Church History and Art
Rachel K. Pannabecker, Kauffman Museum, North Newton, Kansas
Jonathan Prown, Colonial Williamsburg Foundation
Paula B. Richler, Peabody Essex Museum
Rodney Rowland, Strawbery Banke Museum, Portsmouth, New Hampshire
Jeni Sandberg, The Metropolitan Museum of Art
Hank Schnabel, Historic Southwest Ohio, Cincinnati, Ohio
Gail Stanislow, Winterthur Museum, Gardens & Library
Kevin Stayton, The Brooklyn Museum
Kathleen Stocking, New York Historical Association, Cooperstown
Neville Thompson, Winterthur Museum, Gardens & Library
Katya Ullman, Museum of American Folk Art
Stephen Van Dyk, Cooper-Hewitt, National Design Museum
Catherine Hoover Voorsanger, The Metropolitan Museum of Art
Deborah Dependahl Waters, Museum of the City of New York
Gregory R. Weidman, Maryland Historical Society
Gerry Wertkin, Museum of American Folk Art

INSTITUTIONS, AUCTION HOUSES, AND PUBLICATIONS

Abby Aldrich Rockefeller Folk Art Center, Williamsburg, Virginia

Atlanta Historical Society
The Baltimore Museum of Art, Baltimore, Maryland
The Bayou Bend Collection
The Brooklyn Museum
The Bybee Collection, Dallas Museum of Art
Christie's
Colonial Homes Magazine
Colonial Williamsburg Foundation
Cooper-Hewitt, National Design Museum
The Dietrich American Foundation
The Stephen Girard Collection at Girard College, Philadelphia, Pennsylvania
Good Books
Hampton National Historic Site
High Museum of Art, Atlanta
Historic Cragfont
Historic Southwest Ohio
Independence National Historical Park, Philadelphia, Pennsylvania
Kaufman Americana Foundation, Norfolk, Virginia
Kauffman Museum
The Library Company of Philadelphia
Lyman Allyn Museum
The Magazine Antiques
Maine State Museum
Maryland Historical Society
The Metropolitan Museum of Art
Minneapolis Institute of Arts, Minneapolis, Minnesota
Mount Clare Museum House, Baltimore, Maryland, Collection of the National Society of the Colonial Dames of America in the State of Maryland
Museum of American Folk Art
Museum of Church History and Art, Salt Lake City, Utah
Museum of the City of New York

Museum of Early Southern Decorative
  Arts
Museum of Fine Arts, Boston
Museum of International Folk Art
National Gallery of Art
The Newark Museum, Newark, New
  Jersey
New York Historical Association,
  Cooperstown
New-York Historical Society
New York Public Library
New York State Museum, Albany
Peabody Essex Museum
The People's Place
Philadelphia Museum of Art
Prestwould Foundation
Redwood Library and Athenaeum,
  Newport, Rhode Island
San Antonio Museum Association, San
  Antonio, Texas
Shelburne Museum, Shelburne,
  Vermont
Sotheby's
Southern Accents Magazine
St. Louis Museum of Art
The Tennessee State Museum
Vesterheim: The Norwegian-American
  Museum
Virginia Museum of Fine Arts
Westmoreland Museum of Art
Winterthur Museum, Gardens
  & Library
Witte Museum, San Antonio, Texas

DEALERS, COLLECTORS, AND FRIENDS

Jack and Pat Adamson
Patrick Bell and Edwin Hind,
  Olde Hope Antiques
Carswell Rush Berlin
Deborah Bigelow
John Bly
Mr. and Mrs. Joseph Briggs
Norma and Richard Bury
Stiles Tuttle Colwill
Suzanne Courcier and Robert W.
  Wilkins
Didier, Inc., New Orleans
Karen Downs: *Southern Accents* Magazine
Nancy Druckman
David Dunton
Joel and Linda Einhorn
Ralph Esmerian
Nancy Goyne Evans
Ken Farmer

Mr. and Mrs. Stuart Feld
Helaine and Burton Fendelman
Mitch Fetterholf
Susan Filosa
Gale Frederick and Daniel Overmeyer
Elizabeth Donagy Garrett
Wendell Garrett
Sidney Gecker
Sally and Bill Gemmill
Harriet Gold
Stacy Glass Goldstone
Ned and Sheri Grossman
Jane Sikes Hageman
Dr. Hugh Halsey
Connie Hayes
Sam Herrup
Robert M. Hicklin Jr.
Frederick Hill, Berry-Hill
  Galleries, Inc.
Peter Hill
Joan and Victor Johnson
Margot Johnson
Alan Katz
George M. and Linda H. Kaufman
Kelter-Malce Antiques
Leigh Keno, Leigh Keno Antiques
Robert E. Kinnaman & Brian A.
  Ramaekers, Inc.
Talia Klein
Joel and Kate Kopp, America Hurrah
Peggy Lancaster
Evelyn Lauder
Barbara Laux
Pauline M. de Lazlo
Allison Eckardt Ledes
Deanne Levison
Dean Levy, Bernard & S. Dean Levy, Inc.
John Ward Wilson Loose, Lodge #43,
  F. & A.M., Lancaster, Pennsylvania
Charlie Lynes
Daniel J. McCauley III
Millie McGehee
Gael Mendelsohn
Roddy and Sally Moore
Lauren and Keith Morgan
Charles Muller
Marie Purnell Musser
Robert D. Mussey Jr.
Mr. and Mrs. Charles W. Newhall
Carla Ochiogrosso
Julie Paley
Laura A. W. Phillips
Anthony P. Picadio
Frank and Barbara Pollack
Jodi Pollack

Scott Ponemone and
  Michael Frommeyer
Dr. Jeffrey H. Pressman
Shari Rosenbaum
John Keith Russell
Albert Sack, Israel Sack, Inc.
Olenka and Charles Santore
David A. Schorsch
Stephen Score
James Allen Smith
Stephen F. Still
Doris and Stanley Tananbaum
Vickie Leeds Tananbaum
Robert Trent
Don Walters, Walters Benisek
Warner Collection of the Gulf States
  Paper Corp.
Pastor Frederick S. Weiser
Typhaine Zagoreos

To our photographer, Schecter M. Lee, to whom we are deeply grateful for all of the time and dedication he devoted to this project.

Other photographers who provided shots include John Chew, Jeff D. Goldman, Richard Goodbody, Tom Grimes, Alex Jamison, Eric Kvalsvik, Hans Lorenz, Richard S. McWerter, Mark Saxton, David Stansbury, and Greg Vaughn. We thank each of them.

We are most appreciative of Ellen Blissman Gould's creative suggestions and designs that got us started, and the invaluable insight and guidance from our agent, Alice Fried Martell.

We are very grateful to everyone at Clarkson Potter, especially our editors, Roy Finamore, Lenny Allen, Eliza Scott, and Pam Krauss; Lauren Shakely, editorial director; Laurie Stark, managing editor; Liana Parry, production editor; Joan Denman, production manager; Maggie Hinders, design supervisor; and Donna Agajanian, book designer.

Finally, we are indebted to our families, whose lives were disrupted for the long months of research, travel, and writing. Thank you, Bob, for all of your insights and support; thank you, Hilary, for your constant good humor. To Bob E., whose enthusiasm has helped to keep this project alive, and to Andy and Jeffrey, whose support and love were much appreciated.

PREFACE

THIS SURVEY OF PAINTED and gilded furniture explores the decorative surfaces produced by American cabinetmakers and decorative painters from 1790 to 1880. It consists of two parts, which are organized by geographical location. The first part examines the major style centers of the East Coast—Boston and Salem, Philadelphia, Baltimore, and New York City. The second part features painted furniture produced in areas outside these great port cities— New England, the South, the Middle Atlantic states, and the western frontier. Outstanding and unique examples of painted and gilded furniture from each region are discussed within the context of the social, economic, cultural, and stylistic changes that occurred during the nineteenth century. Special emphasis is placed on period painting and gilding techniques, the ways in which this furniture was incorporated into the overall decorative scheme of the home, and the ornamenter's relationship to both the cabinetmaker and the patron.

Our exploration of painted and gilded furniture grew out of a long association with the Museum of American Folk Art, as well as through a deep appreciation of the skills and craftsmanship inherent in the largely empirical creation of folk art. The impetus for writing a comprehensive overview of painted and decorated furniture was seeing our dog-eared pages of Dean A. Fales Jr.'s 1972 publication *American Painted Furniture: 1660–1880* finally fall apart. It seemed easier at that moment to write a new book on American painted furniture rather than find a copy of the original. (How wrong we were!) Fales's book served as the benchmark for our research. At first we sought to find works discovered after its publication. We then decided that if we included masterworks of American painted and gilded furniture represented in Fales's book in our own, then we would place them in a new context. Our task in finding superb new examples of painted furniture was made easier because Fales's book helped end what was a prevailing tendency to "clean up" furniture by stripping "old" painted surfaces. In the years since the publication of *American Painted Furniture,* the painted surfaces of furniture have come to be regarded with the same reverence long afforded easel painting, painted panels, and frescoes.

Pioneering research on painted surfaces has been conducted by Jean Lipman, Nina Fletcher Little, and Esther Stevens Brazer. The publications of the Historical Society of Early American Decoration, founded by Mrs. Brazer, provided us with invaluable information on decorative painting techniques. Additionally, there are a number of superb exhibition catalogs from regional and state studies of painted furniture. These include Edwin A. Churchill's study of the painted furniture produced in Maine for the 1983 exhibition at the Maine State Museum, *Simple Forms and Vivid Colors: An Exhibition of Maine Painted Furniture, 1800–1850; Neat Pieces: The Plain-Style Furniture of Nineteenth-Century Georgia,* a 1983 exhibition at the Atlanta Historical Society; and Brian Cullity's publication, *Plain and Fancy: New England Painted Furniture,* for the Heritage Plantation of Sandwich, Massachusetts. The publications on Baltimore painted furniture, *Baltimore Painted Furniture, 1800–1840* by William Voss Elder III and *Furniture in Maryland, 1740–1940: The Collection of the Maryland Historical Society* by Gregory R. Weidman and colleagues, advanced the understanding of painted furniture of the 1790 to 1840 period in this city. Most recently, Kenneth Joel Zogry's research for *The Best the Country Affords: Vermont Furniture, 1765–1850* and Nancy Goyne Evans's monumental study *American Windsor Chairs* represent two other fine discussions of painted furniture.

Regional studies for Pennsylvania painted furniture include Pastor Frederick S. Weiser's research on Mahantango Valley (also known as Schwaben Creek Valley) furniture, Monroe H. Fabian's *The Pennsylvania-German Decorated Chest,* and Daniel J. McCauley III's examination of Amish culture and furniture, *Decorative Arts of the Amish of Lancaster County.* J. Roderick Moore's research on Wythe County, Virginia, chests; Donald Walters's research on the painted furniture of Johannes Spitler from Shenandoah County, Virginia; and Marie Antoine de Julio's research on New York–German painted chests are also noteworthy additions to the field. *Made in Ohio: Furniture 1788–1888,* the 1984 exhibition and publication for the Columbus Museum of Art and independent research on Ohio furniture makers by Jane Sikes Hageman and Edward M. Hageman both helped to bring a frame of reference and identity to the furniture of this state.

The research by Marion J. Nelson on the material culture and folk art of the Norwegian communities of the prairie states of Illinois, Iowa, Minnesota, and Wisconsin helped to identify the immigrant craft traditions of this group just as the research of Lonn Taylor had in the Far West. Taylor and David B. Warren's *Texas Furniture: The Cabinetmakers and Their Work, 1840–1880* presented local production for the first time and identified the pervasive German influence on Texas furniture forms and decoration. Taylor and Dessa Bokides's *New Mexican Furniture, 1600–1940: The Origins, Survival, and Revival of Furniture Making in the Hispanic Southwest* defined the work of skilled and specialized artisans and demonstrated the incorporation of Anglo-American motifs to create a Hispanic vernacular furniture tradition. The painting and graining traditions of the Mennonites and the Mormons are represented in two other new books: *Mennonite Furniture: A Migrant Tradition, 1766–1910* by Reinhild Kauenhoven Janzen and John M. Janzen and *The Legacy of Mormon Furniture* by Marilyn Conover Barker.

In our own study, we sought to bring together much of this research by placing together furniture from every region of the country in order to provide a broad overview of the nineteenth century. We explored the techniques used by decorative painters in the context of their own time. To do this, we delved into the largely neglected body of period literature written by and directed to the decorative painter and varnisher of the nineteenth century. The authors of these books are quoted throughout our discussions of painting and gilding techniques. (A discussion of this primary source material is found in Appendix A and Appendix B.) Illustrations from the plates, drawings, and designs of these period books also appear in our book in order to further clarify the nature of the information presented by these sources. We sought to understand the shop practices of ornamental painters, chair makers, and cabinetmakers by reading nineteenth-century newspaper advertisements and craftsmen's daybooks. Period illustrations of shops in operation, trade cards, and several pattern books helped us to draw conclusions about the process of painting furniture.

To help facilitate an understanding of the complexity of the production, manufacturing, and properties of paint and gilding, we drew on the research of furniture conservators and the current research of historic preservationists who have studied architectural paints. (This is summarized in Appendix A and Appendix B.)

The primary consideration in the choice of the painted and gilded furniture represented in this book was a desire to see the hand of the ornamental painter. Because of this emphasis, the manufactured furniture produced in Chicago, Cincinnati, Grand Rapids, and St. Louis is largely underrepresented. Rather, the works represented here exhibit artistic and highly expressive designs produced by craftsmen drawing on traditional methods of decoration using hand-prepared paints. Known schools of ornamenters are represented as well as anonymous painters and individuals who signed their work. We chose pieces in superb condition; some exhibit original untouched surfaces and others have been cleaned and conserved to stabilize the paint. Just as furniture conservation and connoisseurship have benefited from the technology first developed for the treatment of easel painting, we have sought to combine beauty and science to present furniture with the very best original surface treatments.

The role of European design sources, émigré craftsmen, importing of European objects, and the use of traditional folk art designs in the production of American furniture is explored. The incorporation of these influences into the American design vocabulary was of particular interest to us. While the nineteenth century is characterized by its numerous revival styles, the adapted forms and decoration of European sources seldom result in a literal interpretation. Rather, American craftsmen created visually interesting and superbly crafted furniture, resulting in uniquely American nineteenth-century styles.

Ultimately, the goal of this book is to encourage a better understanding of the beauty and creativity of American nineteenth-century painted and gilded furniture. It illuminates the rich cross-fertilization of cabinetmakers, ornamental painters, and design ideas. Paint can turn the most ordinary furniture into decorative sculpture. It is the hand-painted embellishments, the remnants of the flourish of a natural bristle brush, the depth of handmade colors produced by hand-ground pigmented paints, and the pattern of wear resulting from years of use that are celebrated in the furniture shown here. We hope that these remarkable achievements of nineteenth-century decorative painters and gilders will continue to be studied and preserved for years to come.

Cynthia V. A. Schaffner
Susan Klein

THE FASHIONABLE double parlor filled with gleaming elegant furniture, imported porcelain, gilded looking glasses, alabaster urns, and elegantly dressed men and women that is depicted in Henry Sargent's *The Tea Party* (c. 1824) was a recognizable interior to the citizens of Boston and Salem, Philadelphia, Baltimore, and New York City during the second decade of the nineteenth century (figure 1.1). Likewise, Eliza Susan Quincy's diary entry depicts a stylish party given in Boston in April 1818: "Our guests numbered about 150, comprising the elite of fashionable society of that day. . . . The ladies were all in full dress; gold and silver muslins, lace & jewels of all descriptions gave brilliancy to the party. . . . Our rooms were universally admired & it was pronounced the most brilliant and successful party of the winter."[1] It was for the fashionable patrons depicted in Sargent's painting and described in Eliza's diary that furniture makers in the major port cities produced exquisitely crafted and masterfully embellished furniture.

The furniture produced in these thriving nineteenth-century port cities reflected not only the taste of the local gentry but also the mix of native-born and émigré craftsmen, along with the availability of imported English and French furniture, pattern books, and other design sources. Boston, the dominant colonial city, was superseded by Philadelphia in both population and furniture production in the 1750s. It was here that the Chippendale, or rococo, style reached its pinnacle in the years before the American Revolution. During the war, cabinetmaking came to a standstill as craftsmen traded in their tools for arms. The signing of the Treaty of Paris in 1783 and the ratification of the United States Constitution in 1790 brought a new era of optimism to the country and renewed prosperity to the great seaport cities, and furniture-making styles reflected this change.

As the country's temporary capital, Philadelphia maintained its dominance and welcomed the French cabinetmakers immigrating to the United States to escape the French Revolution. With its close proximity to Philadelphia, the city of Baltimore emerged as an elegant city with a unique painted furniture production. By the second decade of the nineteenth century, New York City superseded Philadelphia as the dominant furniture-making center. With the opening of the Erie Canal in 1825, which connected New York to the Great Lakes and the West, New York remained the center of cabinetmaking until the last decades of the nineteenth century.

Despite the supremacy of high-style furniture production moving to New York City, the cabinetmakers in each of these other port cities produced unique painted and gilded furniture. Boston's closely knit and insular cabinetmaking community was the center for elegant and exquisitely painted and gilded looking glasses and clocks. An array of fashionable painted furniture was produced here during the Federal era. Philadelphia was the home of the first Windsor chair makers. With an influx of French craftsmen at the beginning of the century, this city was also the center of the American production of high-style painted and gilded furniture in the Louis XVI style. The cabinetmakers of Baltimore produced a distinct regional style of finely painted furniture during the city's greatest years of prosperity from 1800 to the 1840s. New York's premier cabinetmakers became decorators for the wealthy patrons whose opulent homes placed the city at the very center of high-style furniture production. The finely executed, elegantly painted and gilded furniture produced in these cities is a testament to the skills of the artisans whose handcrafted embellishments remain one of the greatest accomplishments of American high-style furniture of the nineteenth century.

OVERLEAF, LEFT
FIGURE I.I: THE TEA PARTY, *circa 1824, Boston; painted by Henry Sargent; oil on canvas; 64³/₈ x 52³/₆ inches.* COURTESY OF THE MUSEUM OF FINE ARTS, BOSTON, GIFT OF MRS. HORATIO A. LAMB IN MEMORY OF MR. AND MRS. WINTHROP SARGENT, 19.12.

OVERLEAF, RIGHT
FIGURE I.2: *Dressing box with looking glass, circa 1790–1800, probably Boston; mahogany and eastern white pine with mahogany, satinwood, and ebony veneers and gesso and gold leaf gilding; 30³/₄ x 13³/₄ inches.* COLLECTION OF THE MUSEUM OF FINE ARTS, BOSTON, COURTESY OF M.M. KAROLIK.

CHAPTER ONE

BOSTON

AND

SALEM

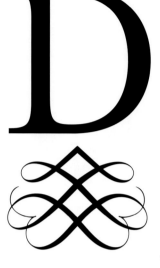

URING THE OPENING DECADES of the nineteenth century the colonial town of Boston was transformed into the most harmoniously neoclassical city in the new Republic. The opening of direct trade with China in 1790 stimulated an era of unprecedented prosperity, revitalizing old fortunes and creating new ones. Between 1790 and 1830 the city's population increased almost 30 percent, from 18,038 to 61,392.[1] Thomas Jefferson's embargo on trade with Britain and France, the War of 1812, and the depression that followed between 1815 and 1819 changed the economic base of the city, transforming the port of Boston into a center for textile manufacturing, railroads, banking, and real estate. A new "aristocracy of money," as Abigail Adams described it, built and furnished elegant homes and strove to cultivate an aura of cultural appropriateness, emulating the social decorum of the old Boston aristocracy.

The Boston-born architect Charles Bulfinch (1763–1844) designed many of the Federal-style mansion houses, public buildings, hospitals, churches, and theaters that became the style of Federal Boston. Bulfinch's design for the Massachusetts State House (figure 1.3), completed in 1797 on the crest of Beacon Hill, heralded an exemplary new public architectural style. The brick facade and classical proportions of the colonnaded portico suggested America's reverence toward the ancient ideals of civic humanism and classical republicanism.

Bulfinch studied mathematics and perspective at Harvard and traveled through France, England, and Italy for two years, from 1785 to 1787. Of his

HIGH-STYLE FURNITURE

grand tour of architectural and ancient sites, he wrote, "I was delighted in observing the numerous objects and beauties of nature and art that I met with on all sides, particularly the wonders of Architecture, and the kindred arts of painting and sculpture."[2] After touring the Roman ruins at Nîmes, Bulfinch wrote that "the present inhabitants show with exultation the remains of a very extensive Roman amphitheater, and several temples; one of which is entire, and is esteemed a perfect model of Corinthian architecture."[3] Presumably this is a reference to the Maison Carrée, the first-century-A.D. Roman temple at Nîmes, which Thomas Jefferson called "one of the most beautiful, if not the most beautiful and precious morsels of architecture left to us by antiquity."[4] During his trip, Bulfinch absorbed the architecture of the past as well as the current trends in taste of furniture and interior design. Both are reflected in his public and domestic architecture.

While in London, Bulfinch likely visited some of the grand houses designed by the Scottish-born architect-designer Robert Adam (1728–1792) and his brother James (1732–1794). The Adam brothers helped revolutionize the English design vocabulary in the 1760s with their interpretation of classical motifs for the exteriors, interiors, and furniture designed for English country estates. Bulfinch's interior architecture drew from the classical vocabulary espoused by the Adam brothers, and he became a major exponent of their style in America.

The Bulfinch-designed Federal Street Theater demonstrated his mastery of classical proportion and restrained opulence. According to a contemporary description of the theater, the walls were light blue; the fronts of the boxes and the columns were painted straw and lilac; and the moldings, balustrades, and fretwork were gilded. A crimson silk drapery was suspended from the second boxes, and twelve elegant brass chandeliers, each with five lights, completed the decoration. This pastel color palette accented with glistening gold and brass chandeliers recalled the Adams' interpretation of the frescoed walls of the ancient cities of Herculaneum and Pompeii. The theater also included "a noble and elegant dancing room . . . richly ornamented with Corinthian columns and pilasters" and "a ceiling *en berceau,* elegantly finished with stucco in compartments," reminiscent of Adam-designed ballrooms for English country houses.[5]

Boston's new aristocracy sought to emulate the neoclassical style espoused by Bulfinch and others. They adorned their homes with imported silver, looking glasses, and porcelain from England, France, and the Far East, but shipping records reveal that very little furniture was imported.[6] Bostonians favored furniture made in their

1.3

own city by the creative and tightly knit community of cabinetmakers, chair makers, carvers, ornamental painters, gilders, and clockmakers whose shops were clustered throughout the city. Despite the conservative proclivities of Bostonians, the Federal-era cabinetmakers of Boston and the neighboring city of Salem produced innovative and elegant painted furniture and magnificent examples of gilded clocks and looking glasses. During the first three decades of the nineteenth century, Boston was also a major center for ornamental painting.

FIGURE 1.3: *Elevation of the New State House, 1787, Boston; Charles Bulfinch; pen and ink; 11½ x 8⅞ inches.* PRINTS COLLECTION OF MIRIAM AND IRA D. WALLACH DIVISION OF ART, PRINTS, AND PHOTOGRAPHS, THE NEW YORK PUBLIC LIBRARY ASTOR, LENOX, AND TILDEN FOUNDATIONS.

PAINTED FURNITURE

The architectural designs of the Adam brothers were transformed into styles of furniture in illustrated pattern books published by George Hepplewhite, Thomas Sheraton, and Thomas Shearer. The line drawings in these portfolios displayed linear furniture with geometric forms and thin veneers with delicate inlaid patterning, low-relief carving, or fanciful painted surfaces. George Hepplewhite in his *The Cabinet-Maker and Upholsterer's Guide* wrote: "For chairs, a new and very elegant fashion has risen within these few years, of finishing them with painted or japanned work, which gives a rich and splendid appearance to the minuter parts of the ornaments."[7] Nathaniel Whittock in his *Decorative Painters' and Glaziers' Guide* reiterated this statement, adding that chairs in this new taste opened "a source of pleasing and profitable employment to the decorative painter."[8] With a rich history of eighteenth-century japanned furniture in imitation of Oriental lacquerware, Boston's ornamental painters adopted new japanning techniques, producing some of the most beautiful surviving specimens of this genre.

Japanning was defined by Thomas Sheraton in his *The Cabinet Dictionary* of 1803 as "a kind of painting."[9] A fuller explanation is a period source that states: "by japanning is to be here understood the art of covering bodies by use of opaque colors in varnish, which may be either afterward decorated by painting or gilding, or left in a plain state."[10] Both Sheraton and Hepplewhite devote several plates in their volumes to chairs, valances, commodes, and other furniture forms for which paint and gilt are recom-

mended as an alternative to carving. The effect of painted furniture, Hepplewhite wrote, allows "a frame work less massy than is requisite for mahogany." Painted furniture, he continued, was to be ornamented in accordance with the colors throughout the room "to make the whole accord in harmony."[11]

The skillfully embellished painted surfaces of furniture highlighted delicate elements that would have been lost in carved mahogany or walnut pieces. The intricate shadings of the feathered plums, foliated vines, bowknots, and delicate berries and the long slender vases of roses at the top of the central splat of the chairs in figures 1.4 and 1.7 were executed by ornamental painters using a variety of long, thin camel's-hair brushes called pencils. Sheraton recommends focusing on the use of light: "take a view of the whole, and consider in what point the light is to strike on the ornament; and on that edge of the leaves and roses opposite to it, retouch and strengthen the outline in such a way as to give relief and effect to the whole."[12] As Hepplewhite wrote, painted furniture should be executed to have "a pleasing and striking effect to the eye."[13] Such attention to detail is the hallmark of paint-decorated chairs of the 1790–1800 period.

The oval feather-back chair (figure 1.4) inspired by Plate 8 in Hepplewhite's *The Cabinet-Maker and Upholsterer's Guide* (figure 1.5), has a history of ownership in the family of Elias Hasket Derby. While long attributed to a Philadelphia maker, furniture historians now believe the chair to be by a Salem maker. The Salem attribution is based on the chair's similarity in form and construction to another Salem-carved mahogany side chair (figure 1.6) and to the fact that no other examples of Philadelphia chairs made in this form have come to light. Additionally, a 1796 bill of sale to Derby from his agent, Joseph Anthony and Co. of Philadelphia, for

FIGURE 1.6: *Side chair, circa 1798, Salem; mahogany, ebony, birch, ash, white pine; height, 39^3/$_8$ inches. Carved chairs from Salem, such as this one with oval carved back with plums and bowknot, help to identify the painted examples as produced in Salem rather than Philadelphia.*
COURTESY OF THE WINTERTHUR MUSEUM, GARDENS & LIBRARY, 57.799.1.

FIGURE 1.7: *Side chair, 1790–1800, Salem; maple and painted decoration; 38^1/$_2$ x 21^1/$_2$ x 22 inches.*
COURTESY OF GEORGE M. AND LINDA H. KAUFMAN.

FIGURE 1.8: *Set of fancy chairs, 1800–1810, probably Massachusetts; birch and painted and gilded decoration; height, 35^1/$_2$ inches.*
PHOTOGRAPH COURTESY OF HIRSCHL & ADLER GALLERIES, INC.

11

FIGURE 1.9: *Detail of a fancy chair, circa 1800, New England; ash and maple with painted and gilded decoration; 34 x 18 x 15½ inches. Part of a set of six chairs and one settee descended through the Harrison family of Charles City, Virginia.*
PHOTOGRAPH COURTESY OF BERNARD & S. DEAN LEVY, INC.

FIGURE 1.10: *Fancy chair, circa 1812, Salem; birch with painted decoration and painted cane seat; dimensions unknown.*
COURTESY OF THE PEABODY ESSEX MUSEUM, SALEM, MASSACHUSETTS. PHOTOGRAPH BY MARK SAXTON.

FIGURE 1.11: *Fancy chair, circa 1800, Salem; possibly by J. Seymour; pine or birch with painted decoration; height, 34 inches.*
COURTESY OF THE PEABODY ESSEX MUSEUM. PHOTOGRAPH BY MARK SAXTON.

1.9

"24 oval back chairs, stuffed seats covered with haircloth, 2 rows brass nails," upon which the Philadelphia attribution is based, is no longer felt to accurately describe this set of chairs. Recent restoration of the upholstery on one of the chairs from this set revealed no evidence of holes along the seat rail caused by the "two rows of brass nails" described in the bill. Finally, the term "oval back" has been found to be a description of Philadelphia bow-back Windsor chairs of the period rather than a reference to the shape of the backs of these chairs.[14] Further research by historians of furniture will help to confirm this new attribution.

The delicately fashioned and elegantly painted English-style chairs of the 1790–1800 period became very popular and acquired the period term "fancy chairs," referring to their decoratively painted surfaces. The origin of the term "fancy" pertaining to Federal-era furniture is hazy—an expression of the aesthetic and fashion of its time, perhaps. Neither Hepplewhite nor Sheraton ever refers to painted furniture as "fancy furniture." Sheraton writes of seven "Japan Chair mfg." but does not mention any fancy chair makers.[15] Yet in a New York advertisement of 1798, predating Sheraton's publication of 1803, William Challen calls himself a "Fancy Chairmaker from London" offering "every article in the fancy chair line."[16]

References in American newspaper advertisements to fancy furniture become more frequent after 1800. By this date, decorative high-style furniture was being produced by chair makers, many of whom also made Windsor chairs. Chairs were now advertised as "plain" or "fancy," in reference to their ornamentation, which followed the fashion. There were fancy ground colors—poppy, green, yellow, cream, white, and black—as well as grain-painted grounds in imitation of rosewood or walnut. Fancy furniture displayed a specific painting technique, described in one advertisement as being laid on "in a new and pecu-

1.10   1.11

liar method" that rendered it "superior to those executed in the usual way."[17] The backs, legs, and arms of fancy chairs and the flat surfaces of fancy furniture displayed a specific vocabulary of neoclassical motifs—trophies of music, clusters of shells, scrolling vines and foliated branches, lions' heads, classical urns (figure 1.9), landscapes and seascapes, bows and arrows, and spread eagles. Specific forms were used by countless fancy chair makers. The first had delicate turned members, slightly vase-turned legs, square or trapezoidal thin rush seats with narrow banding, and back stiles ending in mushroom points (figures 1.11 and 1.12). The second form had turned front legs splaying outward just above the floor and a rounded seat made of painted rush. The rear legs of these chairs engaged the seat and then continued upward to support the crest and stay rails, as in figures 1.13 and 1.14. While these characteristics prevailed throughout the manufacture of fancy chairs, variations were countless.

With prodigious numbers of fancy chairs being produced, an ingenious method of using interchangeable standardized parts and prescribed painted patterns became widely adapted. This preindustrial production system is illustrated by the painted chair pattern book in the collection of the Redwood Library and Athenaeum in Newport, Rhode Island, shown in figure 1.16. Here one basic chair pattern is

require it." He concluded that "the third coat should be ground up in spirits of turpentine only, and diluted with hard varnish, which will dry quick." To make the seat firm, Sheraton suggested that it be given two coats, and he admonished the cabinetmaker who might be tempted to use watercolor for rush bottoms, "for it rots the rushes, and by the sudden push of the hand upon the seat, the colour will frequently fly off."[19] Although most rush seats have been replaced over the years, remains of drips from the original rush seat paint can occasionally be discovered on the underside of fancy chairs.

1.12   1.13   1.14

FIGURE 1.12:
Fancy chair, 1800–1810, New England; maple or birch with painted and gilded decoration; height, 34 inches. Neoclassical motifs prevail on chairs; the variations in the size and shape of the ornamentation attest to the hand decoration.
COLLECTION OF SALLY AND BILL GEMMILL.

FIGURE 1.13: Fancy chair, circa 1816, probably Salem; maple and ash with painted decoration and rush seat; $33^{1}/_{4}$ x 18 x $15^{3}/_{4}$ inches. A nearly identical set of chairs in the Peabody Essex Museum was made for George Crowninshield of Salem for use on his yacht, Cleopatra's Barge. It has been suggested that the painted decoration on these chairs was done by Samuel Bartoll of Marblehead and Salem, but no definite proof exists.
PHOTOGRAPH COURTESY OF PETER HILL, INC.

FIGURE 1.14: Fancy chair, 1815, New England; unknown wood and painted and gilded decoration; height, 35 inches.
COLLECTION OF SALLY AND BILL GEMMILL.

featured on fourteen different chair backs in fourteen different paint techniques. This allows for 196 different painted chair variations—a sizable output for any chair maker.

Hepplewhite suggested that "japanned chairs should have cane bottoms, with linen, or cotton cases over cushions to accord with the general hue of the chair."[18] Painted rush seats are also common on American fancy chairs as a less expensive alternative to cane seats. Sheraton recommended that rush seats be "primed with common white lead, ground up in linseed oil, and diluted with spirits of turpentine," and painted a soft straw color or oyster white. This first priming "preserves the rushes, and hardens them; and, to make it come cheaper, the second coat of priming may have half Spanish white in it, if the price

Period documentation confirms that most fancy chairs were bought in even-numbered sets with two armchairs and one or two matching settees, filling a room (figures 1.8 and 1.15). Painted and gilded cornices for windows and four-poster beds were also part of the fancy furniture milieu (figure 1.19). Hepplewhite gives nine designs for "Cornices for Beds or Windows," which he advises "may be executed in wood painted and japanned, or in gold." He further suggests that "the foliage may be gilt, and the ground-work painted; or, the reverse."[20] This is just the combination of decorative elements in the bed cornice depicted in figure 1.18. The dark ground is embellished with flowers, perhaps inspired by a glazed chintz bed covering, and accented with gilded trim and a reeded basket filled with

1.15

FIGURE 1.15: *Fancy settee, circa 1800, New England; ash, maple, and painted and gilded decoration; 34¹⁄₄ x 44¹⁄₄ x 20 inches.*
PHOTOGRAPH COURTESY OF BERNARD & S. DEAN LEVY, INC.

FIGURE 1.16: *Pattern book of fancy chair maker, 1800, England; hand-painted design on lacquered board folded within a tooled and gilded leather binding. The booklet has fourteen numbered designs. All the chairs exhibit similar parts, only the green klismos-form chair would have needed a different set of templates to cut the chair pattern.* COLLECTION OF THE REDWOOD LIBRARY AND ATHENAEUM, NEWPORT, RHODE ISLAND.

HIGH-STYLE FURNITURE

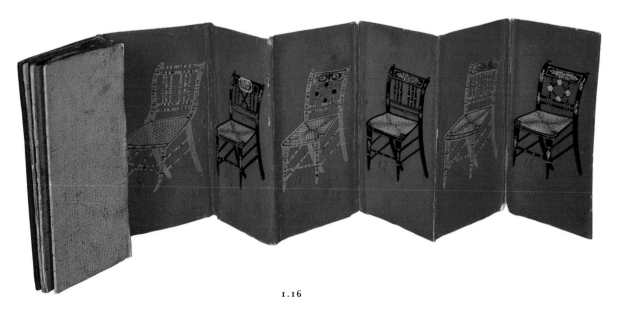

1.16

FIGURE 1.17: *Plate 9 from Sheraton's* The Cabinet-Maker and Upholsterer's Drawing-Book *(London, 1793) may have served as an inspiration for the bedstead in figure 1.18. Sheraton recommended that cornices be painted and gilded, often to match window cornices of the same design.* PRIVATE COLLECTION.

FIGURE 1.18: *Bedstead, 1808–1812, Boston; attributed to the workshop of Thomas Seymour; mahogany with painted and gilded cornice; height, 106¾ inches. The painting and gilding on the cornice of this bedstead represent the creative and skillful artistry of an ornamental artist as well as a gilder.* COURTESY OF THE METROPOLITAN MUSEUM OF ART, JOHN STEWART KENNEDY FUND, 18.110.64. PHOTOGRAPH © 1984 BY PAUL WARCHOL.

OPPOSITE

FIGURE 1.19: *Interior of bedroom in Rundlet–May House, Portsmouth, New Hampshire. The painted fancy chairs were made by Josiah Folsom in 1806. Folsom may also have painted the window cornices.* PHOTOGRAPH COURTESY OF THE SOCIETY FOR THE PRESERVATION OF NEW ENGLAND ANTIQUITIES.

1.17

1.18

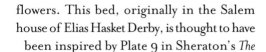

flowers. This bed, originally in the Salem house of Elias Hasket Derby, is thought to have been inspired by Plate 9 in Sheraton's *The Cabinet-Maker and Upholsterer's Drawing-Book* (figure 1.17). The gilding on the cornice is attributed to John Doggett. The bed may have been produced in the workshop of Thomas or John Seymour, who created much of the Derby furniture.[21] The ornamental painter of this masterfully embellished cornice remains unknown, but it is often attributed to John Penniman.

TIMEPIECES AND LOOKING GLASSES

Highly ornamented carved and gilded looking glasses and brilliantly innovative timepieces also provided shimmering and luxurious ornamentation in the homes of Bostonians. No other American geographic region produced such adventuresome and talented clockmakers. Chief among them were the Willard clockmakers, whose shops were located in Roxbury, an area adjoining Boston. Simon Willard (1753–1848) and his brothers, Benjamin (1743–1803) and Aaron (1757–1844), handcrafted the mechanisms for many of the banjo, lyre, and girandole clocks produced in the Boston area during the first four decades of the nineteenth century.

Among the masterful achievements produced

FIGURE 1.20: *Classical bridal lighthouse clock, 1826–1830; signed in oval "Simon Willard's, Patent, Roxbury"; painted and gilded decoration; height, 26½ inches. The finely painted reserve on the door depicts a scene probably copied from a print.* PHOTOGRAPH COURTESY OF ISRAEL SACK, INC.

1.20

by Simon Willard were his "patent timepieces," decorative banjo-shaped clocks with a square box for the pendulum and a circular face connected by the long throat as in figure 1.22. The decorative reverse-painted glass panels on the front of the box and on the throat of Simon Willard's clocks were painted by Boston's ornamental painters Charles Bullard, John Ritto Penniman, Spencer Nolen, and an Englishman identified as John Morris, who may have been Simon Willard's teacher.[22] These designs were typically a combination of delicately worked arabesques and scrollwork, with cross-hatching, done in gold leaf on a white or pastel ground, resembling the finest lacework.

The banjo-shaped clock in figure 1.21 displays exquisitely rendered painted panels signed and decorated by the ornamental painter John Ritto Penniman. Clocks were often commissioned as gifts, and tradition suggests that clock cases with white grounds were given as wedding presents. One of the rarest of Simon Willard's achievements is the bridal lighthouse clock in figure 1.20, signed in the oval: "Simon Willard's, Patent, Roxbury." The reverse-painted scene, probably derived from a print, reflects the hand of a skilled but as yet unidentified ornamental painter.

Aaron Willard, the youngest of the clockmaking brothers, is known for his creativity in developing a variety of smaller mantel clocks like the one shown in figure 1.24. The upper glass panel is painted with repetitive patterns of foliage in gold with stylized cartouches on red in the corners. Below is an oval reserve inscribed in gold on a red ground: "Aaron Willard/Boston." The lower glass, decorated with a pastoral scene, is bordered with foliage and stars. The entire clock case is gilded except for a gold-stenciled base and top, which is surmounted by a brass finial with a spread eagle.

Another Boston clockmaker, Lemuel Curtis (1790–1857), produced the magnificent girandole clock shown in figure 1.23. This original American form, which he patented in 1816, represents the combined

FIGURE I.21: *Patent timepiece, 1811, Boston; works by Simon Willard; reverse-painted panels by John Ritto Penniman; mahogany, gilded wood, and glass; 43 x 10½ x 4 inches. The clock is inscribed twice by John Penniman: in pencil on the back of the throat panel, "Painted by John R. Penniman, Boston, May 1st, 1811"; and on the back of the door glass, "Enamelled by John R. Penniman, Boston, May 1, 1811."* PHOTOGRAPH COURTESY OF STRAWBERY BANKE, PORTSMOUTH, NEW HAMPSHIRE, ON LOAN FROM RONALD BOURGEAULT. PHOTOGRAPH BY BRUCE ALEXANDER.

FIGURE I.22: *Banjo clock, 1808, Boston; works by Aaron Willard, reverse-painted panels by Aaron Willard Jr. and Spencer Nolen; gilded wood, reverse-painted glass panels; 45 x 10 x 4 inches. The square glass panel in the door is signed in reverse by Aaron Willard Jr. and Spencer Nolen. The two men were in partnership as ornamental painters from 1805 to 1809.* PHOTOGRAPH COURTESY OF ISRAEL SACK, INC.

FIGURE I.23: *Girandole clock, 1811–1821, Massachusetts; works by Lemuel Curtis; mahogany veneer, white pine, gilded, églomisé panels; 46 x 13¾ inches.* COLLECTION OF THE MUSEUM OF FINE ARTS, BOSTON, GIFT OF MRS. CHARLES C. CABOT IN MEMORY OF DR. AND MRS. CHARLES J. WHITE, 1991.241.

1.24

FIGURE 1.24: *Mantel clock, 1820–1830, Boston; Aaron Willard; mahogany and brass with églomisé panels; 35 x 13 x 6¹/₈ inches. Stencils may have been used for the repetitive flowers and leaves on the reverse-painted glass panels of this clock.* PHOTOGRAPH COURTESY OF ISRAEL SACK, INC.

FIGURE 1.25: *Label of John Doggett, circa 1802–1817. Engraving based on a drawing by John Ritto Penniman; Boston.* PHOTOGRAPH COURTESY OF ISRAEL SACK, INC.

talents of clockmaker, painter, gilder, carver, and cabinetmaker. The carved and gilded mahogany case supports a convex glass displaying a reverse-painted glass tablet partially covered with gold leaf, which is burnished and surrounded by gilded balls. The throat enframes another reverse-painted glass tablet and is flanked by brass standards. The clock face is surrounded by gilded balls and topped with a carved and gilded eagle. The skillful rendering of the reverse-painted glass tablets, combined with the carved gilded cases, represents the highest artistic achievement in clockmaking of this period—a testament to the unique talents of Boston's ornamental painters.

Reverse-painting, or back-painting, on glass is a technique explained in Stalker and Parker's treatise of 1688. This volume describes a method used in the seventeenth and eighteenth centuries of transferring mezzotints to glass. The mezzotints were soaked in water and laid facedown on a glass covered with a coat of

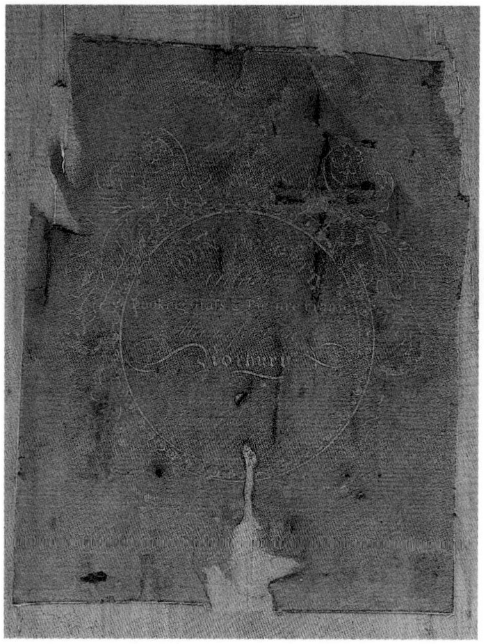

1.25

1.26

Venice turpentine, then removed by gently rubbing the paper with a wet sponge, leaving the outline of the printed design. The artist needed to understand pigments and varnish and how to conceive the work backward as he painted the image by laying on the colors in reverse of the order used for painting on canvas—that is, the highlights and details of the foreground were painted first and were later covered with background color.[23] In the nineteenth century, Rufus Porter, in *A Select Collection of Valuable and Curious Arts,* explains an adaptation of this technique more commonly used in the nineteenth century:

> Set up the glass on its edge, against a window, or place a lamp on the opposite side that the light may shine through, and with a fine hair pencil, draw the out lines of your design on the glass with black; afterward, shade and paint in with the above-mentioned colours, observing to paint that part of the work first, which in other painting would be done last. If transparency is not required, a greater variety of colours may be used, and laid on in full heavy coats. Any writing or lettering in this work, must be written from right to left contrary to the usual order.[24]

Reverse lettering was done in Boston on the glass mats that framed needlework pictures executed by young women who attended Boston-area seminaries. The student's name, the academy, name and the title of the picture

I.2

for the embroidery, and the date are lettered by this method (figure 1.26). Rufus Porter outlines the procedure for creating letters on glass, advising the painter to take a clean, slightly damp glass and "immediately lay on a leaf of gold and brush it down smooth. When this is dry, draw any letters on the gold with Brunswick blacking, and when dry, the superfluous gold may be brushed off with cotton leaving the letters entire. Afterward the whole may be covered with blacking, or painted in any color, while the gold letters will appear to advantage on the opposite side of the glass."[25]

The ornamental painters working in Boston executed reverse-painted glass panels not only for the clockmakers but for looking-glass makers as well. The looking-glass and picture-frame gilding factory operated by John Doggett (1780–1857) in Roxbury was one of the largest such enterprises in America during the first four decades of the nineteenth

1.28

FIGURE 1.27: *Girandole mirror, 1802–1815, possibly Boston; John Doggett; gilded pine, mirror, glass; 41 x 25 x 3⅛ inches.*
PHOTOGRAPH COURTESY OF PETER HILL, INC.

FIGURE 1.28: *Pillar looking glass, circa 1810, Boston; gilded wood and reverse-painted glass panel.*
PHOTOGRAPH COURTESY OF ISRAEL SACK, INC.

FIGURE 1.29: *Detail of pillar looking glass in figure 1.28; the design source for this reverse-painted panel is probably* The Triumph of Liberty, *an engraving published in America after 1797.*
PHOTOGRAPH COURTESY OF ISRAEL SACK, INC.

1.29

century. Some of Boston's most elaborate and masterfully executed surviving looking glasses were produced for the home of Elizabeth Derby West. Doggett's label (figure 1.25), depicting a girandole looking glass with spread eagles holding a festoon of gilt balls with intertwining dolphins at the base, may assist in the attribution of other Doggett girandoles (fig-

ure 1.27). The display of circular and convex girandole looking glasses such as this were recommended by George Smith in *A Collection of Designs for Household Furniture and Interior Decoration* (1808): "In apartments where an extensive view offers itself, these Glasses become an elegant and useful ornament, reflecting objects in beautiful perspective on their convex

1.31

1.30

FIGURE I.30: *Penniman
family coat of arms, July 3,
1830, Boston; painted by
John Ritto Penniman; oil on
wood panel; 17 x 13 inches.*
PHOTOGRAPH COURTESY OF
PETER HILL, INC.

FIGURE I.31: *Looking
glass, 1805, Roxbury,
Massachusetts; attributed to
John Doggett; gilded white
pine and reverse-painted glass
panel; 56⁷⁄₈ x 31 x 5⁵⁄₈
inches.*
PHOTOGRAPH COURTESY OF
ISRAEL SACK, INC.

FIGURE I.32: *Detail of
looking glass in figure 1.31,
inscribed "Painted by John
Ritto Penniman."*

1.32

1·33

surfaces; the frames, at the same time they form an elegant decoration on the walls, are calculated to support lights . . . in general, they will admit of being executed in bronze and gold, but will be far more elegant if executed wholly in gold."[26] After visiting the country home of Elizabeth Derby West, the wife of Nathaniel West, in South Danvers (now Peabody), the famous Salem diarist the Reverend William Bentley wrote, "The Mirrors were large & gave full view of everyone who passed, & were intended for the house in Town but were exchanged as those for this Seat were too large."[27] Bentley's sharp eye for propriety—finding the large looking glasses more appropriate for city dwellings than for country houses—is an allusion to the rarity and expense of looking glasses during the opening decades of the nineteenth century. An inventory taken of Mrs. West's home in 1814 includes eleven looking glasses, two of which

were valued at \$100 and two others at \$115 and \$150 each, putting them among the most expensive items in the inventory. By comparison, a large Turkey carpet was valued at \$100 and a large mahogany sideboard at \$150.[28]

The other popular neoclassical form was the rectangular pillar looking glass with reverse-painted glass tablets inserted within a frame of thin twist moldings. In the example seen in figure 1.33, from Doggett's workshop, the reverse-painted glass tablet depicts a romantic seascape with castellated ruins in a limited palette on a white ground. The designs for reverse-painted tablets were taken from contemporary prints, etchings, and drawing books, and were usually of an allegorical, mythological, patriotic, or historical nature. Idealized feminine figures in the guise of goddesses representing youth, love, fertility, and beauty are seen in the painted glass tablet shown in figures 1.28 and 1.29. Other

FIGURE 1.33: *Detail of a looking glass, 1800–1815, Roxbury; labeled by John Doggett; eastern white pine, gilded, with églomisé panel; 56⅞ x 31 x 5⅝ inches. The Doggett label shown in figure 1.25 is on the back of this looking glass.* PHOTOGRAPH COURTESY OF ISRAEL SACK, INC.

I.34

Boston-area looking glass makers include the partnership of Paul Cermenati and G. Monfrino; Paul Cermenati and John Bernarda; and Charles and Spencer Nolen and the firms of Stillman Lothrop, William Leverett, and James M'Gibbon.

One of the most important surviving documents for historians of Federal-era Boston craftsmen is John Doggett's daybook, now in the collection of the Winterthur Museum, Gardens & Library, in Wilmington, Delaware. Written in longhand, it records in detail Doggett's financial transactions for the years 1802 to 1809, as well as shop practices and important information about the interrelationships of Boston craftsmen and ornamental painters.[29] The daybook also records thirty-six transactions with the ornamental

painter John Ritto Penniman, who executed the panels for a looking glass (figures I.31 and I.32) as well as the engraved label for Doggett.[30]

John Ritto Penniman is the best known of Boston's ornamental painters. He began his apprenticeship at the age of eleven and established a business in 1803, on becoming twenty-one. During the next three decades he embellished not only reverse-painted tablets for Simon Willard, Aaron Willard, William Cummens, and John Doggett but also a wide range of items typical of the skilled urban ornamental painters of this period. An ongoing investigation of Penniman's oeuvre by Carol Damon Andrews has uncovered a vast array of documented Penniman works, including oil paintings, watercolor and oil portraits, drawings for engravings, landscapes,

HIGH-STYLE FURNITURE

1.35   1.36

shop signs, name boards for pianofortes, floor
cloths, designs for frontispieces, trade cards,
certificates of membership, and his family's
coat of arms (figure 1.30).[31] On the trade card
Penniman designed for his own use, he listed
himself as a painter specializing in Masonic
painting, standard painting, drawing, fancy
painting, sign painting, transparencies, and
designs for diplomas. This diversity of talents
was typical of the ornamental and decorative
painters whose livelihood was dependent on
their ability to fulfill many tasks; specialization
would come only after the 1830s.

Penniman's decorative style, like that of
most ornamental painters, is characterized by
his strong use of color and design. Few ren-
derings are taken directly from life; most are
derived from print sources such as drawing

instruction manuals, book illustrations, frontispieces, and contemporary engravings. His
surfaces are highly finished and heavily pigmented with a minimum of modeling and an
emphasis on two-dimensionality. As the
scenes in ornamental painting are taken from
printed sources, rather than from life, they are
often weak in perspective and dimension. To
compensate, ornamental painters use sharp
contrasts of light and dark, white accents, and
clear, bright colors.[32] These characteristics are
seen in the detail of the glass panel in the looking glass in figure 1.32, painted by Penniman;
here, too, is an example of Penniman's
signature.

Penniman is best known for the painted
shells on a demilune commode that belonged
to Elizabeth Derby West, produced in the

FIGURE 1.36: *Side chair,
1810–1820, Boston; made
by Samuel Gragg, branded
"S. GRAGG/BOSTON/
PATENT"; ash and hickory,
painted; 34⅛ x 18 x 20
inches. This is one of a set of
six chairs displaying the same
form, construction, and
ornamentation. Two other sets
are known, with variations
such as round front legs with
goat's hoof feet.*
COLLECTION OF THE MUSEUM
OF FINE ARTS, BOSTON,
CHARLES HITCHCOCK TYLER
RESIDUARY FUND, 61.1074.

1.37

1.38

FIGURE 1.37: *Center table, circa 1836, painted by Sarah D. Kellogg; Amherst, Massachusetts; maple with hand-painted decoration. The reserve on the table base reads: "Amherst Mass. July 9 . . . Sarah D. Kellogg b. 1823."* PRIVATE COLLECTION. PHOTOGRAPH COURTESY OF DAVID A. SCHORSCH.

FIGURE 1.38: *Detail of center table in figure 1.37.*

workshop of Thomas Seymour. The small box shown in figure 1.34 is attributed to Penniman based on its similarity to the rendering of the shells on the top of the commode. Among Penniman's belongings auctioned in 1827 was a "Sportman's Basket containing a variety of Marine Shells," suggesting the shells on the commode and box may have been drawn directly from life rather than from a print source.

While very few other pieces of furniture can be documented as having been painted by Penniman,[33] recent research suggests a new avenue for inquiry. One of a pair of ornamented side chairs attributed to Asa Holden of New York City has been reattributed to the Boston chair maker Joshua Holden (figure 1.35). According to the *Boston Directory,* Joshua Holden's shop was located at Washington and Orange Streets, in close proximity to Penniman's shop, from 1810 to 1835. Since both were involved in the artisan community, it seems likely that a working association was established between them. The painting technique on these chairs exhibits a sense of trompe l'oeil in the outlining to the seat, suggesting a puffed cushion, a reflection of a sophisticated ornamenter.[34]

The most innovative of the painted chairs produced in the early decades of the nineteenth century are the Greek klismos-form bentwood chairs of the Boston chair maker Samuel Gragg (1772–1855). The son of a New Hampshire wheelwright, Gragg was familiar with the techniques of bending wood, and he knew which woods were best suited for this purpose. After arriving in Boston around 1800, Gragg began making Windsor chairs, which he branded "S. GRAGG/BOSTON." Between 1805 and 1807 he is listed in partnership with his future brother-in-law, William Hutchins, and in August of 1808, Gragg took out a patent for his "elastic chair" (figure 1.36). Surviving examples of Gragg's high-style chairs for parlors and drawing rooms are rare and coveted today. While the

HIGH-STYLE FURNITURE

actual patent application has never been found, Gragg's chairs after 1808 are often branded "S. GRAGG/BOSTON/PATENT." Some of Gragg's chairs use a single wooden member in a continuous sweep from the stile to the side seat rail and down through the front leg to the foot. Other surviving examples include chairs with a continuous rear stile and side seat rail with separate turned front legs. Gragg advertised in the *Columbian Centinel* (Boston) on May 10, 1809, that his chairs could be "furnished in sets of any number and of any degree of elegance in ornamental painting and gilding and at a very reasonable price."[35] Surviving side chairs, armchairs, and settees are ornamented with a ground coat and a limited vocabulary of motifs such as peacock feathers, acanthus leaves, and honeysuckle, with striping along the members and, on some chairs, hooved feet. Gragg's chairs are some of the most elegant and creative examples of American high-style fancy chairs.

ACADEMY WORKTABLES

Furniture ornamenters, both professional and amateur, practiced the art of japanning and painting on furniture. In 1804, Archibald Robertson, founder of the Columbia Academy of Painting, stated that "those who cultivate the graphic arts for instruction and pleasure, particularly ladies, whose performances are not only the admiration of the present day, will very probably be held up as models at a future period."[36] Indeed, the sewing tables and worktables ornamented by the young women who attended the New England ladies' academies are among the most compelling and coveted examples of Federal-era furniture. The decoration on these delicate light-colored bird's-eye and tiger maple tables adheres to prescribed methods of painting on wood taught by instructors at the academies (figures 1.39, 1.40, 1.42, and 1.43).

Like watercolor painting on paper, the paint decoration on these tables is drawn from period etchings, engravings, and drawing books such as *The Drawing Book for the Amusement and*

1.39

1.40

FIGURE 1.39: *Worktable, 1810–1815, New Hampshire; artist unknown; painted maple; 29 x 19 x 18 inches. Preliminary sketches with images corresponding to those on tables have been found.* COLLECTION OF THE MUSEUM OF AMERICAN FOLK ART, PROMISED ANONYMOUS GIFT.

FIGURE 1.40: *Detail of worktable in figure 1.39.*

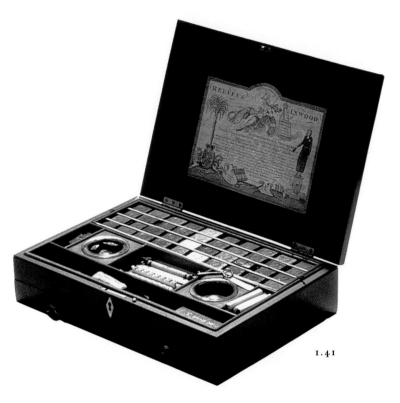

1.41

1.42

Entertainment of Young Ladies and Gentlemen of 1816.
Instructors collected portfolios of images reflecting the prevailing Anglo-American taste for decorative arts drawn from classical imagery and naturalistic forms, such as allegorical scenes, foliated vines, paired birds, castles, and baskets of shells. No manuals have come to light that describe the techniques used by students who attended the academies that offered courses in drawing and painting on wood. However, one of the earliest and most important treatises on painting of the period gives clues to how watercolor painting was taught. In his *Elements of the Graphic Arts* (1802) Archibald Robertson recommends using a box of Reeves watercolors (figure 1.41). Invented by William Reeves in England, these paints were imported to America by the last decade of the eighteenth century. Robertson also lists the following implements for watercolor painting: a soft sponge, black lead pencils, raven-quill pens, plates and cups for holding water and mixing paints, an Indian rubber to remove pencil lines, and four pairs of assorted camel's-hair brushes with pointed, straight, and diagonal ends.[37]

Students of watercolor painting on tables purchased their own table from a cabinet-maker. Choosing from a teacher's portfolio of designs, a student made preliminary drawings on separate templates, one for each surface of the table to be decorated—usually the top and four sides. These drawings were then traced onto the tabletop using the age-old method of covering the back of the paper with chalk. Alternatively, Rufus Porter, in his manual *A Select Collection of Valuable and Curious Arts*, suggests rubbing the back with "plumbago [graphite], or red ochre." The manual provides directions for tracing: "then lay the picture on the ground that is to receive the copy, and trace the lines with a smooth pointed steel or piece of hard pen."[38]

After removing the tracing paper, the student drew the visible outlines over in India ink using a quill pen. Once the ink dried, students used watercolors to fill in the design, one color

HIGH-STYLE FURNITURE

at a time. To keep the colors distinct, it was important to wait for each color to dry before applying the next. Using thin brushes called pencils, students applied a wash of color by dipping the wet brush into the tint, wiping it gently on the edge of the saucer to remove any excess, and dipping it again for more tint. To apply the paint, pressure on the brush had to be heavy at first, with two-thirds of the hair length laid on the paper. As the stroke progressed, the student lifted the pressure along with the brush, so that at the finish of the stroke only a tiny tip of the brush remained in contact with the paper.[39] To finish the work students could add highlights or details with India ink. Once the table was ornamented, it was returned to the cabinetmaker to be professionally varnished. Most tables were also sent to an upholsterer who constructed the pleated pouches that fall between the long, slender legs of the table. Made of the finest silks and imported trims, the pouches held needlework in progress (figure 1.43). Access to the pouch was through a bottom drawer that, when open, revealed a large opening directly into the bag.

Tables ornamented in this manner represented a semester of classes and were much prized by proud parents, who often placed the tables in the front parlor to be admired during the daily rounds of visiting. Often casters were added so the sewing tables could be drawn close to a chair and moved around to capture the best light. Period literature is filled with descriptions of young women punctuating conversations with their needles and casting flirtatious glances while pretending to concentrate on their embroidery. The sewing table is a mirror of this time, a symbol of the beginnings of female formal education.

COTTAGE FURNITURE

Paint-decorated fancy furniture, particularly fancy chairs, remained popular until the 1830s. It was later demoted from parlor to kitchen or was combined with newer style furnishings in a confluence of styles often found

1.43

FIGURE 1.41: *Paint box, 1780, London, England; made by Reeves & Inwood. Each of the ready-to-use colors in cake form is labeled with a period name for the color.* WINTERTHUR MUSEUM, GARDENS & LIBRARY, 67.1828 A–DDD.

FIGURE 1.42: *Chamber table, 1816, Bath, Maine; inscribed "Elizabeth Paine Lombard Feb 1816" on the drawer front; birch, maple, and white pine with hand-painted decoration; 33 x 31 x 16 inches. The top of this table bears lines by Alexander Pope entitled "Hope."* COLLECTION OF THE SHELBURNE MUSEUM.

FIGURE 1.43: *Worktable, 1800–1810, Boston; bird's-eye maple, maple, and pine with hand-painted decoration; 30½ x 18 x 14 inches. The silk-embroidered bag that hangs from a frame in the drawer was used to store needlework. The hand-painted reserve on the tabletop is a rendering of Mount Vernon.* PHOTOGRAPH COURTESY OF BERNARD & S. DEAN LEVY, INC.

I.44

FIGURE I.44: *Cottage fall-front desk, circa 1840, Boston; pine, marble top, free-hand painted reserves and striping on painted ground; 44$\frac{1}{2}$ x 44 x 20 inches. This is part of a six-piece bedroom set.* PRIVATE COLLECTION, COURTESY OF ROBERT E. KINNAMAN & BRIAN A. RAMAEKERS, INC.

FIGURE I.45: *Cottage footboard from the set described in figure 1.44.*

FIGURE I.46: *Cottage bedstead, 1840–1850, Boston; birch with free-hand painted reserves and striping on painted ground; 73$\frac{1}{2}$ x 60$\frac{1}{2}$ x 4 inches (headboard), 39$\frac{1}{2}$ x 58 x 4 inches (footboard). This is part of a set consisting of six pieces.* PRIVATE COLLECTION, COURTESY OF ROBERT E. KINNAMAN & BRIAN A. RAMAEKERS, INC.

　　HIGH-STYLE FURNITURE

1.45

1.46

1.47

HIGH-STYLE FURNITURE

in Boston and Salem homes inhabited by consecutive generations of the same family. The painted furniture tradition was reborn in the 1850s with the introduction of cottage furniture. This simple, charming furniture was painted decoratively in light, bright colors with floral and foliage motifs. It was closely allied with the forms of the mid-century Renaissance Revival styles. The market for this style of furniture can be credited in part to Mrs. Sarah Josepha Hale, editor of the very popular *Godey's Lady's Book*. Mrs. Hale instituted a "Cottage Furniture Department" in the magazine beginning in 1849, which featured line drawings of cottage furniture for different room settings. The trend became exceedingly popular, and furniture manufactories were quick to pick up on it and produce inexpensive machine-made sets of paint-decorated furniture in a variety of mid-century furniture forms.

Cottage furniture was targeted for the middle-class market, and A. J. Downing, the mid-century tastemaker, in *The Architecture of Country Houses* (1850), recommended the products of Edward Hennessey, of 49 and 51 Brattle Street in Boston. Downing wrote that cottage furniture "is remarkable for its combination of lightness and strength, and its essentially cottage-like character. It is very highly finished, and is usually painted drab, white, gray, a delicate lilac, or a fine blue—the surface polished and hard, like enamel. Some of the better sets have groups of flowers or other designs painted upon them with artistic skill. When it is remembered that the whole set for a cottage bed-room may be had for the price of a single wardrobe in mahogany, it will

be seen how comparatively cheap it is."[40] (See figures 1.44 to 1.46.)

One of the best examples of cottage furniture is the 1850s bedstead shown in figure 1.47, which was made by Heywood Brothers of Gardner, Massachusetts, for the president of their company. It is thought to have been decorated by two Heywood employees, the English-born brothers Thomas and Edward Hill. The Hills, who had been trained as coach painters, later became distinguished painters of the American West and the White Mountains. Cottage furniture was produced throughout the country and remained popular well into the twentieth century.

In the years between 1790 and 1830, six hundred painters have been recorded as practicing the various arts of painting in the city of Boston. Though there were professional artists, portrait painters, and miniature painters among them, they were primarily craftsmen. They listed their occupations as house painter, fancy chair painter, ornamental painter, sign painter, dial painter, coach painter, painter and glazier, painter and gilder, and painter and engraver.[41] Within Boston's close-knit community of cabinetmakers, these painters were often commissioned to embellish furniture, fancy and Windsor chairs, looking glasses, and clock faces. While Bostonians clung to the familiar and never fully embraced the robust gilded furniture of the Empire period to the excess found in New York and Philadelphia, the craftsmen of Boston, Salem, and Roxbury made significant contributions to the painted and gilded furniture legacy of the American Federal era.

CHAPTER TWO

PHILADEL

PHIA

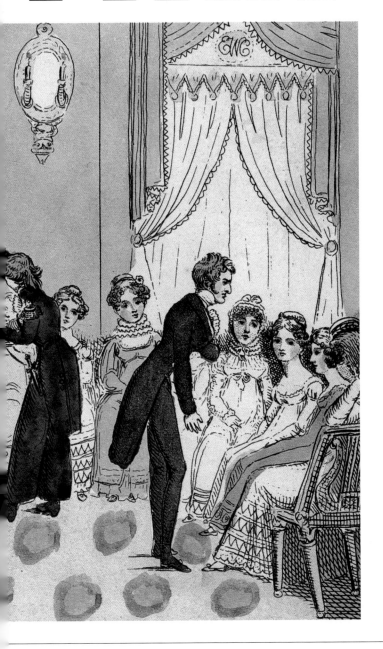

I N 1790 PHILADELPHIA, THE NATION'S temporary capital flourished, becoming a sophisticated, cosmopolitan city where politicians and entrepreneurs flocked to take up residence. Just as the leaders of the newly formed democracy emulated the government of ancient Rome, so too did the residents attempt to emulate classical architecture in their homes. Classical styles reflected the ideals of democracy, and elegant homes epitomized the prosperity of the city.

Descriptions of the home of Anne Willing Bingham (1764–1801), wife of Federalist merchant and U.S. senator William Bingham, underline the grandeur of this era. After returning from a two-year stay in England, Mrs. Bingham oversaw the construction of a Regency-style town house. The house, modeled after the London home of the Duke of Manchester, exuded sophistication and became a haven for aristocratic French émigrés, English entrepreneurs, politicians, and intellectuals, who gathered there for dances, receptions, and dinners. Abigail Adams appropriately described the hostess as "the Dazzling Mrs. Bingham."[1] Her drawing room was furnished with English chairs with lyre-shaped backs decorated with colorful festoons of yellow and crimson silk, reflecting a style popular during this time.[2] Although not an actual reenactment of a scene at the Binghams', *The Tea Party* (figure 2.1), an etching by Edward W. Clay, humorously depicts a gathering similar to her salons. Indeed, the chairs with the lyre-shaped backs in the etching may have been drawn to resemble Mrs. Bingham's chairs.

Philadelphians garnered their wealth from shipping and farming, with flour

HIGH-STYLE FURNITURE

FIGURE 2.2: *Boyd family portrait, circa 1828, Philadelphia; artist unknown; watercolor on paper; 7 x 12¹/₄ inches. Inscribed in pencil on the original white pine backboard in ink: "Mr. Boyd." A period label reads: "Mr. and Mrs. John Boyd and daughters, painted in Philadelphia, 1828." The blue–painted interior paneling is set off by the collection of yellow paint–decorated Windsor chairs of various forms.* PRIVATE COLLECTION. PHOTOGRAPH COURTESY OF DAVID A. SCHORSCH.

being the main exported commodity. Shipping, which extended to Europe, the Baltic countries, and China, formed the foundation of Philadelphia's economy. A stabilized national economy, a strong central bank, and funding of national and state debt encouraged growth. This era ended in the nineteenth century when Philadelphia lost its economic stature as the leading American city to New York and its political dominance to Washington when the capital was moved to that city.

With the coming of the industrial age and the advent of the steam engine, Philadelphia, the mercantile city of the eighteenth century, was transformed into the manufacturing town of the nineteenth century. Simultaneously, the manufacture of furniture developed into a multifaceted industry of which painted furniture was an important aspect. Since colonial times, Philadelphia had been the center for paint supplies and materials used by craftsmen. Eighteenth-century newspapers advertised the availability of pigments and a selection of imported colors and varied materials for the artisan. John M'Elwee had for sale "white lead, Spanish brown, yellow ochre, Venetian red, English lamp black, Prussian blue, verdigrease, and vermilion, dry and ground in oil; also, patent yellow, Dutch pink, red lead, litharge, chalk, and whiting; gold & silver leaf; copall and turpentine varnish, spirits turpentine, linseed oil, boiled and raw; brushes, tools, and camel hair pencils."[3]

Products such as these had been introduced in Europe, but within a few months they made their way to America where they were sent along the eastern seaboard. The nineteenth century witnessed the introduction of the

2.3

pigment industry in America when Samuel Wetherill and Sons opened the first lead-white factory in Philadelphia in 1804. John Harrison opened another such factory in 1810, and soon major cities such as New York and Boston followed with factories of their own.[4] Mixing paints involved a tedious process of buying and combining materials such as pigment, binder, and solvent. The pigment needed to be crushed with a slab or muller, then mixed with a binder such as linseed oil. Paints could not be saved, so each artisan prepared enough for only one day's work. Ready-mixed paints did not emerge until the second half of the nineteenth century.

In the eighteenth and nineteenth centuries, pure white was popular, as was a combination of white paint with gilt decoration inspired by the rococo and neoclassical furniture of London and Paris. Unfortunately, many pieces of white-painted furniture from Philadelphia were painted over with gilt, leaving few discernible original surfaces. Embellishing furniture with gilt was a popular surface treatment inspired by France and England. Equally sought after were pieces stenciled with gilt and verd antique, which complemented the robust furniture of the Empire period. In addition, faux wood graining adorned fancy furniture during the first half of the century. Cottage furniture, inexpensive painted sets of furniture, became equally popular by mid-century. Gilded scrolls and floral designs on plain or grain-painted backgrounds often highlighted these pieces. The availability of this vast variety of painted furniture techniques placed Philadelphia, along with Boston and New York, in a position of importance as a major center of stylish furniture.

FIGURE 2.3: *Tilt-top center table, circa 1825, Philadelphia; maker unknown; bronze, gilt, and tricolored stenciled design on pine and poplar with central chinoiserie surrounded by floral and leaf design with eagle heads, stars, and an elaborate cornucopia; height, 29¹/₂ inches. Only two other similar tables are known. One example is in the Bybee Collection at the Dallas Museum of Art.*
PHOTOGRAPH COURTESY OF DIDIER, INC.

CRAFTSMEN AND CULTURE

By 1800, Philadelphia had become the largest metropolis in America, with a population of 70,000.[5] Scientists, intellectuals, politicians, merchants, and craftsmen flocked to the city. Between 1800 and 1805, directories showed abundant listings of merchants, shipbuilders, and ship owners. The city boasted a diverse cultural environment suitable to the development of academies, libraries, and art institutions. French immigrants made up a large percentage of the city's population. Craftsmen, artists, merchants, and aristocrats spread the Gallic influence, especially in the decorative arts. Consider the Philadelphia directory of 1798, where the Duc d'Orleans, future king of France, was listed as a merchant on Fourth Street and Talleyrand as a resident of South Second Street.[6] William Dubocq, another transplanted Frenchman, became a china merchant while Simon Chaudron worked as a goldsmith and silversmith.[7] Joseph Bonaparte, Napoleon's brother, was yet another Frenchman who came to Philadelphia after his brother's empire fell. His home in Bordentown, New Jersey, known as Point Breeze, and his town house in Philadelphia displayed his taste for fine European art and furniture.[8]

The influence of French-style furniture and decorative arts spread throughout the nineteenth century. Philadelphians, especially those involved in the government or in business, traveled to France and returned with wallpapers, porcelain, tapestry, and window glass as well as furniture and other objects. Thomas Jefferson, a Francophile, returned from France after five years of political service and brought back fifty-nine chairs of the Louis XVI style with gilt or white-and-gilt frames.[9] Benjamin Franklin sent his wife gold-and-white furniture from Paris. Robert Morris, a successful businessman and tobacco broker, negotiated a monopoly with the French Farmers-General so that all the tobacco sold in France went through his company. Morris's newfound wealth allowed him to import French furniture and decorative arts

for his home. He attempted to build a French-style Louis XVI hotel that encompassed the entire block at Chestnut Street and Ninth. The hotel was never completed, but Morris persevered and hired a French cook.[10]

An increased demand for the latest styles led to an influx of well-trained craftsmen into the prosperous city of Philadelphia. Rococo and neoclassical styles of the French and English influenced these craftsmen and their patrons. Although many French- and English-trained furniture makers and ornamenters had emigrated to Philadelphia in the eighteenth century, many more came as a result of the French Revolution and the overthrow of Napoleon. Between 1800 and 1815, some 470 cabinetmakers and 130 chair makers worked in Philadelphia.[11] Some of these English and French craftsmen brought with them printed designs and mental images of their homeland's most popular styles.

FIGURE 2.4: *Wardrobe, part of a set, circa 1850, Philadelphia; Hart, Ware Co.; polychromed wood with gilt floral decoration as well as landscape scenes.* COLLECTION OF MARGOT JOHNSON, INC. PHOTOGRAPH BY RICHARD GOODBODY.

2.4

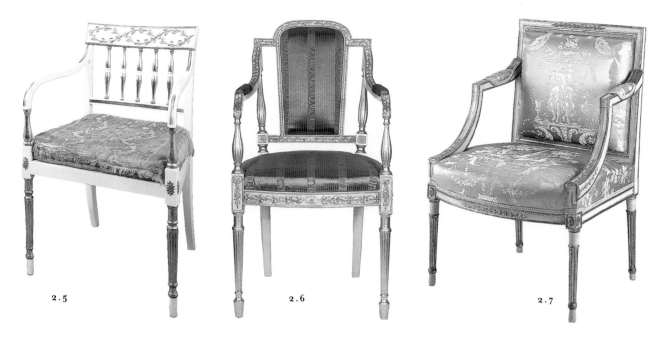

2.5   2.6   2.7

FIGURE 2.5: *Armchair, circa 1800, Philadelphia; maker unknown; gilt, gessoed, and painted ash with secondary woods of cherry and white pine; 32⅝ x 21¾ x 17¾ inches.* PRIVATE COLLECTION. PHOTOGRAPH COURTESY OF LEIGH KENO ANTIQUES.

FIGURE 2.6: *Armchair, circa 1800, Philadelphia; maker unknown; ash as primary wood with composition ornament, painted and gilded; 36½ x 20½ x 21¼ inches.* COLLECTION OF THE WINTERTHUR MUSEUM, GARDENS & LIBRARY, 60.331.

FIGURE 2.7: *Armchair, part of a suite of existing furniture consisting of a sofa and twelve armchairs, circa 1790, Philadelphia; maker unknown; ash, paint, and gilt.* COLLECTION OF THE PHILADELPHIA MUSEUM OF ART, BEQUEST OF MARIE AND FISKE KIMBALL, 55-86-4.

2.8   2.9   2.10

FIGURE 2.8: *Side chair, one of a set of eight, 1830–1840, Philadelphia; possibly by John W. Patterson; painted and gilded wood; 32½ x 17⅞ x 16⅜ inches.* COLLECTION OF THE WINTERTHUR MUSEUM, GARDENS & LIBRARY, 88.697.

FIGURE 2.9: *Side chair, circa 1815, Philadelphia; possibly by John Mitchell; wood stenciled and painted; 32 x 17 x 15½ inches.* COURTESY OF THE STEPHEN GIRARD COLLECTION AT GIRARD COLLEGE, PHILADELPHIA.

FIGURE 2.10: *Windsor armchair, 1840–1850, possibly New Jersey; maker unknown; pine with original cream-yellow paint with gilt, red, and black decoration; height, 10 inches.* COLLECTION OF OLENKA AND CHARLES SANTORE.

FIGURE 2.11: *Arrowback Windsor side chair, 1810–1840, Lancaster County, Pennsylvania; maker unknown; poplar and maple with polychromed decoration on green-yellow background, stenciled silver grapes, bronze leaves, and green fillips with gray banding; 33¹/₄ x 18 x 15¹/₄ inches.* COLLECTION OF THE PHILADELPHIA MUSEUM OF ART, TITUS C. GEESEY COLLECTION, 58-110-16.

FIGURE 2.12: *Rod-back Windsor armchair, one of a set, circa 1811, Lancaster, Pennsylvania; made by Frederick and Jacob Fetter, decorated by James Williams for Masonic Lodge Number 43; polychrome wood with gilt and paint decoration of a Masonic insignia; height, 41 inches.* COURTESY OF LODGE NUMBER 43, F. & A. M., LANCASTER, PENNSYLVANIA.

FIGURE 2.13: *Fanback Windsor side chair, 1780–1800, Lancaster County, Pennsylvania; mixed woods with nineteenth-century red paint over original green paint; height, 36³/₄ inches.* COLLECTION OF GEORGE W. SCOTT JR. PHOTOGRAPH COURTESY OF DAVID A. SCHORSCH.

FIGURE 2.14: *Side chair, one of six, circa 1830, Philadelphia; possibly by John W. Patterson; wood painted faux maple with freehand paint and gilded classical motifs; height, 32¹/₂ inches.* COURTESY OF DAVID DUNTON.

FIGURE 2.15: *Slat-back Windsor side chair, 1820–1830, Pennsylvania; maker unknown; maple, ash, and tulip, painted yellow with freehand decoration; height, 35 inches.* COLLECTION OF THE WINTERTHUR MUSEUM, GARDENS & LIBRARY, 93.82.

FIGURE 2.16: *Birdcage Windsor armchair, one of a set, 1802–1806, Philadelphia; labeled Robert Taylor; maple and mahogany painted, with mahogany arms unpainted; 34⁵/₈ x 19³/₁₆ x 16¹⁵/₁₆ inches.* COLLECTION OF INDEPENDENCE HISTORICAL NATIONAL PARK.

After the American Revolution, books such as George Hepplewhite's *The Cabinet-Maker and Upholsterer's Guide,* published by his widow in 1788, and Thomas Sheraton's *The Cabinet-Maker and Upholsterer's Drawing-Book* of 1793 and 1794 were available in Philadelphia.[12] In addition, *Collection des Meubles et Objets de Goût* by Pierre de La Mésangère (Paris, 1801–1835) and *Household Furniture and Interior Decoration* by Thomas Hope (London, 1807) influenced furniture styles in Philadelphia, as did the 1796 version of *The Cabinet-Maker's Philadelphia and London Book of Prices.*[13] The detailed descriptions in the 1796 price book served as a helpful reference source for cabinetmakers and their clients. In fact, financier Stephen Girard commissioned Ephraim Haines to make a set of ebony parlor furniture based on the designs in that book. The fine work of dedicated craftsmen satisfied the stylish needs of their sophisticated clientele.

NINETEENTH-CENTURY SURFACE TREATMENTS
GOLD LEAF

Craftsmen provided a wide variety of surface treatments to please their clients' sophisticated tastes. Gold ornamentation, applied in leaf or powder form, highlighted carved and recessed areas. An essential element in gilding was gold leaf, which was produced by goldbeaters. A goldbeater was a specialist within the gold-mining community who produced packets or books of twenty-five thin squares of 14-karat or 24-karat gold leaves. Pieces of fine calfskin vellum separated the gold leaves. Originally, England was the primary source for gold leaf used in America, but by the nineteenth century, goldbeaters were practicing their craft in Philadelphia.

Inspired by and competing with the designers from England and France, Philadelphia's furniture makers popularized gold-and-white-painted furniture in America. Locally, furniture influenced by the designs of Thomas Sheraton gained popularity, as did pieces demonstrating fine European influ-ences, especially French. An advertisement placed in a Philadelphia newspaper in 1787 offered "French chairs," which were made and sold in Philadelphia. One inventory included "2 settees in burnished gold, 12 chairs and a fire screen in burnished gold." Governor Penn's town house boasted decorations that included gilded neoclassical furniture. Other Philadelphians purchased French furniture from William Long of London, who advertised in the 1787 *Pennsylvania Packet* that he made "French sofas in the modern taste."[14] The French style also influenced the neoclassical designs of Thomas Sheraton from the late 1780s to the 1830s. The armchair in figure 2.6 is one of several known Philadelphia armchairs with the original paint being white and the composition ornaments and other highlighted areas being gilded.[15] This armchair (1795–1810) represents an Anglicized version of the Louis XVI style. A molded composition rather than a carved decoration was used on the seat rails, arms, and crest of this chair. Originally painted white with water gilding on the composition ornaments and other elements, this armchair reflects the designs for drawing room chairs illustrated in the 1802 *The Cabinet-Maker and Upholsterer's Drawing-Book* by Thomas Sheraton. Donald L. Fennimore, curator at the Winterthur Museum, Gardens & Library, Winterthur, Delaware, has described the remaining original water gilding as "a patchwork of gold leaf on the composition ornament, the bead that flanks it on the arms, and the reeded elements."

Another armchair, circa 1790, from a set of furniture also in the Louis XVI style was owned by Edward Shippen Burd (figure 2.7). This set may have been purchased for the Burd home at the time of his marriage. Originally painted and gilded, the set consisted of a sofa and twelve armchairs. Thought to be of French origin, it was sold at auction in 1921 as French in the Louis XVI period of the sixteenth century.

The catalog stated: "The Marie Antoinette Drawing-Room Suite, Louis XVI Period of

Sixteenth Century. Consisting of a large settee and twelve armchairs. The frames carved
with branches of laurel leaves and berries tied
with looped ribbons, and finished in green
and white enamel enhanced with gilding. All
of the pieces are upholstered in fine Beauvais
tapestry of the period."[16]

When this set arrived in France for resale,
it was sent to the Beauvais factory, where the
tapestry was removed. At this point the factory
craftsmen discovered that this sophisticated set
of furniture was American-made, evidenced
by the wood (black ash) and the American
construction techniques. Although rare, furniture of the Louis XVI style was crafted in
Philadelphia while similar pieces were
imported from France.

ÉGLOMISÉ

Églomisé, another technique borrowed
from the French, utilized the rear of glass
panels as a surface on which to draw the decorative or pictorial design with paint or gilt.
Églomisé panels appeared on furniture from
Baltimore and New York, on some secretary
bookcases from the Boston-Salem area, and
on nineteenth-century looking glasses.[17]
Figure 2.17 shows an exceptional example of
a mahogany-veneered secretary with numerous églomisé panels, circa 1800. The use of
different-colored backgrounds of pale blue,
pink, and green on the églomisé panels dis-
tinguishes this piece of furniture. Note the
exceptional foliate-scroll and swag motifs in
the églomisé panel bands at the pediment,
above the cupboard doors, and along the
lower case sides. Images of Truth holding a
mirror and Justice holding scales adorn the
two large oval panels and punctuate this distinguished, beautiful secretary. In an exciting
discovery, *Claypoole's American Daily Advertiser,* a
Philadelphia newspaper, was found under
one of the églomisé panels in the pediment,
helping to identify the origin and date of the
piece. The date of the paper—Saturday, July
26, 1800—suggests that the piece was made on
or about that date.

2.17

2.18

PAINT AND GILT

Another surface technique attributed to Philadelphia's European, English, and American craftsmen was the use of paint and gilt. Among these artisans aiming to develop their own versions of neoclassicism was English-born architect, interior designer, and furniture designer Benjamin Henry Latrobe (1764–1820).

In *Federal Philadelphia*, Beatrice B. Garvan wrote that "Latrobe's style had come from his architectural connections made in London while in the office of Samuel Pepys Cockerell. He knew Sir John Soane and the spectacular remodeling at Carlton House by Henry Holland. Latrobe's house facades, floor plans, and furniture designs are suave renditions of the earliest manifestations of historical classicism, which was just blossoming in London when he departed in November 1795."[18]

In 1799, Latrobe became America's first professional architect when he designed the Bank of Pennsylvania in Philadelphia. After the burning of Washington in 1814, Latrobe reconstructed the nation's capital. His reputation for sophisticated styles also led to com-

missions for private homes. In 1805, William Waln, a wealthy merchant who had amassed a fortune from the China trade, commissioned Latrobe to build a town house in Philadelphia. Latrobe insisted that he have complete control over the entire project, which included architectural and interior design as well as furniture. He completed the house in 1808. Surviving pieces from the furniture made for the Waln house include two window benches,

2.19

2.20

2.21

a pair of card tables, a backless sofa, a pier table, and seventeen side chairs. The classic Greek styles published by English designers Thomas Hope (1769–1831) and George Smith (w. 1804–1828) and French designers Charles Percier (1764–1838) and Pierre François Léonard Fontaine (1762–1853) may have influenced the design and decoration of this spectacular set of furniture.[19] With it, Latrobe demonstrated his ability to combine classical Greek, Roman, and Egyptian motifs, introducing America to a classical Grecian interpretation of furniture.[20] Thomas Wetherill (d. 1824), a house carpenter working at 324 South Front Street, made the furniture. His signature, "Thos. Wetherill," is discernible behind the mirror of the pier table in figure 2.18.

Jack L. Lindsey, curator of American decorative arts at the Philadelphia Museum of Art, describes the paint on the Waln suite in a 1991 article in *The Magazine Antiques*:

> A close examination of the painted and gilded decoration on the Waln Suite reveals a highly skilled, painterly approach to the depiction of shape and shadow. The carefully executed, dimensional modeling of the various figures and scrolls has been achieved with closely spaced parallel lines and crosshatching in red ocher over the gilded shapes. Where appropriate, thin, delicately applied washes of red ocher were introduced to complete the effects of modeling.[21]

The name of the actual decorator is not known, although it may have been George Bridport (before 1794 to 1819), an ornamental painter who had worked with Latrobe. Bridport advertised himself as a "Decorative painter & Paper Hanger . . . Drawing Rooms Decorated in the French, Egyptian, Turkish, Indian, Chinese & Gothic Style."[22] It is equally plausible that the Baltimore shop of John and Hugh Finlay

painted the set. Each of the seventeen side chairs documented to the suite is an American rendition of the Greek klismos chair carrying a different design on the rectangular crest rail. Plate 36 in Thomas Sheraton's *The Cabinet-Maker and Upholsterer's Drawing-Book* (London, 1793) may have influenced the crest rail motifs.[23] The Waln chair in figure 2.21 boasts a crest rail with a pair of gilt female sphinx flanking an urn motif on an ebonized ground. The front legs are tapered, saber-cut, and decorated with a leaf and lyre motif on an ebonized ground. In comparison, the Baltimore klismos chair has a more pronounced curved back with turned and tapered front legs and outward curved rear legs.

FAUX GRAINING

During the 1820s and 1830s, Philadelphia experienced a boom in the furniture market because of a combination of circumstances. The number of cabinetmakers, chair makers, and ornamental painters residing in the city had more than doubled since the turn of the century due to their expansive market and Philadelphia's reputation as a fashion and financial center.[24] In addition, the growth of the West and improved transportation to the South and to foreign ports contributed to the demand for furniture and to the expansion of this industry. The population of Philadelphia increased in the 1830s, leading to a demand for affordable furniture and new ways of selling it. Thus, in addition to the traditional bespoke or special-order furniture, ready-made furniture was sold retail for the first time. Large quantities of furniture were stocked in storerooms or manufactories. Some craftsmen sold their pieces from upholsterers' warerooms where beds, sofas, and chairs had always been displayed; others consigned their wares to auctioneers. In May 1830, John Hancock & Company opened Upholstery Furnishing Rooms, a company that produced a variety of seating, beds, and window furniture. By 1835 a stock of more than 200 chairs and sofas was retailed through the wareroom. Through successful advertising and a growth in the number of middle-class consumers, the firm achieved enviable status as the largest upholstery and decorating company in Philadelphia.[25]

The rosewood grain painted four-poster bed with gilded stencil decoration shown in figure 2.20 is attributed to John Hancock & Company. The middle-class buyer could not afford a bed made from rosewood or mahogany but could afford a similar piece whose painted surface patterns gave the impression of being "real" rosewood. At this time, handbooks published in America and England guided craftsmen in the art of creating faux graining. *The Cabinet-Maker's Guide of 1827* discussed such furniture finishes:

TO IMITATE BLACK ROSE-WOOD

To work must be grounded black, after which take some red lead, well ground, and mixed up as before directed, which lay on with a stiff flat brush, in imitation of the streaks in the wood; after which take a small quantity of lake [a transparent or translucent pigment used in distemper painting and varnish glazes], ground fine, and mix it with brown spirit varnish, carefully observing not to have more color in it than will just tinge the varnish; but should it happen, on trial, to be still too red, you may easily assist it with a little umber ground very fine; with which pass over the whole of the work intended to imitate black Rose-wood, and it will have the desired effect.

If well done, when it is varnished and polished it will scarcely be known from Rose-wood.[26]

PAINTED AND GILDED FANCY CHAIRS
During the first half of the nineteenth century, fancy chairs were among the most popular items of furniture. The fancy side chair with painted and gilded surface (figure 2.8) is possibly the work of John W. Patterson, a fancy chair maker who was active in Philadelphia from 1817 to about 1840. The chair features a still life of fruit set in a large basket on the cross slat of the lower back, with

a smaller basket of fruit on the scalloped crest rail. Gilding is striped on the stiles, the crest rail, and crosspiece. The klismos-form chair that was being made in the urban style centers at this time influenced the form of this chair while the painted decorative motifs were influenced by the painted ornamentation seen on Baltimore fancy chairs. The front legs are saber-shaped, and the rear posts turn backward in the Grecian style. It is believed that the same John W. Patterson, who was listed in the Philadelphia directories from 1817 to 1833, made this chair as a wedding present for a member of the Tasig family of Philadelphia.

Stephen Girard, a successful merchant, banker, and philanthropist, decorated his home with furniture by local Philadelphia craftsmen. Indeed, he owned many fancy chairs, including the one shown in figure 2.9 (1810–20), which simulated tiger maple graining with gold and black decoration. After frequent use, certain areas on painted furniture lost surface paint and gilt. Local newspapers printed advertisements for services to repair painted furniture, and bills attributed to Girard show that even his fine pieces needed occasional touching up. In 1816 the chairmaker John Mitchell painted and gilded fourteen chairs for Girard at two dollars apiece. Eleven years later Joseph Burden, a Philadelphia chairmaker, also painted and gilded fancy chairs for Girard.[27]

2.22

FIGURE 2.23: *Furniture sketch, 1820–1835, Philadelphia; attributed to the workshop of Anthony Gabriel Quervelle; pen, pencil, and ink on laid paper. This is part of a recently discovered sketchbook attributed to the Quervelle workshop. A notation on the bottom of the sketch states: "feet carved with horn of plenty and gilded with different colours to suit the fruit."*
COLLECTION OF THE PHILADELPHIA MUSEUM OF ART, PURCHASED WITH FUNDS CONTRIBUTED BY AN ANONYMOUS DONOR, MR. AND MRS. W. B. DIXON STROUD, DR. AND MRS. ROBERT E. BOOTH JR., JOHN A. NYHEIM, AND ANNE R. AND JOHN F. HALEY JR., 1995-12-3B.

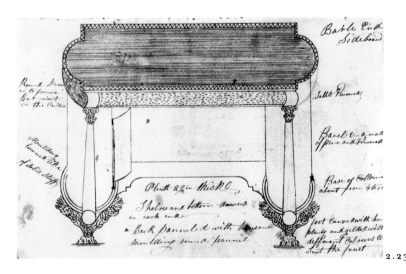

2.23

GILT, POWDERED GOLD, AND VERD ANTIQUE

The list of techniques used by furniture makers during the mid-nineteenth century appears never ending. Was it because of the tremendous influx of craftsmen from England and France or the popularity of richly painted and gilded surfaces? Perhaps it was the result of numerous prosperous consumers searching for the perfect chair or table. The one certainty is that a demand for highly styled furniture existed during this period in America.

Anthony Gabriel Quervelle (1789–1856), one of the most outstanding and creative cabinetmakers of the Empire period, worked diligently to meet the demand. Born and trained as a cabinetmaker in Paris, he emigrated to Philadelphia in 1817. Listed first in the directories as a cabinetmaker, Quervelle became a naturalized citizen in 1823 and opened his United States Fashionable Cabinet Ware House in 1825.[28] During this very creative and productive period, he lived and worked on South Second Street, and his furniture received various prizes at the annual exhibitions of the Franklin Institute.

By 1830, Quervelle's designs had satisfied a large clientele. One of his most prestigious commissions was from President Andrew Jackson for several tables for the White House. The bold sculptural pier table in figure 2.22 is possibly by Quervelle or strongly influenced by him. The dolphins, carved into cherrywood and painted verdigris, stand on their chins with their tails curved backward. The cornucopia beneath the skirt of this table was also painted verdigris, over which metallic powder, probably gold, was applied. A tinted glaze completed the decorative process. The leafy motif on the dolphins' backs is gold leaf on an oil size. Using a stencil, the ornamenter created a stylized leafy design on the rosewood around the looking glass, to which gold leaf was applied with an oil size.[29] Working with gold powder, craftsmen were able to gild hard-to-reach areas of furniture such as carvings and recesses. An ornamenter used a camel's-hair pencil to apply the gold powder, thus accurately highlighting carved areas.

Surface treatments such as gold powder and gilding enhanced the appearance of popular motifs. Dolphins, like eagles, cornucopias, and lyres, became a part of the classical vocabulary used to decorate nineteenth-century furniture. It is not known if furniture makers and their patrons preferred these forms because of their classical meaning; however, books and classical statuary did familiarize people with classical mythology.[30]

Further examples of the use of classical motifs can be found on a suite of furniture believed to have been made by Isaac Jones (w. 1818–1853) for Elijah van Syckel, a wealthy wine and spirits merchant. Originally, the suite consisted of a secretary, a bed (figure 2.24), two wardrobes, a dressing bureau, a washstand, and a set of bed steps. Because Isaac Jones's signature is on the secretary, the set has been attributed to him. Carved lion paws, gilded capitals, floral gilt stencil decoration, gilt borders, and striping embellish the set. The bed in figure 2.24 is distinguished with gilt decoration on a verd antique ground. Like other cabinetmakers in Philadelphia, Jones utilized various techniques such as gilding and verd antique to heighten his furniture designs. By employing combinations of faux-painting and gilding techniques, verd antique results in making wood, plaster, and metal appear to be bronzed. The ultimate appearance was to imitate naturally patinated bronze sculpture.[31] Numerous recipe books of the nineteenth century describe verd antique as bronzing, gold bronzing, or patina antique. Rufus Porter (1792–1884), an itinerant painter of portraits and interior walls of homes, designer of machinery, and publisher, wrote a book in 1825 to aid ornamental decorators in their craft. His recipe for gold bronze follows:

> Melt two ounces of tin, and mix with it one ounce of mercury; when this is cold pulverize it and add one ounce of muriate of ammonia, and one ounce of sulfur, and

OPPOSITE

FIGURE 2.24: *Bed, part of a suite of bedroom furniture consisting of two wardrobes, a dressing bureau, a washstand, and a set of bed steps, circa 1830, Philadelphia; attributed to Isaac Jones; rosewood with verd antique, gilt, and stencil decoration; 112 x 74 inches.* COLLECTION OF THE WINTERTHUR MUSEUM, GARDENS & LIBRARY, 89.12.1.

grind them all together. Put the compound in a flask and heat it in a clear fire (carefully avoiding the fumes) till the mercury sublimes, and rises in vapor. When the vapor ceases to rise, take the glass from the fire. A flaky gold colored powder will remain in the flask, which may be applied to ornamental work in the manner of gold bronze, of which it is a tolerable imitation.[32]

A craftsman trained in the art of gilding more than likely ornamented this set of furniture. In the eighteenth century, gilders were also trained as carvers, but by the nineteenth century gilding and carving had become distinct trades performed by different craftsmen in different establishments.[33]

It is interesting to note that only a few craftsmen in the last quarter of the nineteenth century made handcrafted furniture without the assistance of power-driven machinery. Although the furniture industry became increasingly mechanized, some firms continued to cater to a clientele desirous of handcrafted furniture. "Manufactories" employed twenty-five or more workers to make furniture by hand. Single items or sets of furniture from these firms were sold in warerooms primarily to the middle class.[34]

Allen & Brother handcrafted furniture in its establishment in Philadelphia. The business prospered through the 1870s, and its reputation for high-quality work lasted among a clientele seeking custom work. Indeed, the Allens' shop survived even after mass-produced furniture became the norm. A table attributed to the Allen brothers (figure 2.26) shows the high style and beautiful craftsmanship for which they were known. Made in 1875, this piece displays gilt-incised decoration, a trait of the neo-Grecian style that gained popularity during this time. The table's unusual detail of a cylindrical rod at the apron encircled by gilded rings that end in wheel disks with ball finials may have been inspired by a print of a portiere or by the various design plates of window hangings.[35]

WINDSOR FURNITURE

Philadelphia also developed a reputation as a center for Windsor furniture. Durable, comfortable, and economical, Windsors were made in Philadelphia as early as the 1740s, and by the end of the eighteenth century, manufacturers produced these chairs all over the eastern seaboard.[36] Philadelphia newspapers of the 1740s printed advertisements for them, including one in the *Pennsylvania Gazette* of August 23, 1748, for Windsor chairs made by David Chambers in his shop on Society Hill. In addition, inventories listed Windsors as early as the second half of the eighteenth century. Outside Philadelphia, a Dr. Zachary listed "Ten Windsor arm chairs" in his parlor inventory in 1756.[37] The versatile Windsor became more popular and was used in homes, public meeting places, taverns, and meetinghouses. One convenient feature was that, unlike rush or cane seats, the Windsor seat never had to be replaced.

By the last quarter of the eighteenth century manufacturers were exporting Phila-

FIGURE 2.25: *Music cabinet, 1870–1875, Philadelphia; attributed to Allen & Brother; cherry with opaque white finish, gilded incised decoration, and marble top; 39³/₄ x 25 x 18¹/₂ inches.* COLLECTION OF MARGOT JOHNSON, INC. PHOTOGRAPH BY WILL BROWN.

2.25

delphia Windsor chairs to the entire eastern seaboard, the South, the West Indies, and Europe.[38] By 1810 they were among the top eighty exported goods made in Philadelphia.[39] At that time, Hepplewhite and Sheraton fancy chairs as well as Baltimore fancy chairs influenced manufacturers of Windsors to incorporate paint ornamentation (figure 2.16).

Various types of painted ornamentation, such as freehand and stencil work, complemented the rectangular tablet top at the crest rail of Windsors made in Philadelphia and throughout Pennsylvania by the second decade of the nineteenth century. In figure 2.15, the slat-back Windsor, circa 1820–1830, from eastern Pennsylvania has a beguiling floral design of red roses and strawberries with green leaves on the crest rail. The bamboo joints, rear posts, spindles, legs, and vox stretchers boast dark brown or black paint on the striping. Decorative striping used frequently by fancy chair ornamenters further enhanced many Windsors. The Windsor chair in figure 2.11 shows the use of gilding and stenciling so popular at mid-century. Here, stenciled silver grapes and bronzed leaf designs decorate the chair. At this point, many Windsor makers made the popular fancy chairs; however, these were distinctly different from Windsor chairs. Windsors belonged in less important rooms in the house and on the porch or lawn, whereas fancy chairs graced the parlor, the most important room in the house.

As craftsmen constructed Windsor furniture from a mixture of woods, paint became a unifying element. In addition, it protected the surface from the weather. Early-eighteenth-century Windsors were painted green, but by the nineteenth century different shades of yellow, from pale to a rich golden color, were used. By the middle of the century, however, colors such as black, red, mahogany, white, and yellow appeared alone or in combinations. Mahogany was extremely popular: an ornamenter created the color by applying a mahogany stain or varnish over a pink or salmon base coat.[40] By the twentieth century

FIGURE 2.26:
Center table, circa 1875, Philadelphia; attributed to Allen & Brother; cherry with opaque white finish and gilt-incised decoration and marble top; $31^5/_8$ x $44^3/_4$ x $29^1/_4$ inches.
COLLECTION OF THE BROOKLYN MUSEUM, MARIE BERNICE BITZER FUND, 1994.153.

many Windsors had been repainted, obliterating the original surface. Some acquired scars from the aging process, presenting a crackled surface that resembled alligator skin, adding character and depth to the already distinctive Windsor-style chair.

Philadelphia craftsmen certainly influenced furniture design throughout the eighteenth and nineteenth centuries. At first a limited number of artisans handcrafted furniture that reflected popular classical ideals. Large numbers of experienced craftsmen later utilized their talents and a wide variety of materials to create pieces not only for the wealthy but also for the middle class whose taste may have been sophisticated but whose budget was quite small. Every technique from faux graining to gilding to verd antique brought furniture to sophisticated heights. Whether used on a fancy chair, a Windsor, or a cottage set, these surface techniques adorned each piece in a unique way.

BALTIMORE

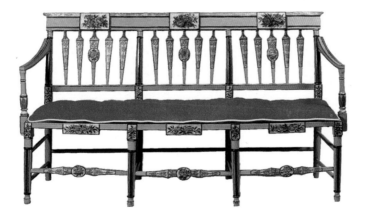

T THE END OF THE EIGHTEENTH century and on into the nineteenth, shipping magnates, merchant princes, and entrepreneurs living in the flourishing inland port of Baltimore displayed their wealth by building town houses and constructing country homes of great size and fine style. Clearly these affluent members of Baltimore society wanted to display in their homes their knowledge of European history, culture, and decorative arts.

One such home, Hampton, was built in the Georgian style by Captain Charles Ridgely (c. 1702–1772) and remained in the Ridgely family for several generations, from the eighteenth through the twentieth centuries. This very large, ornate home stood in Towson, Maryland, several miles from Baltimore, and could accommodate hundreds of people at one time in its massive great hall. One visitor at Hampton in 1812 commented in his diary that "Fifty one People sat down to Dinner in the Hall and had plenty of room." Charles Carroll, another visitor, attended a gathering at Hampton for which three hundred invitations were issued.[1]

A grandnephew who lived at Hampton after the captain's death graced the impressive mansion with sets of fancy furniture. Included in his collection was a set of "15 Yellow & Gilt cane bottom arm chairs with cushions, 2 sofas & 3 window seats to match & 2 different coloured covers for all."[2] Various painted botanical illustrations adorned the crest rail panel, seat rail panel, and front stretcher panel of each piece of furniture. These decorative floral illustrations represent one of the most beautiful and enchanting designs of the period. A

HIGH-STYLE FURNITURE

settee from this suite is shown in figure 3.2.

Other homes similar to Hampton were furnished with elegant and sophisticated pieces embellished with paint and gilt in the neoclassical styles that had gained popularity in America.

The citizens of Baltimore prospered from farming tobacco and wheat. To export these crops, a shipbuilding industry emerged and carried this farming civilization into the age of commercialism. Baltimore evolved from a small tobacco village in 1750 to a town of approximately 13,503 citizens by 1790 and 31,514 by 1800.[3] Throughout this period, shipping magnates, merchant princes, and entrepreneurs utilized the grandeur of their homes to display their wealth. U.S. Attorney General William Wirt in 1822 described Baltimore in a letter to his daughter. He told of walking on a hillside that overlooked the city and witnessing firsthand the expansive beauty of the landscape. Struck by the surrounding magnificence, he wrote that he marveled in "the future grandeur of this city and the rising glories of the nation. . . . No city in the world has a more beautiful country around it than Baltimore. . . . All that could have been expected from wealth and fine taste have been accomplished."[4]

Shipping played a major role in the evolution of Baltimore as a center of affluence and style. Exporting crops and importing goods inevitably led to good fortune in business. Robert Gilmor, a Scotsman who came to

Maryland in 1769 and moved to Baltimore in 1778, is a fine example of one who profited immensely from mercantile trade. At first he was the representative in Amsterdam for sales of wheat and tobacco. He formed his own mercantile house after the Revolutionary War, shipping produce to the West Indies, Europe, and India. Gilmor substantially increased his fortune when he built a powder mill on the Gwynn Falls. The additional profits afforded his son, Robert Gilmor Jr., likewise a merchant prince, the opportunity to become a patron of the arts and an important collector.[5]

By the turn of the century the appetite for anything European grew and was satisfied by travel to London, Paris, and Rome. As Philip Hone, celebrated diarist and onetime mayor of New York, wrote, "All the world is going to Europe."[6] Many of the mercantile community developed an understanding of European classicism through travel abroad. A knowledge of European history, culture, architecture, and decorative arts enhanced the ability of these merchants to bring a new level of sophistication to the United States. Soon elegant and sophisticated furniture embellished with paint and gilt in the European and English neoclassical styles became popular in the United States. Nineteenth-century Baltimore emerged as an important center for sophisticated painted and gilded furniture embellished with ornamentation of the finest quality.

Wealthy Americans who traveled abroad

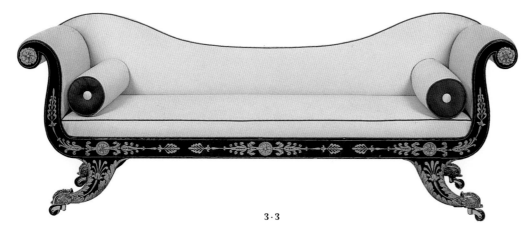

3·3

John and Hugh Finley

HAVE opened a shop at No. 190½, Market-street, opposite Mr Peter Wyant's inn, where they have for sale, and make to any pattern, all kinds of FANCY and JAPANNED FURNITURE, viz.

Japanned and gilt card, pier, tea, dressing, writing and shaving TABLES, with or without views adjacent to the city.

Ditto cane seats, rush and windsor CHAIRS, with or without views.

Ditto cane seats, rush and windsor SETTEES, with or without views.

Ditto Window and Recess Seats.

Ditto Wash and Candle Stands.

Ditto Fire and Candle Screens.

Ditto Ditto. with views.

Ditto Bedsteads, and Bed and Window Cornices, &c.

Which they warrant equal to any imported.

They as usual execute Coach, Sign and Ornamental Painting.

Military standards, drums, masonic aprons, all kinds of silk transparencies, &c. in the neatest manner, and on the shortest notice.

☞ Old chairs repainted.

N. B. Apply as above or at their manufactory No. 3, South Frederick-street.

October 24. d

returned with samples of furniture and decorative arts of the neoclassical period. These pieces inspired the skilled local furniture makers. Foreign-trained furniture makers brought firsthand knowledge of European neoclassical styles and design motifs to Baltimore. It is important to note that the English influence was as strong in Baltimore in the Federal period as the French was in Philadelphia. Additional knowledge was gained from the English design books that were available in Baltimore and helped artisans create superior pieces of quality furniture. Among these texts were George Hepplewhite's *The Cabinet-Maker and Upholsterer's Guide* and Thomas Sheraton's *Cabinet Dictionary*. In her writings, Gregory Weidman, curator of the Maryland Historical Society, attributes the form of some Baltimore pieces to another Sheraton book, *The Cabinet-Maker and Upholsterer's Drawing-Book*; however, no documentation exists to confirm its existence in Baltimore. *The Cabinet-Maker's London Book of Prices* with plates by

3.5

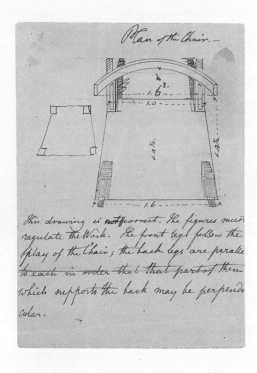

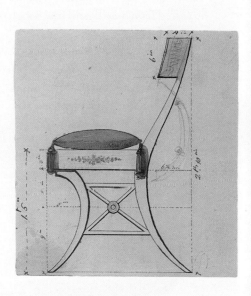

Thomas Shearer also played an important role influencing local furniture.[7] It is clear, therefore, that travel abroad was only one factor that contributed to the style of furniture that emerged in Baltimore during the early nineteenth century. The American approach was not to copy the furniture of Europe and England but to derive a style of its own from the same ingredients, using a new and different approach.

While Baltimore had several shops producing fancy furniture, none equaled the quality and sophistication of John (fl. 1799–1840) and Hugh (fl. 1803–1831) Finlay's establishment. The brothers, born and trained as cabinetmakers in Maryland, produced Federal or early neoclassical furniture between 1790 and 1815 and late classical or Empire-style furniture from 1815 to 1840. John started his career as a coach painter and was joined in 1803 by his younger brother, Hugh. Together they had the good sense to advertise in the *Federal Gazette,* calling attention to the wide variety of painted furniture they made (figure 3.4). By the second decade of the nineteenth century their shop employed more than sixty-eight individuals and boasted not only the most beautiful furniture but also the most extensive inventory and orders.[8]

Clients from Maryland and surrounding areas were proud to own furniture executed by the Finlays. In 1809 the Finlays received their most prestigious commission from Benjamin Henry Latrobe, who commissioned them to execute furniture for the oval drawing room of the White House during James Madison's presidency. Included in the order was a set of thirty-six chairs, two sofas, and four settees. Latrobe created drawings from which this suite was executed, and the Finlays completed it on New Year's Day, 1810. Because this furniture was designed in the Empire style it represented an introduction to the classical Greek styles preferred by the English and French designers. A drawing by Latrobe of the chair shown in figure 3.5 was made for the Madison White House. Unfortunately, the furniture was

3.6

3.7

destroyed when the British burned the White House during the War of 1812. These designs influenced future works of the Finlay shop.

On returning from Europe in 1810, Hugh Finlay advertised in the *Baltimore American* that he was now able to design furniture based on the ideas gathered from his trip. One advertisement read, "A Handsome Collection Of Engravings . . . with a number of Plaster Figures for Mantel ornaments . . . a number of Drawings, from furniture in the first houses of Paris and London [have arrived and will be used to make the finest pieces]."[9] Weidman writes that the drawings Finlay brought back were probably by Thomas Hope and by Charles Percier and Pierre François Léonard Fontaine. The distinguished nature of Finlay's clientele warranted trips to Europe to garner ideas. The Finlays commissioned artists such as English-born Francis Guy (1760–1820) and Dutch-born Cornelius de Beet (c. 1772–1840) to enhance the ornamental design of the furniture.

Besides furniture, the elegant homes of the nineteenth century boasted other items that attest to the wealth and sophisticated tastes of the owners. Mirrors by George Smith (fl. 1797–1820), for example (figure 3.6), emulated English mirrors with fine gilding and

FIGURE 3.4: *Finlay advertisement (in which Finlay was misspelled as Finley), October 24, 1803, from the Federal Gazette, Baltimore.* COURTESY OF THE MARYLAND HISTORICAL SOCIETY, BALTIMORE.

FIGURE 3.5: *Drawings for a chair for President James Madison's White House, circa 1809, Benjamin Henry Latrobe; watercolor, pencil, pen and ink on paper; 5¼ x 5⅛ inches. This chair, part of a suite of furniture consisting of thirty-six chairs, two sofas, and four settees, is the earliest example of the Empire style of neoclassical furniture made in Baltimore. This suite was executed at the Finlay shop in 1809 and influenced the designs of other furniture created by the Finlays.* COLLECTION OF THE MARYLAND HISTORICAL SOCIETY, BALTIMORE.

FIGURE 3.6: *Detail of a mirror, 1800–1820, Baltimore; possibly made by George Smith; carved and gilded yellow pine frame; 72¾ x 48¼ x 7¾ inches. Designed with a projecting cornice and decorated with classical figures, this looking-glass frame represents a style that was popular during this period.* COURTESY OF THE MARYLAND HISTORICAL SOCIETY, BALTIMORE, 18.6.36.

FIGURE 3.7: *Pianoforte, 1825–1835, Baltimore; made by Joseph Hiskey; mahogany, white pine, cherry, oak; height, 36⅞ inches. The hand-colored pastoral scene on the panel above the keyboard was engraved by John Medairy and William Bannerman from drawings by Samuel Smith, an artist living in Baltimore.* COURTESY OF THE MARYLAND HISTORICAL SOCIETY, BALTIMORE, 62.6.1.

The following six chairs are a popular variant of the ancient klismos chair and illustrate the dissemination of this form from the formal, more expensive chair (figure 3.8) to a less expensive version (figure 3.13):

FIGURE **3.8**: *Klismos side chair, 1815–1825, Baltimore; painted decoration attributed to Hugh and John Finlay; cherry, maple, tulip poplar, painted a vibrant chrome yellow and chrome green with gilding, bronzing, and penciling in red, white, black, ochre, and sepia; $31^5/8$ x $20^1/8$ x $21^1/2$ inches. This chair was part of a set of twelve that belonged to Edward Lloyd of Wye House, Talbot County, Maryland.* COLLECTION OF THE WINTERTHUR MUSEUM, GARDENS & LIBRARY, 92.29.1.

FIGURE **3.9**: *Side chair, 1820–1840, Baltimore; painted and gilded wood, front seat rail and crest rail poplar; 34 x 19 x 22 inches.* COLLECTION OF THE MARYLAND HISTORICAL SOCIETY, BALTIMORE, 82.29.

FIGURE **3.10**: *Side chair, 1820–1840, Baltimore; maker unknown; maple, paint decoration in white (now a pale yellow-gray), sepia, forest green, and black; $31^1/4$ x 19 x $21^3/8$ inches. Romantic scenes of ruins, bridges, and towers decorate the crest rail of this chair and the other five chairs in this set.* COLLECTION OF THE MARYLAND HISTORICAL SOCIETY, BALTIMORE, 43.40.5.

FIGURE **3.11**: *Side chair, circa 1820, Baltimore; maker unknown; maple painted to simulate rosewood, gilt and polychrome stenciling with minor freehand ornamentation in black.* COLLECTION OF THE COLONIAL WILLIAMSBURG FOUNDATION, 1993-175.1.

FIGURE **3.12**: *Side chair, circa 1820, attributed to John and Hugh Finlay; wood painted Prussian blue with freehand gilt decoration, chrome yellow caned seat; $32^3/4$ x $19^1/2$ x 20 inches.* COLLECTION OF STILES TUTTLE COLWILL INTERIORS. PHOTOGRAPH BY ERIC KVALSVIK.

FIGURE **3.13**: *Side chair, circa 1825, Baltimore; maker unknown; wood painted freehand in yellow, green, red, gold, and black; $31^1/2$ x 18 x 19 inches. The popular neoclassical design motif of swans was seen on the more expensive fancy furniture and on the cheaper copies as well.* PRIVATE COLLECTION. PHOTOGRAPH COURTESY OF CHEW & CO.

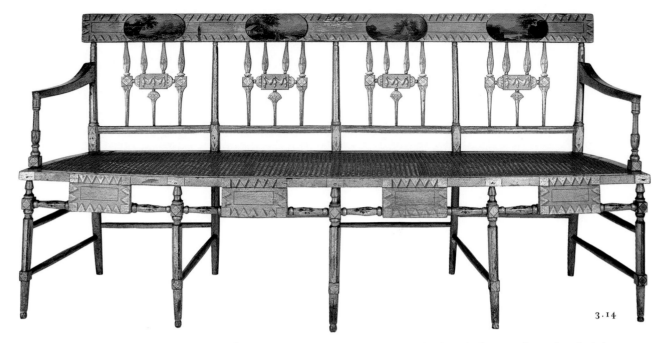

FIGURE 3.14: *Settee, 1814–1815, Baltimore; made by Thomas Renshaw; ornamented by John Barnhart; maple, tulip, and walnut, painted putty color with polychrome and gilt and bronze decoration, cane seat not original; $35^3/_8$ x $75^7/_8$ x $23^3/_8$ inches. This settee was probably part of a set of fancy furniture; two matching chairs are in the Baltimore Museum's collection. Although the ornamenter's name, along with that of the maker, is printed in block letters across the stay rails of the two center backs, it is doubtful that Barnhart executed the landscape scenes on the crest rail. A landscape artist would have been employed to render these panels.* COLLECTION OF THE BALTIMORE MUSEUM OF ART, PURCHASED AS THE GIFT OF ROBERT G. MERRICK, MRS. D'ARCY PAUL, J. GILMAN D'ARCY PAUL, MRS. ALVIN THALHEIMER, AND MRS. MILES WHITE JR., BMA 1950.51.

FIGURE 3.15: *Settee, 1805–1820, Baltimore; poplar, walnut, and maple, polychrome and gilded decoration with landscape scenes on the panels of the crest rail; height, $35^1/_2$ inches. The style and design of the Finlay shop, the premier fancy furniture makers, were frequently imitated by other Baltimore craftsmen. This beautifully ornamented settee was probably the prototype for the labeled Renshaw and Barnhart settee shown in figure 3.14. The landscape scenes may have been painted by Cornelius de Beet, the Baltimore landscape artist.* COLLECTION OF THE MARYLAND HISTORICAL SOCIETY, BALTIMORE.

carving. By the 1830s, pianofortes were also popular additions to the drawing rooms of the affluent. Joseph Hiskey (fl. 1819–1848) of Baltimore produced fine pianos. The one in figure 3.7 is embellished with a landscape scene engraved by John Medairy and William Bannerman from drawings by Baltimore artist Samuel Smith.

In a forty-year magical period, Baltimore reigned as an important center for painted furniture. Affluent citizens had reached new heights of taste and style through travel abroad and desired that this newfound sophistication be a part of their lives. Architects and furniture makers crafted beautiful designs and contributed to making their homes places of grandeur.

BALTIMORE'S FANCY FURNITURE MAKERS

Numerous estate inventories list fancy furniture in middle- and upper-class Baltimore homes. Some people owned entire sets of such furniture. Governor Eager Howard's home, Belvidere, boasted a yellow-and-gold set, a blue set, and a white set.[10] These sets were predominantly made up of chairs and settees, very popular seating furniture. An entire group of chair makers worked in Baltimore to meet the demand for fancy furniture. Among them were Robert Fisher, Thomas S. Renshaw, and John Hodgkinson.

Printed in the seat rails of the polychromed and gilt settee in figure 3.14 are the names Thomas S. Renshaw and John Barnhart. Renshaw and Barnhart were in business for two years, 1814 to 1815, at 37 South Gay Street.[11] The settee shown is painted a putty color with gilt and paint decorations of romantic landscapes on the crest rail. The crest rail is edged with a bold sawtooth design. Another settee is shown in figure 3.15. Although the designs of these two settees are similar, the finish, decorations, and design on figure 3.15 are far more sophisticated, indicating that this must have been the prototype for the piece shown in figure 3.14 and that it was possibly made in the Finlay shop. Like so many other Baltimore furniture makers, Renshaw was definitely influenced by the Finlay shop. The similarities are seen in the crosshatch and sawtooth gilt banding. A table attributed to the Finlay shop, shown in figure 3.16, boasts sawtooth banding and a landscape scene, Finlay trademarks.

Affluent citizens of Baltimore looked beyond the structure of furniture in search of color and exquisitely painted designs. The fancy furniture commissioned by the wealthy complemented their homes. Designs depicted both real and imagined landscapes and neoclassical motifs such as swags, crossed torches within a wreath, bows and arrows, eagles within wreaths, winged thunderbolts, and anthemia.

3.16

3.17

3.18

3.19

3.20

FIGURE 3.19: *Armchair,
1800–1810, Baltimore;
John and Hugh Finlay; maple
and ash with polychrome and
gilded decoration on a black
ground; 33³/₄ x 22¹/₄ x 21
inches. This armchair is part of
a thirteen-piece suite
consisting of ten armchairs,
two settees, and a marble-top
pier table.*
COLLECTION OF THE
BALTIMORE MUSEUM OF ART,
GIFT OF LYDIA HOWARD DE
ROTH AND NANCY H. DEFORD
VENABLE IN MEMORY OF THEIR
MOTHER, LYDIA HOWARD
DEFORD, AND PURCHASE FUND,
BMA, 1966.26.3.

FIGURE 3.20: *Side chair,
one of a pair, 1800–1810,
Baltimore; attributed to John
and Hugh Finlay; mahogany
and maple painted black with
gilt and polychrome
decoration.*
COLLECTION OF THE
METROPOLITAN MUSEUM OF
ART, GIFT OF MRS. PAUL
MOORE. PHOTOGRAPH BY PAUL
WARCHAL, 1974.102.1.

FIGURE 3.21: *Pier table,
circa 1810, Baltimore;
attributed to John and Hugh
Finlay; polychromed
decoration in yellow, green,
and white, with a faux marble
top; 37 x 40¹/₂ x 19³/₄
inches.*
COLLECTION OF STILES TUTTLE
COLWILL. PHOTOGRAPH BY
ERIC KVALSVIK.

FIGURE 3.22: *Card table
with ovolo corners,
1800–1810, Baltimore;
attributed to John and Hugh
Finlay, with architectural
scene by Francis Guy; wood
painted black with gilt and
polychrome decoration; 29⁵/₈
x 35⁷/₈ x 17⁵/₈ inches.*
MOUNT CLARE MUSEUM HOUSE,
BALTIMORE, COLLECTION OF
THE NATIONAL SOCIETY OF THE
COLONIAL DAMES OF AMERICA
IN THE STATE OF MARYLAND.
PHOTOGRAPH BY JEFF D.
GOLDMAN.

The card table in figure 3.17 shows a delicate display of classical motifs, including an imaginary landscape framed with gilt bands in a leafy vine motif. Although no official documents provide information concerning the actual painters employed by the Finlay shop, it is believed that this picturesque scene may have been painted by Francis Guy (1760–1820), an English-born landscape artist.[12] Presumably in reference to Guy's talent, the Finlays advertised in the *American and Commercial Daily Advertiser* on August 11, 1804, that they could provide clients with "views on their chairs & furniture, which they alone can do, as they hold an exclusive right for that species of ornaments, which so much please those who have seen them."[13] Some say that Francis Guy could not establish himself as a landscape painter and therefore turned to painting landscapes and architectural views on fancy furniture for the people of Baltimore.

Besides embellishing furniture with landscape scenes, the Finlays incorporated architectural views of actual Baltimore houses and public buildings into their designs. This creative concept, similar to displaying a family crest on porcelain or silver, highlighted Baltimore's pride in its private and public buildings. An advertisement in the *Federal Gazette and Baltimore Daily Advertiser* of January 31, 1803, describes Finlay tables and cane-seat chairs "painted and gilt in the most fanciful manner, with and without views adjacent to this city."[14] A thirteen-piece suite of painted furniture by the Finlay shop is embellished with paintings of public and private buildings representing Baltimore architecture of the late eighteenth century. It is believed that Francis

3.21

3.22

3·23

FIGURE 3.23:
*Candelabrum, one of a pair,
1804–1820, French; signed
"Rabiat, France"; gilt bronze,
cast; height, 35³/₄ inches.*
COLLECTION OF THE SAINT
LOUIS ART MUSEUM,
DECORATIVE ARTS AND DESIGN,
FRIENDS' PURCHASE WITH
FUNDS DONATED BY THE
MEASUREGRAPH COMPANY IN
HONOR OF HENRY B. PFLAGER,
119:1971.1.

*Pedestal, one of a pair,
circa 1820, Baltimore; white
pine with painted and gilded
decoration; height, 36 inches.*
COLLECTION OF THE SAINT
LOUIS ART MUSEUM,
DECORATIVE ARTS AND DESIGN,
FRIENDS' PURCHASE WITH
FUNDS DONATED BY THE
MEASUREGRAPH COMPANY IN
HONOR OF HENRY B. PFLAGER,
118:1971.1.

FIGURE 3.24: *Drawing
from a sketchbook, circa
1817, Robert Gilmor Jr.;
watercolor on paper; 7 x 9¹/₄
inches.*
COLLECTION OF THE
MARYLAND HISTORICAL
SOCIETY, BALTIMORE.

Guy painted the seventeen architectural views on this set. Since only two of the houses, Homewood and Mount Clare, exist today, the entire set serves as a surviving record of these buildings. Homewood, originally owned by Declaration of Independence signer Charles Carroll, stands today on the campus of Johns Hopkins University. Mount Clare, the home of Charles Carroll, a lawyer, is located today in Carroll Park. Part of this furniture suite is the armchair in figure 3.19, which depicts Rose Hill, built circa 1800 by William Gibson. The card table in figure 3.22 displays the home of Charles Carroll. This house was restored in 1972 by Victor C. B. Covey and Kay Silberfield. At that time the restorers learned how the actual painting was accomplished, and they came to realize the intricacy of the method used by the original painters. The restorers reported that black paint covered the entire surface of the table, including areas underneath the Mount Clare painting. This was followed by an application of copper-colored gilt, which accented the decorative design on the legs and skirt. Yellow striping was also applied on the legs. White paint was applied over the gilt, further enhancing the design, and finally, a thin black border outlined the sides and bottom of the architectural scene. The most significant fact of the restorers' discovery is that the roofline of the building extended past the gilt of the frame, proving that the scroll decoration was applied first.[15]

During conservation it was also learned that a gilder executed the decorative designs, like the gilt paterae—a classical Greek ornament in the shape of a circle or ovoid—while an accomplished artist such as Francis Guy painted the architectural views. Stiles Colwill, in the 1981 exhibition catalog of the work of Francis Guy, compares Guy's canvas landscapes to those on painted furniture. The same brushwork and "overall plein air quality of the two views . . . reflect a single artist's technique."[16] To paint this landscape view onto the apron of the table, Guy used the same method he employed when painting views on canvas. By erecting a tent with a strategically placed window, Guy developed a method of capturing a scene utilizing white chalk on black gauze. He sketched onto the gauze the scene he saw through the window and then transferred it onto a canvas before painting it. When painting scenes on furniture, Guy used a dark background color on which to transfer his sketches.[17]

Another landscape painter who worked with the Finlay shop was Cornelius de Beet. He was listed in the Baltimore city directories from 1810 to 1840 as a fancy painter or ornamental painter. A letter, now in the collection of the Massachusetts Historical Society, was written in 1825 by the painter Rembrandt Peale to Thomas Jefferson. This letter states that de Beet "was engaged in Baltimore ornamenting Windsor chairs for Messrs. Finlay when I became acquainted with him and it is only of late that he has attempted to make pictures or landscapes. I cannot but think his practice on the chairs has been injurious to his taste."[18] The table shown in figure 3.16 has been attributed to both the Finlay shop and de Beet.

Members of the Baltimore elite turned to Europe for the latest in refined taste. Travel abroad heightened their awareness of European culture and classical antiquities and greatly affected the manner in which they decorated their homes. Robert Gilmor Jr., a merchant, patron of the arts, and major force in establishing the Maryland Historical Society, traveled abroad collecting neoclassical artifacts. The excitement and appreciation he felt for European culture and history were captured in his letters, journals, and drawings. A drawing from Gilmor's travel journal (figure 3.24) shows a richly decorated drawing room in a European friend's home. This room could easily have been in the nineteenth-century home of a wealthy Baltimorean.

Considering Europe the epitome of fine taste, affluent Americans developed a keen interest in anything European. It was

3.26

FIGURE 3.25: *Portrait of a Seated Boy, 1825, probably Pennsylvania; painted by Bass Otis; oil on canvas; 20 3/4 x 14 3/4 inches.* COLLECTION OF THE WESTMORELAND MUSEUM OF ART, WILLIAM A. COULTER FUND, 60.91.

FIGURE 3.26: *Window bench (or stool), 1820–1840, Baltimore; attributed to John Finlay and/or Hugh Finlay; cherry and walnut painted to simulate rosewood; 24 x 72 x 21 inches.* COLLECTION OF GEORGE M. AND LINDA H. KAUFMAN.

BALTIMORE | 67

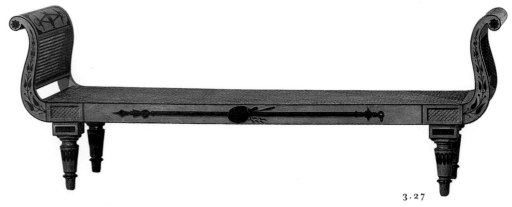

3.27

FIGURE 3.27: *Sofa, circa 1810, Baltimore; wood painted ochre with polychrome neoclassical decorations; 86³/₄ x 30¹/₂ x 24 inches. The decorative motif of an artist's palette alludes to the owner's talent as an artist and also symbolizes the present subject, painted furniture.*
COURTESY OF PETER HILL, INC.

FIGURE 3.28: *Window seat, 1810–1820, Baltimore; attributed to John and Hugh Finlay; pine and poplar, painted, stenciled, and grained; 12⁵/₈ x 47 x 16 inches. This rectangular bench is adorned with palmettes, sheafs of wheat, and griffins, all popular classical motifs seen on Baltimore painted furniture. The gilt designs are painted in ochre, red, brown, and white, with green and yellow panels shaded black. This ornamental scheme was executed freehand.*
COLLECTION OF THE SAINT LOUIS ART MUSEUM, DECORATIVE ARTS AND DESIGN, 1571:1983.

fashionable to import textiles, porcelains, wallpaper, statuary, chandeliers, and lamps. The French gilt bronze candelabrum in figure 3.23 was placed on a polychromed and stenciled gilt pedestal and then embellished by a decorative painter. The manner of displaying this candelabrum is indicative of the way in which the European and American styles were successfully combined.

The nineteenth-century homes of the wealthy were impressive structures. Many had a front parlor or drawing room for formal entertaining and a rear parlor for family. In most houses, the drawing room furniture consisted of chairs arranged along the walls. Catherine Beecher, in *Letters to Persons Who Are Employed in Domestic Service*, stressed the importance of not allowing the chairs to go awry "as if dancing a jig with each other."[19] Equally fashionable were pairs of pier tables or card tables adorned with paint and gilding, sometimes with faux marble tops. These tables were

also placed against the walls so that gilt-framed looking glasses could be hung above them.

Elaborate mirrors were yet another way for affluent homeowners to display their fashionable taste. George Smith, a craftsman in Federal Baltimore, was noted for exquisite gilded mirrors. He was a carver and gilder who also sold framed prints and pictures as well as resilvering glasses, making venetian blinds, gilded cornices, and brackets, etc.[20] The mirror in figure 3.6 is attributed to George Smith.

Gilding not only decorated furniture and accessories but also embellished the interior architecture of homes, making the rooms glitter in the evening when candles and lamps were lit and details on the walls and wallpaper were revealed. Gilding enhanced the woodwork and wallpaper in elegant drawing rooms as well. Other means of embellishing the interior of these fine homes included faux wood treatments, faux marbling, stenciling, and painted floorcloths.

The parlor, decorated in this manner, was meant to impress guests while they were being entertained and was the room that demanded the most constant attention. When guests were received in the late afternoon and early evening, socializing often included music. In the nineteenth century, music demonstrated cultivated taste and refinement. Therefore a piano often graced the parlor and provided an evening's entertainment. Elizabeth Garrett spoke of the importance of musical accomplishment for a young woman when she wrote, "When a daughter sat down to perform for a

3.28

parlorful of guests, such tunes pronounced the genteel education her parents had procured her, and not without considerable expense."[21] Portraits of these cultivated young women performing at the piano serve as documentation of this notion of style. The pianoforte also provided an ideal place for masters of painted furniture to display their talent. Joseph Hiskey of Baltimore made the pianoforte shown in figure 3.7. The romantic landscape above the keyboard was engraved by John Medairy and William Bannerman from drawings by Samuel Smith, another Baltimore artist.

By the early nineteenth century, yet another place for furniture was created in many homes when architects began to build a recessed area under windows where benches or stools could be placed. Robert Gilmor's inventory lists "2 Painted Chintz covered Window seats" in his dining room.[22] Window seats reflected a variety of styles, and some were fashioned to look like the painted window seat in *Portrait of a Seated Boy* (figure 3.25). Another window seat, shown in figure 3.28, is decorated with classically inspired motifs of pal-

mettes, griffins, and sheafs of wheat. The graceful window bench in figure 3.26 has been painted to simulate rosewood, with gilded anthemia and rosettes completing the design.

THE EMPIRE PERIOD

After the War of 1812 a new style of painted furniture influenced by the English Regency style became popular. In 1812 the English designer George Smith wrote *A Collection of Ornamental Designs,* a book that may have had an impact on many local ornamenters.[23] Charles Percier and Pierre François Léonard Fontaine's *Recueil de Décorations Intérieures* (Paris, 1812) also inspired some of the painted motifs found on the furniture of this period.[24]

In the early neoclassical period, furniture was painted a single ground color, but in the new style of the Empire period, the furniture was painted with a grain to simulate rosewood. Some pieces were embellished with stenciling, freehand brushwork, pigment powders, and gold leaf. The card table in figure 3.30, for example, reveals a rosewood-grained top with a scrolled acanthus and anthemion border. The central panel on the apron consists of a

FIGURE 3.29: *Grecian couch, 1820–1840, Baltimore; attributed to John or Hugh Finlay; yellow poplar, cherry, white pine; faux rosewood graining and freehand gilding; 35³/₄ x 91¹/₂ x 24¹/₄ inches.* COLLECTION OF THE MUSEUM OF FINE ARTS, BOSTON, GIFT OF MR. AND MRS. AMOS B. HOSTETTER JR., ANNE AND JOSEPH P. PELLEGRINO, MR. AND MRS. PETER S. LYNCH, MR. WILLIAM N. BANKS, EDDY G. NICHOLSON, MR. AND MRS. JOHN LASTAVICA, MR. AND MRS. DANIEL F. MORLEY, AND MARY S. AND EDWARD J. HOLMES FUND, 1988.530.

3.29

FIGURE 3.30: *Card
table, 1819, Baltimore; made
by Hugh Finlay; painted to
imitate rosewood, gold leaf,
gilt, paint stencil design, and
freehand decoration; height,
29 inches. This rectangular
card table with X-base and
scrolled brackets is a common
form seen on Baltimore
furniture from the Empire
period. The faux rosewood
graining consists of a red
ground, sometimes called
Pompeian red, streaked with
black-umber. Decoration
above the rosewood graining
consists of oil-gilt banding,
pale yellow striping, and gilt or
painted stenciled designs.*
COLLECTION OF THE
PRESTWOULD FOUNDATION.
PHOTOGRAPH BY HANS
LORENZ.

frieze of stenciled fruits, flowers, and foliage artfully laid above a medium brown background and colored with paints ranging from cream to red-brown to dark brown-black. Some shading may have been applied using stencils and pigment powders over a tacky surface. Freehand detail work employed these same muted colors. These techniques produced an illusion of depth and an interesting sepia-toned antique effect. Stencils, oil size, and gold leaf were applied to the scrolled anthemia. This design emanated from the stamped brass rosettes on the shaped brackets of the base and from the anthemia and scrolls on the edges of the top. Here also freehand detail in red-brown and dark brown provided shading.[25] This table is one of a pair of card tables that Humberston Skipwith ordered for $120 in 1819 from Hugh Finlay for his home, Prestwould, in Clarksville, Virginia.[26]

By the 1820s the popularity of imitation rosewood graining had increased, and ornamenters were able to create a rendering of rosewood almost identical to the actual wood. The strong paint strokes on the Grecian couch in figure 3.3 successfully combine faux rosewood graining with gilded neoclassical motifs. The leafy rosettes and elongated anthemia reflect the motifs of the late neoclassical period of Baltimore painted furniture. By painting black shadows around each motif, the artist forced the gilded decorative motifs to stand out. This piece is an excellent example of faux rosewood with gilded decoration imitating ormolu furniture mounts. Unlike the gilded decoration described in Chapter 4, the application of the gilded decoration of the window bench in figure 3.26 and this Grecian couch results in an almost three-dimensional quality. Once again the couch and the window bench are attributed to the Finlay shop.

3.30

HIGH-STYLE FURNITURE

3.31

FIGURE 3.31: *Side chair, 1815–1820, Baltimore; possibly made by John and Hugh Finlay; maple painted gold with black and green decoration, freehand gilt decoration, and stenciling; height, 34 inches. This chair, an adaptation of the Roman version of the Greek klismos chair, is one of a set made for Woodburne, the home of the Abell family of Baltimore. Each chair's crest rail has a slightly different decoration including griffins, unicorns, and other mythological figures set on a black-green background. The curved back of this chair derives its form from the Grecian klismos and its turned front legs from Roman saber legs.* COLLECTION OF THE METROPOLITAN MUSEUM OF ART, PURCHASE, MRS. PAUL MOORE GIFT, 1965, 65.167.6.

3·32

FIGURE 3.32: *Detail of Plate 56 from* The Cabinet-Maker and Upholsterer's Drawing-Book *[1793], Thomas Sheraton. The crest rail design in figure 3.31 is most likely derived from this illustration.* PRIVATE COLLECTION.

HIGH-STYLE FURNITURE

In this same period the ancient Grecian klismos chair was being adapted in Baltimore. Sometimes referred to as a Grecian chair, this style was exquisitely produced for the wealthy, and was copied for the mass market and exported as far away as South America and the Caribbean.[27] A study of the modified version of a Greco-Roman klismos chair in figure 3.31 reveals that it is painted with freehand gilt and polychrome decoration in addition to stencil decoration. The chair, one of a set attributed to the Finlays, was made between 1815 and 1820 for Woodburne, the home of Arunah S. Abell of Baltimore. All the crest designs are different with the use of griffins, unicorns, and classical motifs. Flanking each animal are Grecian scrolls on a field of black-green. The artist most likely derived the design from Plate 56 in Sheraton's *The Cabinet-Maker*

and Upholsterer's Drawing-Book, 1802 edition (figure 3.32).

These chairs show winged thunderbolts and fan-shaped palmettes on the side seat rails above the front and back legs—designs that are repeated on other Baltimore furniture from this period. It is interesting to note that a pier table (figure 3.34) made for Alexander Brown, a shipping and banking entrepreneur, has very similar winged thunderbolts, which were colored in verd antique, as were the palmettes on the apron, the stripes and rings on the column shafts, and the large water leaves on the column bases.[28] Pompeian red paint and the faux marble top and base make this piece outstanding. This table was part of a set attributed to the Finlays, who at the time were the only firm advertising multiform suites.[29] They were also the only firm with knowledge

3.33

FIGURE 3.34: *Pier table, circa 1815, Baltimore; attributed to John and Hugh Finlay; poplar and other woods painted yellow and Pompeian red with polychrome, stenciled, and freehand decoration, with top and base painted to imitate marble; 34½ x 38 x 18¾ inches. Part of a set that included a sofa, a pair of window seats, a pair of card tables, a dozen chairs, and a dining table, made for Alexander Brown, a shipping and banking magnate.* COLLECTION OF THE MARYLAND HISTORICAL SOCIETY, BALTIMORE.

FIGURE 3.35: *Card table, circa 1825, Baltimore; attributed to Hugh Finlay; mahogany, poplar, and other woods painted black with freehand gilt decoration, mahogany top and applied stamped metal bases; 27½ x 35¾ x 17¾ inches. The swan motif was a popular neoclassical design derived from a French design that also decorated Baltimore fancy chairs (figure 3.9) and the Ridgely parlor set pictured (figure 3.33).* COLLECTION OF STILES TUTTLE COLWILL. PHOTOGRAPH BY ERIC KVALSVIK.

of and access to such sources as Thomas Sheraton of England and Percier and Fontaine of France. The strong influence of architect Benjamin Henry Latrobe is seen on this pier table, which incorporates the Egyptian columns that were also seen on the table made for William Waln of Philadelphia. The beautifully executed paint ornamentation was influenced by the designs of Percier and Fontaine and Sheraton.[30]

The Finlays maintained their popularity as quality craftsmen and, in 1832, were commissioned by John Carnan Ridgely and his second wife, Eliza, to make a suite of furniture for Hampton, the family mansion. Ridgely (1790–1867) was the second son of Charles Carnan Ridgely and thus the third generation to occupy the house. He commissioned a set of black-and-gold Empire-style furniture that included a sofa, fourteen chairs, a pier table, and a center table and cost $327. In figure 3.33 this entire set of extraordinary furniture is pictured in the drawing room of Hampton. Unupholstered, the sofa with gilded swans and chimera feet was the most expensive piece.[31] The gilded swans under the armrests are similar to swan motifs found in French Empire furniture by Percier and Fontaine. Eliza Ridgely, who possessed a strong interest in French decorative arts, may have suggested these motifs. It is interesting to note that this

classical motif was incorporated into other pieces of Baltimore furniture (figure 3.35) and was also seen in a New York pier table (figure 4.21).

Led by John and Hugh Finlay, Baltimore's preeminent fancy furniture makers, the craftsmen and artists of nineteenth-century Baltimore created painted furniture and decorative arts for a distinguished, knowledgeable clientele. Within forty-five years, painted furniture in this region reached new heights in artistic representation and quality construction. Stylish designs painted and gilded on furniture were extremely captivating. From the early neoclassical period, craftsmen fashioned real and imagined landscapes, architectural scenes, and classical design forms such as musical trophies and bows and quivers of arrows on crest rails of chairs and settees. In the later Empire period, gilded motifs such as anthemia, rosettes, and winged thunderbolts ornamented faux rosewood graining. Tables, window seats, and Grecian chairs and couches were emblazoned with these popular designs. Baltimore's sophistication combined with the affluence of its citizens to support an atmosphere conducive to artistic creativity. A lack of competition increased the demand for commissioned sets of fancy furniture during the Empire period and enhanced the reputation of the Finlay shop.

3.34

3.35

FIGURE 3.36 : *Pair of side chairs, 1815, Baltimore; made by John and Hugh Finlay; yellow poplar, maple, and walnut painted and gilded, with caning; height, 29 inches. These chairs, part of a set of twelve, are documented as having been made for Richard Ragan (1776–1850), a Hagerstown merchant.* COLLECTION OF MR. AND MRS. STUART FELD.

3.36

NEW
YORK

CITY

O**N APRIL 30, 1789,** a fourteen-year-old Bostonian, Mary Palmer Tyler, was in New York City. Standing on the sheltered stoop of a nearby house, she watched George Washington take the oath of office on the colonnaded balcony of the newly renovated Federal Hall (figure 4.1). "It never rained faster . . . than it did that day," she later recalled. "I saw the Chancellor [Livingston] read from a paper what we all supposed to be the oath; I saw Washington bow himself and kiss the sacred volume. When the Chancellor waved his hat, saying, 'Long live George Washington!,' this was a sign that the ceremony was completed; when all that immense crowd tossed their hats in the air and almost rent their throats with hurrahs for several moments, repeating, 'Long live George Washington!' while he answered their enthusiasm by repeated bows on all sides."[1] A year after this momentous occasion, the federal government moved to Philadelphia and few imagined that the modest port of New York City would soon develop into "the great commercial emporium of America."

The large, deep bay formed by the confluence of the Hudson and East Rivers as they entered the Atlantic Ocean provided Manhattan Island with a natural saltwater harbor that offered easy access in all seasons and sufficient depth of water for the sloops, brigs, and schooners to come right up to the wharves. Given this advantage, New York was truly "a city and a sea port, possessing advantages unequaled in the world."[2] Many of the narrow, winding streets around Federal Hall led to banks of the rivers, where cargoes were loaded and unloaded.

Along Pearl Street wholesale dry goods were sold. Brokers gathered to

HIGH-STYLE FURNITURE

4·3

PAGE 76

FIGURE 4.1: *Federal Hall and Wall Street, 1798, New York; by Archibald Robertson; watercolor; 8⅜ x 11 inches. George Washington was sworn in as first president on the balcony of Federal Hall.* COLLECTION OF THE NEW-YORK HISTORICAL SOCIETY, 1864.14.

PAGE 77

FIGURE 4.2: *Recamier, circa 1825, probably New York; mahogany, poplar, and black ash painted black with gilded penwork, stenciling, and verd antique; 29 x 65 x 22½ inches. This is part of a set that includes the six side chairs in figure 4.13.* PHOTOGRAPH COURTESY OF MILLIE MCGEHEE.

FIGURE 4.3: *Family group in New York interior, 1807; painted by François Joseph Bourgoin (a. 1762–1817); oil on canvas; signed, dated, and inscribed on lower right, "J. Bourgoin, pt/New-york-1807-"; 30 x 42 inches.* PHOTOGRAPH COURTESY OF BERRY-HILL GALLERIES, INC.

speculate in all forms of securities at the Tontine Coffee House at the corner of Wall and Water Streets. And elegant retail shops had begun to line Broadway.

The rapid economic growth following Washington's inauguration prompted Perrin du Lac to write in 1801 that "everything in the city is in motion, everywhere the shops resound with the noise of workers. . . . One sees vessels arriving from every part of the world, or ready to depart, and . . . one cannot better describe the opulence of this still new city than to compare it to ancient Tyre, which contemporary authors called the queen of commerce and the sovereign of the seas."[3]

The census of 1790 recorded only 33,131 residents, but ten years later the population of New York had nearly doubled and by 1810 it had tripled to 96,373.[4] As the city's population exploded, the number of houses increased, and New York cabinetmakers pressed their advantage. An 1805 city directory listed sixty-six cabinetmakers, nineteen chair makers, and fifteen carvers and gilders and declared that "the furniture daily offered for sale equals, in point of elegance, any ever imported from Europe, and is scarcely equal in any other city in America."[5] By 1820, New York's financial and commercial preeminence was firmly established, and the city's cabinetmakers superseded those of Philadelphia in the leadership in design and production of furniture. The completion of the Erie Canal in 1825 and the development of coastal packet boat lines allowed New York furniture makers to expand their market as the population grew and moved west. New York remained in the forefront of furniture design and production until the end of the nineteenth century.

The great trading ships that plied the waters of the Atlantic and Pacific Oceans brought goods and resources from all over the world to New York: mahogany and rosewood from the Caribbean and Latin America; metal mounts, hardware, brushes, and paint pigments from France and England; and upholstery textiles from Europe and Asia. Like the other urban furniture centers, New York absorbed French and English furniture styles through published designs, pattern books, periodicals, and trade manuals as well as through the importation of furniture and other decorative objects. Primarily, though, it was the arrival of skilled and ambitious cabinetmakers and other guild-trained craftsmen that brought European furniture styles to this country. Indeed, nearly every furniture style was produced by one or another of New York's leading immigrant craftsmen.

The Scottish-born cabinetmaker Duncan Phyfe (c. 1768–1854), active in New York from 1792 to 1847, was the most visible progenitor of the first phase of neoclassicism, which lasted from 1790 to 1815. The second half of the neoclassical era, from 1815 to 1825, was led by the French *ébéniste* (cabinetmaker) Charles-Honoré Lannuier (1779–1819), who worked in New York from 1804 until his untimely death in 1819. Lannuier's furniture constituted an original synthesis of the Louis XVI and French Empire styles into an American design vocabulary that has rarely been duplicated. The Gothic Revival (1835–1850) was eloquently interpreted by the French cabinetmaker Alexander Roux (c. 1813–1886), and the Rococo Revival of the 1850s to the 1870s was defined by German-born John Henry Belter (1804–1863), who brought a distinctive American interpretation of French rococo design to mid-century furniture.

The Egyptian Revival of the late 1860s and 1870s had at its forefront the French-born Auguste Pottier (1823–1896) and his partner, William Pierre Stymus, after the formation of their firm of Pottier & Stymus Mfg. Co. by 1859. The Renaissance Revival style of the 1860s and 1870s, manifesting itself in a number of subcategories romantically evocative of the great ages of the past, was led by another French immigrant to New York, Leon Marcotte (1824–1887). Finally, at the end of the nineteenth century, the Aesthetic style of 1875 to 1895, with its intermixed elements of

HIGH-STYLE FURNITURE

4·4

4·5

Far Eastern, Middle Eastern or Moorish, classical, and European designs, found full expression in the furniture of German-born brothers Gustave (1830–1898) and Christian Herter (1839–1883). Their firm, Herter Brothers, which began production in New York in 1851, served wealthy patrons by providing fine handcrafted furniture until the beginning of the twentieth century.

New York's dynamic economy created an eager market for new furniture forms made in the latest fashions from the finest woods, exhibiting skilled craftsmanship and sophisticated decorative techniques. Though it evokes a myriad of historical styles, nineteenth-century furniture is highly original and distinctly American by virtue of its place, style, and materials. New York furniture of the nineteenth century exhibits the use of a full vocabulary of decorative techniques: japanning, gilding, verd antique, bronze powder stenciling, hand-gilt penwork, staining, varnishing and ebonizing of woods were used in the first half of the century; gilded incising, hand-painted plaques, faux graining, and polychrome surfaces represent stylish com-

ponents, both borrowed and original, from the 1860s to the 1880s.

NEOCLASSICAL FURNITURE

Despite their political break with England, Federal-era Americans continued to look to London for models in architecture, furniture, and fashion. The architectural designs and illustrations in Robert and James Adam's *Works in Architecture* (London, 1773–1779), featuring motifs—swags, paterae, urns, fans, bellflowers, honeysuckle vines, beribboned sheaves of wheat, painted dolphins, and armorial devices—were transformed into styles for furniture in illustrated pattern books published by George Hepplewhite and Thomas Sheraton. Inspired by these publications and by imported examples, New York cabinetmakers responded with a distinctly American interpretation of English fancy furniture. The family portrait dated 1807 by François Joseph Bourgoin (a. 1762–1817) in figure 4.3 illustrates the interior of a New York Federal home. Delicate rosewood and mahogany furniture on a patterned Brussels carpet is representative of a front parlor of a town house. The

FIGURE 4.4: *Side chair, 1800, New York; maker unknown; black ash, cherry, and white pine with painted decoration; height, 34½ inches.*
PHOTOGRAPH COURTESY OF HIRSCHL & ADLER GALLERIES, INC.

FIGURE 4.5: *Armchair, 1800–1815, probably New York; birch seat rails, maple legs; 34⅜ x 19¼ x 19¾ inches.*

COLLECTION OF THE MARYLAND HISTORICAL SOCIETY, GIFT OF MRS. VAN SANTWOOD MERLE-SMITH JR. (KATHERINE P. N. SMITH) IN MEMORY OF MR. AND MRS. EDMUND LAW ROGERS SMITH, 78.50.2. PHOTOGRAPH BY JEFF D. GOLDMAN.

4.6

wood mantel with gilded urn and swag patterns is topped with a pair of Argand lamps that are hand-painted red and marble obelisks. Along with the paintings on the walls, the scene is suggestive of a Federal-era New York family of means and cultured intelligence. The yellow-painted side chair drawn up to the desk is an American interpretation of the English Regency paint-decorated chairs that captivated sophisticated patrons in Baltimore, Boston, and New York.

While this room features a single painted chair, surviving sets of early New York painted furniture suggest that whole rooms were filled with suites of painted furniture. The side chair in figure 4.4 is part of a larger set of furniture that includes surviving side chairs and a settee. In these examples, the urn splat of the chairs is flanked by vertical rails embellished with flowers in natural colors on a simulated rosewood ground. The polychrome roses and flowers extend into the crest rails as four-petaled stylized flowers in white, with green foliage adorning the stiles and legs. Like many American furniture forms, this suite of furniture is not a slavish copy of an English exam-

ple; it exhibits a more spontaneous linear form, the pastel colors are lighter, and the flowers are more abstract and freely rendered than on English examples. Chair maker John Mitchell in 1796 advertised that he made "dyed and japanned Chairs in the most tasty manner, and in the now prevailing fashion in London with hair or rush bottoms."[6] This set of New York polychromed chairs on a black ground and the armchair in figure 4.5 on a white ground capture the essence of these sophisticated alternatives to carved mahogany furniture.

The 1805–1806 New York City Directory lists nineteen chair makers, saying of their trade, "The necessary article of Chairs are manufactured in this city in large quantities, and for elegance and strength, no way inferior to the cabinet furniture. That of fancy is carried to an unrivalled degree of elegance."[7] Surviving trade cards, newspaper advertisements, labeled furniture, port manifests, and inventories help to identify a host of New York fancy chair makers, including George W. Skellorn (figure 4.6), Henry Dean (figure 4.9), Thomas and William

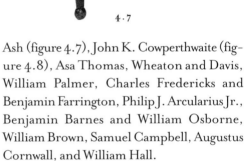

4·7

4·8

FIGURE 4.7: *Fancy side chair, 1815–1825, New York; possibly made by William Ash; maple and painted decoration; $33^{1}/_{4}$ x 18 x 16 inches. This is a landscape chair with a scene in the reserve on the top rail of the back of the chair.* NEW YORK STATE MUSEUM, LONG-TERM LOAN FROM THE WUNSCH AMERICANA FOUNDATION, 3.1972.1-A-B.

FIGURE 4.8: *Fancy armchair, 1810–1820, New York; attributed to John K. Cowperthwaite; maple, tulip, and painted decoration; 35 x 20 x 16 inches. On a white ground decorated with colored drapery, tassels, and shells, this chair is the elegant product of the New York fancy chair industry.* COLLECTION OF THE WINTERTHUR MUSEUM, GARDENS & LIBRARY, 57.973.

FIGURE 4.9: *Advertisement for Bruce & Dean's Fancy Chair Manufactory, circa 1818. Fancy chairs are displayed in front of the windows and inside the open door.* PHOTOGRAPH COURTESY OF THE MUSEUM OF THE CITY OF NEW YORK, THE J. CLARENCE DAVIES COLLECTION, 29.100.1767.

4·9

Ash (figure 4.7), John K. Cowperthwaite (figure 4.8), Asa Thomas, Wheaton and Davis, William Palmer, Charles Fredericks and Benjamin Farrington, Philip J. Arcularius Jr., Benjamin Barnes and William Osborne, William Brown, Samuel Campbell, Augustus Cornwall, and William Hall.

Windsor chair maker John De Witt & Company advertised "Windsor Chairs japann'd and neatly flowered," as did Walter M'Bride, whose chairs were "japanned any colour and neatly flowered." Other Windsor chair makers included Karns and Hazlet; G. Leggett; Isaac Van Dyke, who moved from Philadelphia to New York; Thomas Timpson; and James Always, who advertised Windsor chairs in both plain and fancy colors. The firm of Timpson & Gillihen advertised that their Windsor chairs were "stuffed over the seat, and brass nailed round the edge."[8]

The trade card of Scottish-born William Buttre of W. Buttre's Fancy Chair Manufactory, located at 17 Bowery and 15 Crane Wharf, provides an invaluable resource for understanding the shop practices of the New York fancy chair makers (figure 4.10).

Depicted here is the division of labor used in the production of fancy chairs. The work of six specialists is overseen by the head of the firm, dressed in a suit, directing the activities in the center. One artisan turns the chair members on a lathe, another assembles the chair, and a third canes the seat. Once construction is completed, the chair is sent to the paint room, away from the sawdust created in the production process. Here an apprentice grinds pigments and prepares the paint; a second artisan applies the ground coat. The ornamental painter—wearing a suit, suggesting his elevated status—then lays on the finely painted decorative details. The chair is finished with varnish, presumably added by the artisan who applied the ground.[9] A prodigious number of fancy chairs were produced in New York in this preindustrial production system.

As demand increased for New York fancy furniture, power-driven machinery cut chair parts from templates to increase production. Expansive trade routes and the use of interchangeable standardized parts resulted in New York fancy chair makers presenting stiff competition to chair makers from Maine to Saint

W. BUTTRE'S *FANCY CHAIR MANUFACTORY*.
Wholesale & Retail,
Nº 17, Bowery and Nº 15, Crane-wharf, N.York.

4.10

Louis and south to Buenos Aires. New York fancy chairs could be obtained by special commission by residents of towns and cities throughout the country using a middleman. For example, the Portsmouth, New Hampshire, merchant Jacob Wendell (1788–1865) commissioned a suite of fourteen chairs and one settee of painted furniture from the New York firm of Bailey and Willis (figure 4.11). Bailey and Willis are not listed as chair makers in New York directories; they may have been broad-based retail merchants who provided clients with a variety of New York goods.[10] Indeed, retail merchants and auctioneers became important middlemen for cabinetmakers and chair makers who, with increasingly heavy consumer demands, began to change their marketing practices after the first quarter of the nineteenth century.

The cachet of New York fancy chairs throughout the country is evidenced by advertisements found in other American cities including Portsmouth, New Orleans, Cincinnati, Saint Louis, Columbus, and San Francisco. A Savannah, Georgia, cabinetmaker's advertisement announced that he had "just returned from the north, & has now an opportunity of offering for sale an elegant assortment of the most fashionable CHAIRS."[11] New York chair makers cut chair parts and shipped "knocked down" parts in bundles to agents and cabinetmakers in Savannah, who would then assemble the chairs. Occasionally the chair parts were sent unpainted, accompanied by paint and glue and then decorated by ornamental painters in Savannah.[12] Chairs shipped in this manner were advertised as "possessing the advantages of being finished on the spot, and consequently are not injured by transportation."[13] With chair parts made in New York, then assembled and painted by cabinetmakers and ornamenters in Savannah, establishing the city of origin becomes problematic.

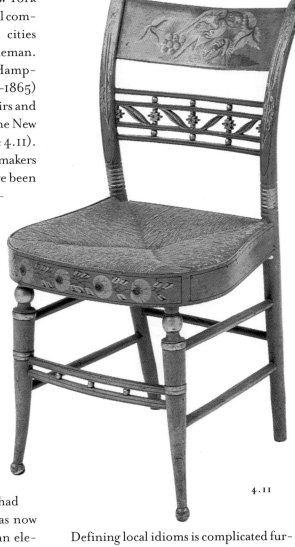

4.11

Defining local idioms is complicated further by the fact that New York ornamenters often moved, taking their New York decorative vocabulary to new cities. Advertisements in cities like Hartford, New London, and Albany offered chairs in the "most approved New York Fashion."[14] An advertisement for a Connecticut fancy chair store announced that they had obtained from New York a first-rate workman at gilding and ornamenting. If a transplanted New York ornamenter decorated a chair made of imported New York chair parts in New Haven for a Connecticut family, is it a New York chair or a Connecticut chair? To further complicate the attribution process, chairs were frequently repainted, as evidenced by both contemporary advertise-

FIGURE 4.10: *Engraved trade card for William Buttre's Fancy Chair Manufactory, circa 1813, New York. This is one of the most visually descriptive images of the manufacturing of early fancy furniture and an important source of information about early-nineteenth-century shop practices.* COURTESY OF THE WINTERTHUR MUSEUM, GARDENS & LIBRARY, JOSEPH DOWNS COLLECTION.

FIGURE 4.11: *Fancy side chair, 1815–1816, New York; hickory, yellow poplar, soft maple, and ash with painted decoration; $33^5/_8$ x 18 x $16^1/_8$ inches. This is one of a set of twelve side chairs, two armchairs, and one settee sent to Jacob Wendell of Portsmouth from the New York mercantile partnership of Benjamin Bailey and Walter Willis, who charged $5.25 for each chair.* COURTESY OF THE STRAWBERY BANKE MUSEUM, PORTSMOUTH, NEW HAMPSHIRE, GIFT OF GERRIT VAN DER WOUDE. PHOTOGRAPH COURTESY OF BRUCE ALEXANDER PHOTOGRAPHY.

ments and the daybooks of ornamental painters and cabinetmakers. New production methods, a highly mobile society, and increasing industrialization make defining regional styles of many nineteenth-century furniture forms a fascinating and ongoing exercise.

The long-held desire for all things English began to change as Federal-era Americans increasingly found political affinity with France and became intrigued by the splendor of French furniture, Parisian fashions, and Bordeaux wines. Writing to his wife, Abigail, from Paris in 1793, John Adams observed that "our countrymen are about to abandon the good old, grave, solid manners of Englishmen, their ancestors, and adopt all the apery, levity, and frivolity, of the French."[15]

While Philadelphia was the center for the production of nearly all identified painted

4.12

and gilded American furniture in the Louis XVI style, New York cabinetmakers drew from the decorative vocabulary of French furniture in other ways. Federal-era neoclassical and Empire New York–made furniture is replete with a variety of different gilding techniques. Water gilding and oil gilding, whereby gold leaf was applied using either an oil or water base, are found on furniture, mirrors, and frames. Gold and metallic powders were applied freehand or stenciled onto the flat surfaces of tables, sofas, and chairs, simulating gold ormolu mounts. Another favored embellishment was verd antique decoration, a method of imitating on wood the green color of patinated or corroded bronze sculpture. Nearly all gold leaf was imported, but by mid-century eighteen goldbeaters worked in New York.[16]

Both oil and water gilding are used in the looking glass in figure 4.12. Typical of New York mirrors is the use of several églomisé panels, seen here between the pilasters, above the columns as a central tablet, and within the triangular plinth. The decorative work in the central tablet, with foliated grapevines, delicate flowers, and entwining cornucopias, is executed in a looser, more abstract style than is found on panels produced in Baltimore and Philadelphia. The elements placed outside the outline of the mirror—including the elaborate crest ornaments above the frame, the pair of gilt wood urn finials, the wire floral springs, and the triangular plinth—are hallmarks of New York pillar looking glasses.

The second phase of America's neoclassical furniture style began around 1815 and lasted until around 1825. The light palette, delicate forms, and straight or elliptical lines of the earlier period, which were derived from Imperial Roman monuments, gave way to more archaeologically accurate adaptations of the forms and motifs of earlier Greek models. Furniture became more heavily sculptured and more deeply carved. Classically derived forms became popular—the Greek klismos chairs, Roman curule chairs with X-shaped

HIGH-STYLE FURNITURE

legs, and Grecian reclining couches. Much of the mahogany furniture of this second neo-classical period was finished with glistening varnishes and polished surfaces. New York furniture is also accented with gessoed and gilded, verd antique, and burnished gilt surfaces, freehand gold leaf gilding and penwork, or gilt-stenciled decoration, and other sophisticated decorative detailing (figure 4.13).

American cabinetmakers incorporated into their vocabulary elements of the new imperial style codified by the French architect and designer employed by Napoleon, Charles Percier (1764–1838) and Pierre François Léonard Fontaine (1762–1853). A French traveler, J. Milbert, described the furniture he saw in North America between 1815 and 1823 as:

FIGURE 4.13: *Set of six side chairs, circa 1825, probably New York; mahogany, poplar, and black ash painted black with freehand gilding and stenciling; height, 44 inches. The recamier on page 77 is part of this set.* PHOTOGRAPH COURTESY OF MILLIE MCGEHEE.

CHAISE.LONGUES.

ORNAMENT.AT.FOOT.ENLARGED

LEG.ENLARGED

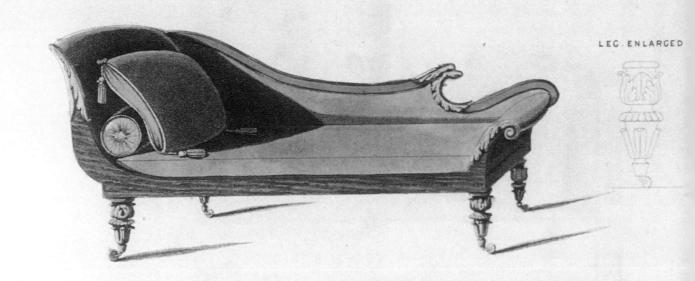

LEG.ENLARGED

4.14

SCALE.   4   3   2   1   FOR CHAISE.LONGUES.

SCALE   1   FOR ENLARGED PARTS.

LONDON. Pub.d by JONES & C.o April 22.1826.

1   2   3

DINING & DRAWING ROOM CHAIRS.

N°82.at R.ACKERMANN'S REPOSITORY of ARTS &c.Pub.Oct.1.1815.at 101.Strand.London.

4.15

FIGURE 4.14: *Plate 10 "Chaise Longues," from* The Cabinet-Maker and Upholsterer's Guide, Drawing-Book and Repository *by George Smith (London, 1826).* COLLECTION OF THE SMITHSONIAN LIBRARIES, COOPER-HEWITT, NATIONAL DESIGN MUSEUM.

FIGURE 4.15: *Plate 21, "Dining & Drawing Room Chairs" from* The Repository of the Arts *(London: Ackermann, 1809–1828).* COLLECTION OF THE SMITHSONIAN INSTITUTION LIBRARIES, COOPER-HEWITT, NATIONAL DESIGN MUSEUM.

4.16

4.17

FIGURE 4.16: *The shop and warehouse of Duncan Phyfe, 1816–1817; by John Rubens Smith (1775–1849); watercolor and pen and brown ink; 15³/₄ x 18⁷/₈ inches.* COLLECTION OF THE METROPOLITAN MUSEUM OF ART, ROGERS FUND (1922), 22.28.1.

FIGURE 4.17: *Pier table, 1820–1825, New York; attributed to Duncan Phyfe; mahogany with gilt penwork decoration; 36³/₄ x 42 x 18 inches. The mate to this pier table is in the collection of the High Museum of Art, Atlanta. The gold leaf and penwork decoration on the aprons of this table displays some of the finest pen-shaded gilt decoration known.* PHOTOGRAPH COURTESY OF PETER HILL, INC.

. . . either manufactured by the Americans or imported from France or England. Beds, tables, chairs, chests of drawers, secretaries, etc. are made here, and they are superior in construction and solidity if not in taste and shape. Elegant but fragile pieces of French furniture can not stand competition with the perfectly filled American products of heavy mahogany. However, to pay our country its due homage, I shall add that French workmen started this business in America and it is they who are developing it most successfully. They use the best models and books on furniture and interior decoration by Messieurs Percier and Fontaine.[17]

Percier and Fontaine produced a stream of publications from 1798 on, the most influential of which was *Recueil de Décorations Intérieures (Collection of Interior Decorations)*, a set of seventy-two plates illustrating the authors' work. The plates appeared in twelve installments of six sheets each, the first of which was issued in 1801, and was completed in 1812, when all seventy-two plates were bound together, along with an introduction and description of the plates. (A second edition appeared in 1827.) These plates displayed bold, archaeologically inspired interiors and were soon known throughout Europe. This French Empire style was reinterpreted by Thomas Hope, an Englishman who published his own book of designs, *Household Furniture and Interior Decoration,* in 1807. The same year another Englishman, George Smith, produced a similar pattern book titled *The Cabinet-Maker and Upholsterer's Guide, Drawing-Book and Repository* (figure 4.14). Other vehicles for the dissemination of this style in America were Rudolph Ackermann's *The Repository of the Arts* (figure 4.15), a widely circulated periodical published from 1809 to 1828 in England, and Pierre de La Mésangère's *Collection des Meubles et Objets de Goût,* published serially in France from 1796 to 1830. Copies of these publications, brought to New York by American travelers and others, found their way into private collections and libraries.

Duncan Phyfe, New York's most celebrated Federal-era cabinetmaker, located his shop,

4.18

warehouse, and showroom at 168–72 Fulton Street (figure 4.16). This well-chosen location, near Broadway just north of Bowling Green, was described by James Fenimore Cooper as "the fashionable mall of the city."[18] In his own adaptation of the French ormolu mounts, Duncan Phyfe's workshop produced exquisite and masterfully executed freehand gilding decoration, often on faux-grained rosewood backgrounds. The pier table in figure 4.17 exhibits freehand gilding and penwork decoration on the apron in a pattern derived from French sources. Executed by applying gold leaf to an oil size painted in a pattern over a varnished surface, the gilding is shaded with India ink using a quill pen to provide a three-dimensional appearance.[19] The final effect of this technique is similar in appearance to etchings or fine copper plate engraving. Phyfe's rendering of the classical designs, using the freehand gilded decoration, differs from those found on Baltimore furniture, which are rendered in a more painterly

fashion. The Baltimore examples create shading with black and red outlines applied with a pencil or very thin camel's-hair brush on a ground of loosely executed rosewood graining. Little is known of the shop practices of Duncan Phyfe, and it remains unclear if this ornamentation was executed in his shop or commissioned to another New York ornamenter.

One of the most popular nineteenth-century furniture forms is the klismos chair, derived from images of chairs found on Greek vases. This style was interpreted into furniture designs by Thomas Hope, Charles Percier and Pierre François Léonard Fontaine and diagrammed in the *New York Book of Prices* of 1817. Referred to as "Grecian" or "skroll back" chairs, they were made in sets for drawing rooms and parlors. The smooth, broad scroll backs, tablet tops, and deeply swept side rails ending in paw feet were embellished in every major city with distinctive decorative motifs. New York klismos chairs are distinguished by their construction and the use of stencils and bronze powders and freehand gilding and penwork on highly imitative rosewood-painted or japanned grounds. The klismos-

FIGURE 4.18: *Side chair, 1815–1825, New York; maple, rosewood-grained ground with gilt and caned seat; 32 1/8 x 18 x 20 3/4 inches. The gilded decoration is derived from a number of common motifs of the period— spread eagles, cornucopias, and lion heads derived from classical motifs with a decidedly patriotic bent.* PHOTOGRAPH COURTESY OF BERNARD & S. DEAN LEVY, INC.

FIGURE 4.19: *Pier table, 1816–1819, New York; Charles-Honoré Lannuier (1779–1819); mahogany, verd antique and gilded, brass die-stamped and string inlay, ebony, ormolu mounts, mirror plate, and white marble top; 35 1/2 x 48 1/2 x 20 inches. Stamped twice at the top of the inside of each front leg: "[1] H. LANNUIER/NEW-YORK/[2] JACOB." The table also bears two of Lannuier's printed labels.* PHOTOGRAPH COURTESY OF HIRSCHL & ADLER GALLERIES, INC.

4.19

4.20

form chair in figure 4.18 exhibits another New York gilding technique. The crest rail, front seat rail, and upper front legs are grain-painted in imitation of rosewood; freehand-painted metallic powders are applied over this ground while it is still tacky. The shading of these areas was achieved by scratching through the gold powders with a stylus or sharp instrument rather than by using India ink as in the Phyfe pier table.[20]

Duncan Phfye's main competitor was the French-born ébéniste Charles-Honoré Lannuier, who arrived in New York in 1803 at age twenty-four. Lannuier was introduced to the commercial milieu of the city by his brother Augustine, a confectioner and distiller located at 100 Broadway. With an astute understanding of his New York clientele, Lannuier placed an advertisement in the *New York Evening Post* of July 15, 1803, in which he characterizes himself as a man who has "just arrived from France, and who has worked at his trade with the most celebrated Cabinet Makers of Europe."[21]

Lannuier's furniture was inspired by French designs in the Louis XVI and Empire styles, which he adapted to the tastes of sophisticated New Yorkers. The stamped and labeled Lannuier pier table in figure 4.19 is one of a pair thought to have been purchased by a French émigré, Armand de Balbi. Gilded and burnished details are used on the winged female figures and the acanthus leaf feet terminals as well as on the acanthus leaf supports at the top of the legs. The dark green on the figures and the feet is an example of verd antique or bronzing decoration.

Lannuier may have apprenticed in Paris with his older brother, Nicholas Lannuier, in a guild tradition with clearly defined areas of specialization. It is thus unlikely that Lannuier executed the gilded and verd antique or bronzing finishes on his furniture. He did maintain ties to the French community in New York, and he employed at least one apprentice of French descent; this suggests that a French-trained specialist in his employ might have been responsible for executing the gilding of Lannuier's New York furniture. The steps taken to produce the verd antique techniques exhibited on Lannuier's furniture have been discovered by conservation done in recent years on several pieces of Lannuier furniture. Lannuier executed verd antique or bronzing techniques that drew from the gilder's tradition. That is, his furniture usu-

HIGH-STYLE FURNITURE

4.21

4.22

ally reveals a gesso base over which two or three layers of dark green or black/brown paint had been applied. Gold powder was used sparingly on top of this layer, and the whole was sealed with a clear spirit varnish. "This technique," concludes conservator Robert Mussey, "is reflective of his [Lannuier's] familiarity with French prototypes of the period."[22] Conservation on other gilded elements of Lannuier's tables reveals gesso-coated figures and swans that are covered with a layer of red bole, water size, and gold leaf with selective burnishing.[23] Because bronzing and gilding techniques are fragile, darken with age, and have to be repainted over the years, there are few nineteenth-century examples in perfect condition. It is thus difficult to know the intended coloration of the originals, and researchers have found that there were a variety of gilding and bronzing techniques with a wide range of coloration.

EMPIRE FURNITURE

The earlier neoclassical style gave way to the bold, imposing forms of the late neoclassical period dating from 1825 to 1840. Rosewood became the preferred wood, and the bold, flat S-curved surfaces of the large and imposing

furniture of this period were often embellished with gold and bronze powders, applied as freehand or stenciled decoration. While the pianoforte was a mechanical challenge for its manufacturers, for the cabinetmakers and ornamental painters it was an opportunity to express creative genius. One of the most masterfully embellished pianofortes from this era is the rosewood and mahogany one in figure 4.20, with its elaborately decorated gold leaf and penwork. Made by Ryder & Tallman of 15 Barclay Street in New York, it is in a rare state of preservation, embodying the entire vocabulary of nineteenth-century gilt stenciling, bronzing, ebonizing, and graining. Pianofortes were placed in the parlors of genteel New York families where young daughters

4.23

FIGURE 4.21: *Pier table, 1820–1830, New York; attributed to Joseph Meeks & Son; ebonized, gilded, and stenciled woods with marble and mirror; 38 x 44 x 18 inches.*
COURTESY OF THE KAUFMAN AMERICANA FOUNDATION, NORFOLK, VIRGINIA.

FIGURE 4.22: *Whitney Family center table, circa 1825, New York; rosewood veneer with stenciled decoration and brass inlay, painted and verd antique pedestal and feet, scagliola top; 29 x 36 inches.*
COLLECTION OF THE MUSEUM OF THE CITY OF NEW YORK, GIFT OF MRS. EGERTON L. WINTHROP, 36.160.

FIGURE 4.23: *Detail of scagliola top in figure 4.22.*
COLLECTION OF THE MUSEUM OF THE CITY OF NEW YORK, GIFT OF MRS. EGERTON L. WINTHROP, 36.160.

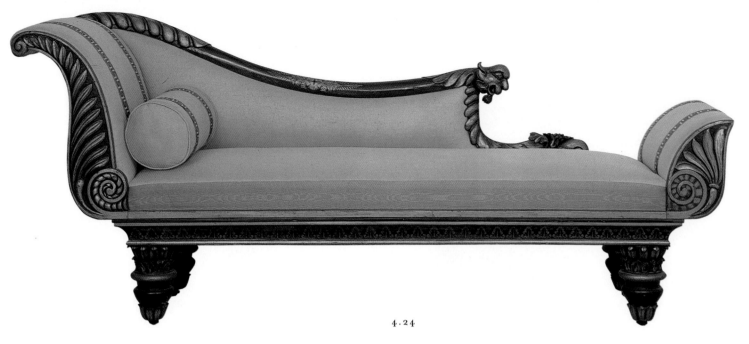

4.24

played melodies from one- and two-page song sheets while entertaining friends. New Yorkers were so accustomed to this kind of performance that the *New York Mirror* on the occasion of pianist Louis Moreau Gottschalk's New York debut in 1852 wrote: "Most people have been subject to so much thrumming of the instrument at home that they become nervous when they see an artist preparing to attack them with one in public."[24]

A host of New York furniture firms made Empire-style furniture to fill the rooms of the newly built row houses constructed by New York's growing legion of merchants and professionals. Surviving examples attest to the power of the machine and the ability of skilled craftsmen to create furniture in a grand and imposing manner for this market. Firms such as Joseph Meeks & Son, manufacturers of cabinet furniture and upholstery, prospered from the early 1830s until the late 1860s.[25] An ebonized, gilded, and stenciled pier table in the Kaufman collection is attributed to Joseph Meeks & Son (figure 4.21). The pier table stood for three generations in a Greek Revival house built in 1840 by Judge Hugh Halsey on Main Street in Bridgehampton, New York. After graduating from Yale in 1814, Halsey established a law practice in his hometown, where he later served as surveyor general for

the state of New York and as a state senator. The convex frieze on this table is stenciled with fruit and foliate motifs in gold. The pair of wood swans on metal lyre strings, the acanthus and fruit-carved legs, and the shaped plinth are stenciled with powdered gilt. This is Empire furniture at its most exuberant. Pier tables were often made in pairs, and fashion dictated that they be placed between two windows. Other furniture forms of the Empire period were center tables, with beautifully painted and gilded decoration. Placed in the middle of a parlor, tables held reading material and art objects (figures 4.22 and 4.23). An exquisitely rendered sofa of the Empire period, with stencil gilding characteristic of New York furniture of this period, is illustrated in figure 4.24.

GOTHIC AND ROCOCO REVIVALS

By 1845 the scrolled form of the Empire period gave way to new revival styles of the Gothic, which were indebted to European sources, according to A. W. N. Pugin, who in 1835 published *Gothic Furniture in the Style of the Fifteenth Century.* In America, the earliest known examples of designs for Gothic revival furniture were published in Robert Conner's *Cabinet Makers' Assistant* of 1842, followed by *The*

Architecture of Country Houses by Alexander Jackson Davis (1850). The furniture of this period and that of the Rococo Revival, a style that dominated the furniture at the London Crystal Palace Exhibition in 1851, reveal little paint decoration, gilt, or other related embellishments. A rare exception is one of a pair of gilded sofas in figure 4.27, attributed to the German-born New York cabinetmaker John Henry Belter. Belter patented and pioneered the use of laminated layers of bent steamed wood to create strong furniture that could be carved with elaborate naturalistic motifs. This furniture defined American rococo with its three-dimensional and naturalistic carving, loosely derived from French eighteenth-century prototypes.

New York increasingly became a city of elegance and creative excesses. For the entrepreneurs of the Gilded Age the cabinetmaking firms established by Leon Marcotte, Alexander Roux (figure 4.25), Pottier & Stymus, Kimble & Cabus, and the Herter Brothers came to represent the upper echelon of cabinetmaking in America. The wealthy patrons who built the Italianate mansions, French châteaux, and Gothic castles along New York's grand residential thoroughfare, Fifth Avenue, sought cabinetmakers who could also serve as decorators. Gifted cabinetmakers, supported by large firms of highly skilled artisans, provided the furniture, upholstery, and furnishings as well as the interior and exterior architectural details of these opulent homes and mansions.

EGYPTIAN REVIVAL

The arrival in New York in 1851 of the first major Egyptian collection to come to America, followed by the opening of the Suez Canal in 1869, sparked a new fascination with ancient Egypt and generated the Egyptian Revival style of the 1860s and 1870s.

The firm of Pottier & Stymus, formed after 1859, which produced some of the most thoroughly Egyptian-style furniture found in America, helped to popularize this style. The

4.25

4.26

FIGURE 4.27: *One of a pair of sofas, 1850–1860, attributed to John Henry Belter, New York; carved, laminated, and gilded rosewood; 42¹⁄₂ x 90 x 36 inches. It is extremely rare to find surviving gilded Belter furniture.*
VIRGINIA MUSEUM OF FINE ARTS, RICHMOND, VIRGINIA, GIFT OF MRS. HAMILTON FARNHAM MORRISON IN MEMORY OF HER PARENTS, ROBERT LETCHER MOORE AND JOSEPHINE LANDES MOORE. PHOTOGRAPH BY RON JENNINGS.

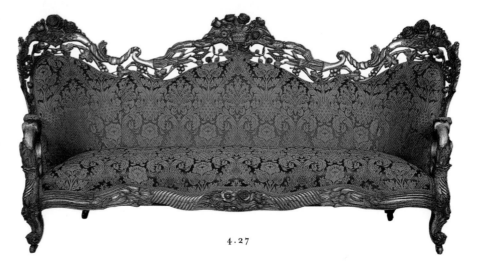

4.27

4.28

FIGURE 4.28: *Cabinet, 1848–1858, New York; attributed to Alexander Roux; ebonized rosewood with veneers and inlays of unidentified woods.* PHOTOGRAPH COURTESY OF MARGOT JOHNSON, INC.

FIGURE 4.29: *Fire screen, 1878–1880, New York; Herter Brothers; gilded cherry, painted and embossed paper, embroidered silk; 53 x 29³/₄ x 22¹/₂ inches.* COLLECTION OF MARGOT JOHNSON, INC. PHOTOGRAPH BY DAVID ALLISON.

HIGH-STYLE FURNITURE

4·29

ebonized, walnut, and gilded armchair from Pottier & Stymus in figure 4.26 is part of a larger set of parlor furniture dating to 1870–1875. Here gilding is used in a new way —as a bold highlight within incised chevrons and palm leaves on the ebonized and walnut frame. This patterning and the gilt brass sphinx heads are only loosely derived from archaeological finds in rather glamorized renditions of motifs borrowed from ancient Egyptian headdresses, jewelry, and costume. The upholstery is original to the chair, which is part of a set of furniture that undoubtedly filled a room in which Egyptian motifs covered the wall, ceiling, and floor. The factory of Pottier & Stymus, at 375 Lexington Avenue, between Forty-first and Forty-second Streets, is documented in *The Golden Book of Celebrated Manufacturers and Merchants in the United States,* which describes the factory in detail. Labor was divided by floors: the artists who painted fresco panels were on the first floor, and the finishers and gilders worked in the basement; the entire fifth floor was devoted to varnishing, modeling, painting, and gilding the architectural woodwork produced by the firm, which created and coordinated entire interiors, including wall and ceiling decoration, woodwork, furniture, and flooring.[26] For many fashion-conscious New Yorkers, Egyptian Revival–style room settings captured the allure of this exotic land.

RENAISSANCE REVIVAL

The furniture that emerged out of the Renaissance Revival style of the 1860s and 1870s evoked numerous furniture forms during the reigns of Henry II, Francis I, and Louis XVI. Harriet Prescott Spofford, author of *Art Decoration Applied to Furniture,* published in 1878, considered "nothing more luxurious" than this style. An advertisement for Alexander Roux appealed to the Gilded Age customer in many ways:

> Every article of Furniture is made under our immediate supervision of superior quality of lumber and from artistic designs.

Special attention is paid to the blending of the substantial and artistic. We have now on hand a large and splendid assortment of Plane and Artistic Furniture, such as Rosewood, Buhl, Ebony, and Gilt and Marqueterie of foreign and domestic woods, and are now prepared to execute all orders for the Furnishing of Houses, such as Wood Mantel-Pieces, Wain-scoting, Mirror-Frames, Cornices, and Cabinet-Work in general, in the best manner and at the lowest rates.[27]

The editorial note at the conclusion of the advertisement states that "the reputation of the above house is at the head of the list. Mr. Roux, to whom we refer you, is always ready to serve visitors." By this date Roux had acquired premises at 479 and 481 Broadway and, according to the 1855 New York City census, employed 120 workers in that year.[28] The furniture of Alexander Roux displayed decorative accents of delicate gold mounts, drops and incised gilded outlines, paint-decorated porcelain plaques, ebonized woods and veneers, and inlays in patterns of climbing vines and flowers (figure 4.28), reflecting his interpretation of the Louis XV and Louis XVI styles.

THE AESTHETIC MOVEMENT

In the 1870s the Aesthetic movement in America was inspired by a similar movement in Great Britain, which was a reaction to what was perceived as the vulgarity of mid-nineteenth-century design. The goals of the movement were conveyed to Americans in an outpouring of art advice and pattern books by British authors, beginning in 1868 with Charles Locke Eastlake's *Hints on Household Taste.* The movement stressed the beautification of useful objects—furniture, glass, ceramics, wallpaper, carpets, metalwork. The emphasis was on stylized surface ornamentation, which frequently consisted of geometrical floral patterns, delicate inlays, burnished gilded details, polychromed accents, and faux grains.

The firm headed by Christian Herter and his brother, Gustave, became New York's premier comprehensive decorating and furniture firm. Herter Brothers created settings and one-of-a-kind masterworks of Aesthetic era furniture for an elite clientele that included William H. Vanderbilt; LeGrand Lockwood of Norwalk, Connecticut; Darius Ogden Mill of Milbrae, California; Milton Slocum Latham of Menlo Park, California; Mark and Mary Frances Sherwood Hopkins of San Francisco; and J. Pierpont Morgan. Their furniture mixed a large vocabulary of painted and gilded decorative motifs: incised lines and reeding were highlighted with gilding or polychrome; carved details received vivid coloration executed in paint; case furniture was enlivened with polychrome panels. The artists of these decorative applications remain unknown, but examples of their work speak to their imagination and superlative skills.

The Herter brothers freely borrowed and adapted motifs and forms from a wide range of historical periods and exotic cultures, particularly new influences from the Far East, especially Japan. This marriage of Europe and Japan is evident in the fire screen made for Mark Hopkins's San Francisco mansion by the Herter brothers (figure 4.29). This gilded screen with hand-painted and embossed paper reserves of the four seasons is one of the most perfectly preserved objects of the Gilded Age. A Herter Brothers cabinet (figures 4.30 and 4.31) draws from the Japanese aesthetic in a different manner. Oil-gilded carved flowers with three shades of gilding highlight the sideboard.

The superb craftsmanship and innovative furniture produced by the city's cabinetmakers kept New York in the forefront of furniture design and production throughout the nineteenth century. In a city driven by a desire for elegance, cabinetmakers created furniture styles derivative of past styles yet highly original in the use of decorative details resulting in superb new furniture styles. This sense of innovation made New York the center of high-style furniture throughout the nineteenth century.

4.30

4.31

COUNTRY

FURNITURE

OUTSIDE THE MAJOR style centers of the East Coast, furniture makers had a long tradition of painting much of what they produced. Documentary evidence reveals that both eighteenth- and nineteenth-century American homes were filled with vivid colors and lively patterns. Faux-grained woodwork has been found under layers of paint in historic restorations from New Hampshire to Charleston and from the hills of Tennessee to the mountains of Utah. Richly pigmented paints—Venetian red, yellow ochre, Prussian blue, and blue-green verdigris—have been found on the walls of two-room cabins, as well as in the homes of America's merchant princes and presidents. The furniture in these rooms was painted, finished, and polished to complement the decorative scheme.

The rural cabinetmaker adopted paint as an effective alternative to the more costly carving, gilding, inlays, or woods used in high-style furniture. While a mahogany side chair produced in the New York City workshop of Duncan Phyfe might exhibit an intricately carved spread eagle on the midrail, rural chair makers like Lambert Hitchcock produced equally fashionable chairs for their patrons.

The country chair maker painted inexpensive woods to imitate mahogany and decorated the midrail with bronze powders using a stencil to convey the shape of a spread eagle.

At the beginning of the nineteenth century, most Americans lived on self-sustaining isolated farms. They might have made their own furniture during the winter months, but most commissioned local cabinetmakers to produce the furniture for their new homes, adding more furniture as the families grew. When the great migration of settlers from Europe and the East moved west, cabinetmakers and ornamental painters packed up their tools and brought their skills to the plains and prairies to help furnish new houses. In so doing, they reinvented the styles that they knew, and used them long after they had gone out of fashion in the East. Many wished to recreate their old homes, others made do as a result of little time and energy to devote to furnishing with fashionably styled furniture.

The vast array of paint-decorated furniture shown in the chapters that follow displays techniques that are inherent in the skills and traditions of the craftsmen. The form and decoration of country furniture is sometimes an interpretation of the styles of the urban centers, and at other times it draws heavily from the ethnic and folk traditions of its craftsmen. It also reflects the needs of the client and the tastes of the community; it conveys a purposeful desire for simplicity and a uniquely nineteenth-century self-consciousness to have one's furnishings reflect fashionable taste at a good price.

The hand of the ornamenter speaks loudly in the best of painted country furniture. The fluidity of paint allowed for the rapid and creative transformation of a plain piece of furniture into a pleasing and colorful addition to a room. Some country furniture exhibits highly expressive designs and patterns. Other examples masterfully employ a varied vocabulary of motifs. These can be derived from traditional design sources or from a symbolic iconography drawn from religion, fantasy, or other decorative arts such as textiles and printed sources. Paint was not a ready-made product until the 1860s; painters prepared their own paints from dry pigments, linseed oil, natural resin varnish, and other materials on a daily basis or as needed. Grinding and producing paint was a skill as complex as that of graining

and the laying on of paint. The most common types of paint in the nineteenth century were oil-base paints, casein or milk paints, and distemper paints. Each was used for different purposes—with oil-base paints being more expensive to produce—and each of these painted surfaces is represented here.

Painted furniture is nearly always made of soft woods, which are less expensive than hard woods but easily covered by paint. The use of paint to enhance simply crafted furniture by simulating more expensive hardwood furniture or as a camouflage for poor workmanship is only one part of the painted furniture story. Examples of finely crafted furniture reflecting the same workmanship in mahogany as in a painted and stenciled soft wood have increasingly been found. In many communities, grained painted furniture was the height of fashion and reflected highly skilled and valued craftsmanship. Some of the most visually exciting of America's nineteenth-century painted furniture are the product of nonurban artisans. It was often in small workshops that cabinetmakers and ornamenters carefully, freely, and exuberantly expressed natural talents and an unerring eye for color and design.

OVERLEAF, LEFT
FIGURE 5.1: *Centerpiece of a friendship book, 1823–1838, by Celestia Bull, dated "September 27th 1826," Winchester, Connecticut; 8 x 6¹/₂ inches. This friendship book was created by Celestia Bull for her friend Sarah Sawyer. The centerpiece depicts a New England parlor interior of the period.* COURTESY OF WALTERS–BENISEK ART AND ANTIQUES. PHOTOGRAPH BY DAVID STANSBURY.

OVERLEAF, RIGHT
FIGURE 5.2: *Tall-case clock, circa 1820, Winchester, Connecticut; attributed to Riley Whiting; pine, painted and grained; 82 x 17¹/₂ x 10¹/₂ inches. The white-painted dial is decorated with flowers and leaves; the grain-painted case in black, brown, and yellow on a brown ground simulates figured veneers in an exaggerated and precisely executed manner.* PHOTOGRAPH COURTESY OF HELAINE AND BURTON FENDELMAN.

Winchester September 27th 1826

NEW

ENGLAND

THE CONNECTICUT PARLOR IN THE 1826 watercolor (figure 5.1) has much in common with the fictional New England parlor described by Nathaniel Hawthorne in *The House of the Seven Gables*, published in 1851. In the parlor of the "rusty wooden house, with seven acutely peaked gables" there was "a carpet on the floor, originally of rich texture, but so worn and faded, in the latter years, that its once brilliant figure had quite vanished into one indistinguishable hue. In the way of furniture, there were two tables; one, constructed with perplexing intricacy, and exhibiting as many feet as a centipede; the other, most delicately wrought, with four long and slender legs, so apparently frail, that it was almost incredible what a length of time the ancient tea-table had stood upon them." In the convention of the period and as depicted in the watercolor, "half-a-dozen chairs stood about the room, straight and stiff, and so ingeniously contrived for the discomfort of the human person, that they were irksome even to sight." On the walls of the Pyncheons' parlor hung "ornamental articles of furniture," which Hawthorne describes as "a map of the Pyncheon territory . . . the handiwork of some skillful old draftsman" and a "portrait of old Colonel Pyncheon, at two thirds length."[1]

These two rooms illustrate what nineteenth-century New England probate inventories suggest—a remarkable similarity of furnishing.[2] The "noble looking mansions" that rose "like Magic"[3] in the port cities of Newburyport, Salem, and New Bedford, Massachusetts, and Portsmouth, New Hampshire, were furnished in a convention similar to the houses built by merchants in

COUNTRY FURNITURE

Burlington, Vermont, and Hartford, Connecticut. Visitors to the white clapboard houses of sheep and dairy farms in the Connecticut River valley would find rooms furnished much like those in the manufacturing towns along New England's other rivers and streams, where swift rapids and tumbling waterfalls turned mill wheels. The parlor or front room usually had a richly figured carpet, a table for serving tea or for reading and conversation, a pair of comfortable chairs, a set of fancy or Windsor chairs arranged around the perimeter of the room or in groupings to suit the occasion, and walls hung with portraits, needlework, maps, and etchings.

This consistency emanated from the desire of both urban and rural New Englanders to furnish their homes in a fashionable manner, to conform to the aesthetics of their own community, and to purchase well-made, reasonably priced furniture and furnishings.

Recalling his own past, H. Hudson Holly wrote in 1878 that "heretofore it has been the custom to buy new furniture in accordance with the latest caprice of fashion, just as a lady

selects a new bonnet."[4] Astute New England cabinetmakers composed newspaper advertisements replete with promises of furniture designed "in the newest taste" or "in the latest styles" (figure 5.3). Cabinetmaker Thomas Boynton advertised in the *Vermont Republican and American Statesman* (Windsor) on March 16, 1818, that his "establishment employed an 'experienced workman' who has worked many years in Boston and New-York [and] can furnish those who like the fashions and taste of the Metropolis, with the newest patterns. . . ."[5] The town of Hampshire, Vermont, had enough demand for cabinetmakers trained in urban centers to support both Julius Barnard, who had "worked sometime with the most distinguished workmen in New York," and Oliver Pomeroy, who had "worked two or three years in the city of Philadelphia."[6] The other theme that pervades period advertisements and correspondence is the desire of New Englanders to get good workmanship at a fair price. Knowing their patrons, cabinetmakers advertised furniture "at moderate prices" and offered "[the most] reasonable

FIGURE 5.3:
Advertisement of Dickinson & Badger. From the Middlesex Gazette, *Middletown, Connecticut, December 5, 1815.*
PRIVATE COLLECTION.
FIGURE 5.4: *Parade banner, 1841, Portland, Maine; painted by William Capen Jr.; oil on silk; 34 x 40 inches. Depicting an artist's palette encircled by a floral and foliage wreath emanating from a cornucopia with brushes and pencils under the motto "OUR LIFE is one of LIGHTS & SHADOWS."*
PHOTOGRAPH COURTESY OF THE MAGAZINE ANTIQUES.

5·3

5·4

terms as can be purchased at any other Store in this city, or in the city of New-York."[7]

Not all New Englanders sought to furnish their homes in the latest taste from cabinetmakers lately of New York, Boston, or Philadelphia or in the convention of the time. In *Walden*, Henry David Thoreau cried out against overadornment, the love of the superfluous, and the loss of simplicity seen in the houses of his Massachusetts neighbors. When building his cabin at Walden Pond, Thoreau borrowed tools, recycled old materials, and filled the cabin with furniture "part of which I made myself,—and the rest cost me nothing of which I have not rendered an account." Thoreau's furniture "consisted of a bed, a table, a desk, three chairs, a looking glass three inches in diameter, a pair of tongs and andirons . . . and a japanned lamp. . . . Furniture! Thank God, I can sit and I can stand without the aid of a furniture warehouse."[8]

Throughout the nineteenth century, New Englanders sought ways to adjust to the changes brought on by the movement from a traditional agrarian economy to a larger commercial market economy. The part-time farmer-cabinetmaker whose shop was attached to his farm now found full-time employment in the shops of cities, towns, and villages which were prospering from whaling, shipbuilding, foreign trade, or the manufacture of textiles. The specialization of trades that had occurred in Boston during the middle of the previous century was now evident throughout New England. Surviving trade cards, advertisements, and city directories indicate the emergence of well-established communities of ornamenters, painters, and glaziers. Partnerships were established for "Painting, Glazing, and Chair-Making," or "Sign and House-Painting" firms, "Windsor and Fancy chair manufactories," "painters," and "fancy chair ornamenters."

Local Charitable Mechanic Associations were formed with a selective volunteer membership of master workers, owners, or superintendents of workshops. Associations were composed of divisions of cabinetmakers, chair makers, silversmiths, carvers, printers, gilders, and other mechanics, providing a visible political and social force in cities and towns throughout New England. Members often marched in local parades carrying silk banners like the one executed by William Capen Jr. for the October 8, 1841, parade in Portland, Maine (figure 5.4). The Painters and Glaziers and Brush Makers division carried a banner adorned with an easel and brushes and the motto "OUR LIFE is one of LIGHTS & SHADOWS."

The richly embellished furniture and highly figured carpets in watercolor portraits by Joseph H. Davis, who worked from 1832 to 1837, represent an aesthetic that appealed to many New Englanders of the period. Over 160 portraits by Davis are known, nearly all featuring grain-painted chairs and tables in a setting of exuberant color and movement (figure 5.5). The rectilinear, flat surfaces of Federal-era furniture, with an emphasis on two-dimensional decoration, provided a ready surface for paint decoration. It can be seen on the blanket chests, bureaus, bedsteads, tables, fireboards, and chairs that filled the orderly rooms of New England homes.

The painted surfaces of New England furniture run the spectrum from high-style forms with grain painting simulating mahogany, rosewood, or bird's-eye maple to simply constructed case pieces decorated with imaginative swirling designs displaying a natural spontaneity and creativity and to stained surfaces over simply constructed furniture. This variety of paint-decorated surface decoration reflects varying degrees of expertise and availability of tools and pigments by the ornamenter. All decoration reflects the taste of the client, of course. Some wanted furniture patterned like that of the urban centers. Others, unwilling or unable to pay for stylish pieces, sought simple, practical furniture that became a New England style of its own. Nineteenth-century New England painted furniture is thus

5·5

often made of local wood and is plain in shape and simple in construction—a less expensive alternative to high-style hardwood furniture. Some examples of painted furniture, however, are expertly constructed, with fine joinery and surface embellishments reminiscent of their urban counterparts.

GRAIN-PAINTED FURNITURE

Imitating the colors, veins, grains, and figures of fancy hardwoods, some contended, required the facility, talent, and perceptive powers of a fine artist portraying a human face. To encourage mastery of grain painting, John W. Masury suggested in his manual that the ornamenter travel "the long road of patient study, close observation, and practice, practice, practice." Masury recommended that the artisan collect samples of wood to study, selecting "the best which nature offers; those which are most pleasing to the eye, and most interesting as objects of study and observation. Natural deformities, except as curiosities, are

not worth perpetuating."[9] Nathaniel Whittock's manual went so far as to include color plates of hand-grained examples for each of these woods (figure 5.6).

Grain painting was called two-toned finish or veining in the opening decades of the nineteenth century. It began with a priming coat followed by one or two layers of a ground color. When dried, this layer was smoothed with a pumice stone. A glaze was applied and, while wet, manipulated with one or more graining tools to create the desired effect. Graining tools listed in period manuals included badger-hair brushes, natural sponges, washed leather, goose quills, sticks, feathers, bristles, putty, chamois, and buckskin. When the decorative layer dried, coats of protective varnish were applied. The final finish saturated the colored layers beneath, lightening the decorative effect, protecting the paint from moisture, abrasion, wear, dust, and soot. Often apprenticed from age fifteen to eighteen, the decorative painter ground and

FIGURE 5.5: *The Tilton family, 1837; Joseph H. Davis; watercolor, pencil, and ink on paper; 10 x 15¹/₆ inches. This room is replete with patterned and grained tables and chairs.* COLLECTION OF THE ABBY ALDRICH ROCKEFELLER FOLK ART CENTER, WILLIAMSBURG, VIRGINIA.

5.6

mixed his own pigments, formulated his own paints and varnishes, and collected his own tools while perfecting a wide range of wood-graining techniques.

IMITATIVE GRAINING

Painted wood graining that is so close to nature as to trick the eye can be seen in the New Hampshire console table in figure 5.7. Paint was ingeniously employed to imitate both fine-grained mahogany and delicate inlay, as seen in the border of swags on the apron. The conceit was heightened by the use of a real gray-and-white cyma-scalloped marble top to create a unique masterwork of graining and ingenuity. Mahogany, a rich imported wood, was the most popular wood imitated by graining. Hezekiah Reynolds provided recipes for the paints used in mahogany graining:

> Prime with spruce yellow; when thoroughly dry, add to the yellow a small quantity of

white Lead, say four ounces lead to one pound yellow, and lay the second coat. For the third coat take a sufficient quantity of Stone yellow pulverized; heat it on coals in iron; taking care to stir it constantly untill it changes to a red color; then let it cool; mix and grind it with clarified or boil'd oil; and it will be fit for use. Then for shading the work take umber pulverized, and prepare it by heating as before untill it changes to a darker color; then mix and grind it in oil. When both are prepared lay the third coat; and immediately shade it with the umber, that the colors may more easily blend together.[10]

Rufus Porter describes in his manual, *A Select Collection of Valuable and Curious Arts,* the tools and brushes needed to produce the graining of mahogany: a "short stiff brush for the glaze," "a small flat brush" for applying dark shades to the graining, and a "pencil" (a very thin brush) to imitate the shading of the wood (figure 5.8). He further suggests that balls of

5·7

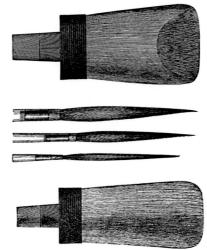

5·8

cotton be used to wipe off the stain, creating a light effect, and that "light stripes or lines may be produced by drawing a piece of cork or soft wood over the work, thus taking off, or removing the dark colours, that the original ground may appear."[11]

Nathaniel Whittock's manual provided the most comprehensive method of executing mahogany graining:

[T]ake a large tool [brush] and well filling it with colour, but not too wet, draw it over the panel you intend to grain firm so not in a straight line, but in a slanting and in some cases a wavy direction, letting the hand press heavily upon the brush so that the hairs may spread . . . giving the appearance of various grains according to the handling of the brush. As soon as the colour is by this means spread over the panel, take a large dusting brush, lightly beat the work with the points of the hairs . . . against the grain; this must be done very quickly with a light hand, and at the same time using proper judgment to

vary the beating. . . . When the panel is all blended together, the colour will have nearly become set, or what the gilders call tacky. At this time take a piece of damp washed leather folded to an edge, and take out the large masses of light . . . the grain beauty of this work consists of its being done with quickness and spirit.[12]

Precise in his description, Whittock touches on the artistry of graining when he writes of the movements of the hand, which should be quick, light, spirited, and practiced. The sweep of the lines in the glazes, the extra care taken to finish each stroke, and the subtle understanding of the natural graining of wood combine to produce the precision and beauty of wood graining at its best.

Around 1820, as cabinetmakers fashioned furniture in the more archaeologically correct Empire style, glistening rosewood supplanted mahogany as the preferred wood. Maine joined the Union in 1823, and much of the

FIGURE 5.7:
Grain-painted console table, 1790–1800, Portsmouth, New Hampshire; grain-painted maple and pine with cyma-scalloped marble top; 33½ x 40½ x 17¾ inches.
PHOTOGRAPH COURTESY OF DAVID A. SCHORSCH.

FIGURE 5.8:
Illustrations from The Complete Carriage and Wagon Painter *by Fritz Schriber (New York, 1887) depicting paintbrushes.*
PRIVATE COLLECTION.

5.9

5.10

state's surviving furniture reflects Empire-style rosewood-grained furniture with red-on-black or black-on-red ornamentation (figure 5.9). The ornamental painters produced long, wide horizontal striations with a quick strong sweep of the hand across the flat surfaces of the Sheraton dressing table and washstand in figure 5.10. The yellow striping outlining the drawers and back splat and the dabs of paint on the legs mimicking the cross section of rosewood complete the conceit.

One of the most enduring forms of the Empire period was the klismos-form side chair (in the portrait in figure 5.11), derived from images found on Greek vases. The klismos chair, with its curved back and tapering legs, was a high-style form seen in painted, gilded, and stenciled chairs produced in Baltimore, New York, and Philadelphia. Reinterpreting the form to suit the taste of its patrons, the Portland fancy chair manufactory of Walter Corey Company produced rosewood-grained side chairs with gold striping until the middle of the century. The chair in figure 5.12 dates to the 1840 or 1850s and is stenciled on the rear seat rail with "W. COREY. PORTLAND, ME." At its height, the company employed over one hundred men in a six-story building in Portland, using machinery run by a sixty-horsepower engine.[13] While the furniture was cut with the aid of machinery, the ornamentation was executed by specialists with a time-saving innovation that all but eliminated the skilled ornamental painter. The ground coat was laid on by one mechanic while the rosewood graining was executed in a quick, cursory manner by another who specialized in graining. After the graining dried, a striping specialist added the gold lines that outline the vase-shaped splat, the scrolled crest rail, the center line of the front stretcher, and the saber-shaped legs. The final step in the finishing process was the application of one or more coats of varnish.

Wood graining could be accomplished not only with the smooth strokes of a brush but

5.11

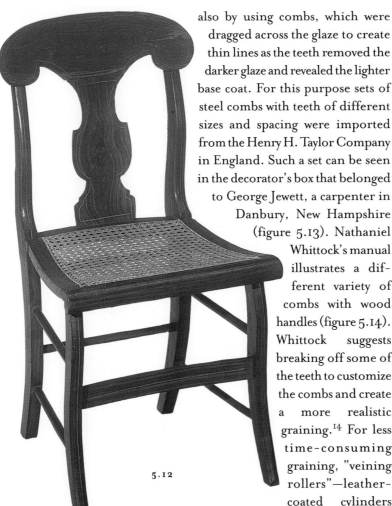

also by using combs, which were dragged across the glaze to create thin lines as the teeth removed the darker glaze and revealed the lighter base coat. For this purpose sets of steel combs with teeth of different sizes and spacing were imported from the Henry H. Taylor Company in England. Such a set can be seen in the decorator's box that belonged to George Jewett, a carpenter in Danbury, New Hampshire (figure 5.13). Nathaniel Whittock's manual illustrates a different variety of combs with wood handles (figure 5.14). Whittock suggests breaking off some of the teeth to customize the combs and create a more realistic graining.[14] For less time-consuming graining, "veining rollers"—leather-coated cylinders with incised lines duplicating the knots and grains of wood—could be rolled onto long flat surfaces prepared for graining. The veining rollers in figure 5.13 were used for the wood graining on coffins, an important source of income for many ornamental painters.

IMAGINATIVE GRAINING

Some New England ornamenters were more interested in capturing the character of the wood than exact imitation. They produced some of the most masterful and coveted pieces of nineteenth-century painted furniture. The techniques used in imaginative graining are referred to in period sources as vinegar painting, mottling, sponging, strippling, scumbling, feather painting, and finger painting. A remarkably well preserved sample box belonging to New Hampshire ornamenter Moses Eaton exemplifies the splendid array and variety of imaginative graining. Nine of the ten panels display finished graining techniques using green, burnt umber, and raw umber glazes. The tenth panel provides a sample of the ground color.

The town of Shaftsbury in the southwest corner of Vermont is regarded as the center of a distinctive school of imaginative grain-painted furniture from 1803 to 1825. Using a variety of graining tools the craftsmen mimicked the mahogany, figured satinwood, flamed birch, rosewood, and bird's-eye maple veneers of Federal-era high-style furniture. The six-board chest in figure 5.16 loosely resembles real woods, while the single-drawer chest in figure 5.15 uses mustard, green, red, and black paint to create vivid and highly figured graining framed by imitative string veneers. A third example from this school is the bureau exhibiting a faux veneering around the drawer fronts and an outline on the sides and legs (figure 5.17).

Composed of primarily two-drawer chests and six-board blanket chests, this group of furniture has intrigued and puzzled historians of furniture for many years. Chests decorated in this style have been attributed to the Mattesons of Shaftsbury, based on five signed examples bearing these inscriptions: "By J. Matteson/August I A.D. 1803"; "Thomas G. Matison/South Shaftsbury/Vt/1824"; "Thomas Matteson/S. Shaftsbury, Vermont/1824"; "Benonia Matteson to B. Burlingame Dr. [debit]/To paint $2.70/

5.12

FIGURE 5.12: *Side chair, 1840–1850, Portland, Maine; made by Walter Corey; maple and grain painted; 33¹/₂ x 20⁵/₈ x 18¹/₂ inches; inscribed "W. COREY. PORTLAND. ME." on rear seat rail.*
COURTESY OF EARLE G. SHETTLEWORTH JR. AND MAINE STATE MUSEUM, AUGUSTA, MAINE.

FIGURE 5.13: *Decorator's box with ornamental painting tools, 1810–1850, New Hampshire; unknown wood; /⁹/₄ x 17¹/₄ x 10¹/₂ inches.*
PHOTOGRAPH COURTESY OF SOTHEBY'S.

5.13

To Paint & Grain Chest $2.00/$4.70"; and "W.[?] P. Matteson/S. Shaftsbury."[15] The Vermont Folklore Center in Middlebury examined estate inventories of members of the Matteson family and found that none of them owned painters' tools.[16] Kenneth Joel Zogry, curator of collections at the Bennington Museum, has concluded from his research that "repeated attempts to identify specifically the craftsmen in the extensive Matteson family who built or decorated this furniture has failed." Zogry suggests rather that "these simply constructed case pieces were made in Shaftsbury, possibly by various members of the Matteson family."[17] While the overall form and shape of the skirts are similar, the surface treatments of the labeled chests are different in both coloration and design execution. Other chests with this distinctive style of ornamentation have surfaced throughout New England. Until more definitive evidence comes to light regarding the ornamenter, this furniture can only be regarded as a regional style.

The pioneer collectors of American painted furniture, Jean and Howard Lipman, are credited with discovering another school of decorative painting on the flat surfaces of two-drawer blanket chests from Massachusetts, created between 1825 and 1835 (figures 5.18, 5.19, and 5.20). These chests display a common construction with turned, detachable legs, and a highly creative decorative style that is at once imaginative and controlled.[18] The carefully organized patterning on these chests employs a variety of techniques reminiscent of the hardwood-veneered surfaces of the period, yet totally original in coloring. A technique often called

vinegar painting was created by rolling putty with a little oil and a glaze containing vinegar. The rolled putty was stamped onto the glaze, and as the glaze dried, the oil and vinegar separated, creating a seaweedlike appearance. The patterning on the chest in figure 5.20 is highlighted by the use of base coats in three shades. The extra care taken in positioning the flowerlike images so that they are not interrupted by the lines of the drawers exemplifies the imaginative skill and assured hand of a fine ornamental painter.

In the hands of some ornamental painters,

FIGURE 5.14: *Graining combs, circa 1820; Plate II from Nathaniel Whittock,* Decorative Painters' and Glaziers' Guide *(London, 1828). Different arrangements of teeth can be placed in the handle to create graining of different widths and patterns.* COLLECTION OF THE SMITHSONIAN INSTITUTION LIBRARIES: COOPER-HEWITT, NATIONAL DESIGN MUSEUM.

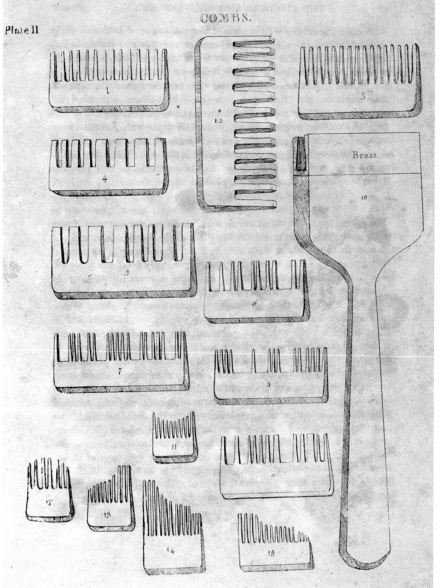

5.14

FIGURE 5.15: *Single-drawer blanket chest, circa 1824, South Shaftsbury, Vermont; Matteson school; paint-decorated pine; 36 x 40 x 18 inches. The vivid grained and stripple decoration in mustard, green, red, and black recalls the patterning of chests signed by various members of the Matteson family of South Shaftsbury, but this chest is not signed.*
PHOTOGRAPH COURTESY OF LEIGH KENO.

FIGURE 5.16: *Six-board blanket chest, circa 1825, South Shaftsbury, Vermont; Matteson school; pine and paint decoration.* COLLECTION OF MABEL WILSON ANTIQUES.
PHOTOGRAPH COURTESY OF DAVID A. SCHORSCH.

FIGURE 5.17: *Chest of drawers, 1825, South Shaftsbury, Vermont; Matteson school; wood unknown with imaginative graining; $42\frac{1}{2}$ x 42 x 18 inches.*
COLLECTION OF SHERI AND NED GROSSMAN.

FIGURE 5.18: *Two-drawer blanket chest, 1825–1835, Massachusetts; unknown wood with grain-painted decoration; $39\frac{3}{4}$ x $42\frac{1}{4}$ x $18\frac{1}{4}$ inches.*
COLLECTION OF THE MUSEUM OF AMERICAN FOLK ART, NEW YORK, GIFT OF JEAN LIPMAN IN HONOR OF CYRIL I. NELSON, 1994.5.1.

FIGURE 5.19 : *Two-drawer blanket chest, 1825–1835, Massachusetts; softwood with grain-painted decoration; 40½ x 41 x 18¼ inches.*
ALAN KATZ COLLECTION. PHOTOGRAPH COURTESY OF GIAMPIETRO GALLERY.

FIGURE 5.20 : *Two-drawer blanket chest, 1825–1835, Massachusetts; unknown wood with grain-painted decoration; 40 x 42 x 18 inches.*
PHOTOGRAPH COURTESY OF DAVID A. SCHORSCH.

FIGURE 5.21 : *Chest of drawers, 1830–1850, Maine; birch, pine, and painted decoration; 39¾ x 43 x 17½ inches.*
PRIVATE COLLECTION, COURTESY OF ROBERT E. KINNAMAN & BRIAN A. RAMAEKERS, INC.

FIGURE 5.22 : *Six-board blanket chest, 1820–1840, Maine; pine with a thin orange-red stain over a yellow ground; 61 x 18¼ x 24 inches. The swirling broad strokes*
accent this unusually long chest in an exuberant sweep of the ornamenter's brush across the front, side, and top of this chest.
COURTESY OF ROBERT E. KINNAMAN & BRIAN A. RAMAEKERS, INC.

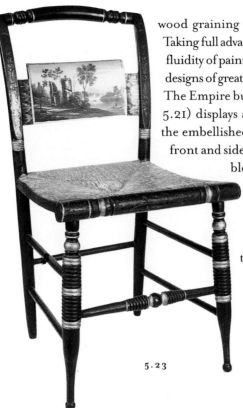

wood graining was a highly creative art. Taking full advantage of the properties and fluidity of paint, they created free-flowing designs of great exuberance and character. The Empire bureau from Maine (figure 5.21) displays an independent spirit in the embellished painted surfaces on the front and sides. Broad sweeping strokes blend to give highly exaggerated wood grains in the unusually long blanket chest in figure 5.22. The unintended abstraction in this example is what often attracts the contemporary eye to nineteenth-century decorative graining.

5.23

LANDSCAPES ON FIREBOARDS, WALLS, AND FURNITURE

Thomas Sheraton, in his *Cabinet Dictionary* of 1803, defined landscape in painting, as "the view or prospect of any country extended as far as the eye can see."[19] Landscape painting was the province of the decorative artist, not the fine artist, at the beginning of the nineteenth century. In America, painting or sculpting was considered an occupation like any other, not an elevated calling set apart. Painting as a fine art was regarded as frivolous, unworthy of a man who was capable of more serious pursuits. "There is, in America," declared Francis Grund in 1837, "no deficiency of talent either for drawing or painting; but there is little or nothing done for their encouragement."[20] With so few outlets in a nation still finding itself, many fine

artists became artisans and mechanics in order to make use of their gift. Self-taught or apprenticed, they made a living creating a wide range of visual ornamentation.

Two highly skilled ornamental landscape painters—Rufus Porter (1792–1884), who worked in New Hampshire and the upper Connecticut River valley, and Michele Felice Cornè (1752–1845), who worked in Salem, Boston, and Newport—might have become fine artists if the circumstances of their lives had been different. Rufus Porter, an inventor, a journalist, and the founder of *Scientific American,* painted murals, landscapes, miniature portraits, and boxes as well as furniture, overmantel panels, and fireboards. He learned his craft as a house and sign painter and is known to have painted sleighs and drums. He played the drums, in fact, and even taught drumming and drum painting.[21] Today he is best known for the landscape murals he painted on the walls of well over a hundred New England houses and taverns from 1824 to the mid-1840s (figure 5.27). Porter wrote a series of articles for *Scientific American* between September 11, 1845, and April 9, 1846, in which he gave directions for landscape painting on walls.[22]

Michele Felice Cornè came to Salem in 1800 from Naples, Italy. Cornè painted ship portraits, naval actions, scenic murals on paper, overmantels, fireboards, portraits, and large panoramas of current events. The attack on Tripoli in 1805 was one such commission. Cornè assisted in the painting of a 10- by 60-foot view of the attack in 1805. It was displayed so that citizens of Salem, for a fee, might see a visualization of events unfolding across the ocean. The overman-

5.24

5.25

tel in figure 5.25, by Cornè, is believed to have come from the Simon Forrester House at 188 Derby Street in Salem. This imaginary harbor view of 1805 is typical of the work of decorative artisans, in that it was composed not on the spot "from nature," but presumably as an adaptation of an engraving. Cornè draws picturesque landscapes of the rolling hills of Italy in which he replaces toiling peasants with strolling ladies and gentlemen dressed in costumes typical of the period.[23]

The tablet tops and back splats of fancy chairs also provided flat surfaces for landscape scenes. Though inspired by English fancy chairs with romantic views of castles, arched bridges, crumbling ruins, sunlit seascapes, and thatched cottages, American ornamental painters often turned to scenes closer to home. While Baltimore fancy chair painters depicted local buildings and New York ornamenters favored Hudson River views, New England painters turned to the forested landscapes and seascapes of their region. The portrait of Mrs. Harrison in figure 5.34, for

5.26

5.27

FIGURE 5.25: *Overmantel, imaginary harbor view, circa 1800, Salem; attributed to Michele Felice Cornè; oil on wood panel; 39 x 59 inches.* COLLECTION OF THE PEABODY ESSEX MUSEUM, SALEM, MASSACHUSETTS, 129.155.3.

FIGURE 5.26: *Detail of a serving table, 1810–1825, New England; pine with hand-painted decoration on a blue ground.* PRIVATE COLLECTION. PHOTOGRAPH COURTESY OF DAVID A. SCHORSCH.

FIGURE 5.27: *Detail of a mural, 1825–1830, Hancock, New Hampshire; attributed to Rufus Porter.* PHOTOGRAPH COURTESY OF *THE MAGAZINE ANTIQUES.*

FIGURE 5.28: *Portrait of a woman sitting in a yellow fancy chair, 1820–1830, New England; oil on panel; 22 x 24 inches. The young woman rests her arm on a beautifully decorated fancy chair with red and green decoration on a yellow ground.* COLLECTION OF ROBERT E. KINNAMAN & BRIAN A. RAMAEKERS, INC.

COUNTRY FURNITURE

FIGURE 5.29: *Fancy dressing table, circa 1820, Salem; pine with painted decoration on a painted white ground; 47 x 37¹/₄ x 17 inches. Delicately hand-painted sprays of leaves, birds, a lion, and a unicorn decorate this bold Empire form, which is highlighted with striping.*
COLLECTION OF FRANK AND BARBARA POLLACK. PHOTOGRAPH COURTESY OF HELAINE AND BURTON FENDELMAN.

FIGURE 5.30: *Fancy worktable, circa 1820, Salem; pine and painted decoration on a painted white ground; 28 x 17¹/₄ x 15³/₄ inches.*
COLLECTION OF THE PEABODY ESSEX MUSEUM, SALEM, MASSACHUSETTS. PHOTOGRAPH COURTESY OF HELAINE AND BURTON FENDELMAN.

FIGURE 5.31: *Dressing table, 1820, New England; pine, painted ground with freehand, sponged, and stenciled decoration; dimensions unknown.*
PHOTOGRAPH COURTESY OF AMERICA HURRAH ARCHIVES.

FIGURE 5.32: *Dressing table, 1815–1825, Portsmouth, New Hampshire; eastern white pine, original brass hardware, painted and gilded decoration; 36¹/₈ x 36⁷/₈ x 18⁵/₁₆ inches. This is one of the most outstanding pieces of painted furniture to survive from Portsmouth. Its original vibrant decorative scheme is intact, but the varnished surface has yellowed over time, giving the blue decoration a green cast.*
COLLECTION OF THE ABBY ALDRICH ROCKEFELLER FOLK ART CENTER, WILLIAMSBURG, VIRGINIA.

example, shows her sitting on a chair beside an open window, through which you can see a landscape that closely resembles her real-life landscape. The ornamental painter of a set of four side chairs and a serving table created a panoramic sweep of one town, using the chair backs and back splat of the table to duplicate an entire town (figures 5.24 and 5.26).

ful patterning on this furniture, providing visual accent to rooms painted in complementary colors.

Throughout New England, Windsor chair manufacturers produced large numbers of fancy chairs. The Newburyport Chair Factory, advertising in the *Newburyport Herald* in the spring of 1829, touted "Chairs, of every

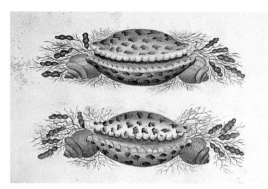

5·33

FIGURE 5.33: *Watercolor drawings, 1811–1812, from Christian M. Nestell, drawing book, New York; 9½ x 15 inches. Christian Nestell's design book contains over seventy-five watercolors done while he was a student in New York City.* WINTERTHUR MUSEUM, GARDENS & LIBRARY, JOSEPH DOWNS MANUSCRIPT COLLECTION.

FIGURE 5.34: *Portrait of Mrs. Harrison, 1810–1830, New England; artist unknown; oil on canvas; dimensions unknown.* COLLECTION OF THE LYMAN ALLYN MUSEUM, 1939.11.

Fancy furniture with freehand decoration on a ground of white, yellow, vermilion, green, and tan captivated urban and rural homeowners. In the many surviving portraits of New Englanders posed wearing their best clothes, fancy chairs can be seen decorated with trophies of musical instruments, garlands of flowers, eagles, and cornucopias (figure 5.28). The fashion for Adam-inspired English painted chairs began around 1790 in Baltimore, Boston, and New York, and by 1810, fancy furniture had become popular throughout the country. Fancy chairs were sold in sets with an even number of side chairs, a pair of armchairs, and one or two sofas. Suites of fancy furniture included bedsteads, cornices, dressing tables, and washstands (figures 5.29 to 5.32). This furniture could be commissioned with ornamentation in imitation of textiles. The daybook of ornamental painter and cabinetmaker George Davidson records that he painted "a set of window cornices in Imitation of Calico" for $5 in February of 1793 and two years later painted a set of bed and window cornices for $20."[24] The colored cushions recommended for fancy chairs further enhanced the fanci-

description, . . . viz:—Cane bottom Chairs, of a superior quality, worth from $2.50 to $4.00 each—Fancy Chairs, Windsor Chairs, and Box Chairs for Shipping. Any pattern or color, made to order WASHSTANDS—CHAMBER TABLES. Bureaus, and Work stands, of every description, always on hand, at wholesale or retail."[25] Jacob Wendell, a successful Portsmouth, New Hampshire, merchant, purchased three sets of fancy furniture for his house on Pleasant Street between 1816 and 1817.[26] The Wendell household also contained one of the most outstanding surviving pieces of painted fancy furniture—the dressing table in figure 5.32. The blue ground of this piece is enhanced by a deep blue mottled imitation-marble-patterned top, gilded spiral stripes on the legs, and stenciled clusters of grapes with fine detailing on the apron. Surviving dressing tables in this form attest to their popularity and a diverse range of patterning.

Little documentary evidence has come to light on the exact method of ornamentation of fancy furniture. However, the design book of Christian Nestell, a fancy chair ornamenter, suggests that ornamenters had a variety of practiced motifs that they executed freehand on furniture (figure 5.33). In his manual, Nathaniel Whittock states that "it must be obvious to all, that the painter who has some knowledge of drawing and the rudiments of perspective, will have great advantage over the man who has not attained this knowledge." He suggests that the decorative

finishing." His directions for the ornamentation begin:

The ornaments should be sketched in with a black lead pencil, very light, and so as not to exceed the outline of the colour. And as the leaves and flowers are proceeded with, they should be nearly finished at the first painting; particularly when the colours are

painter "become acquainted with the rudiments, at least, of this the highest, most lucrative, and at the same time, most pleasing department of his art." He does, however, hold out the "possibility of becoming a furniture painter, to a certain extent, without being able to draw," and he outlines the "proper method of decorating furniture, without a knowledge of drawing" by explaining the elements of drawing light and shade and perspective.[27] Thomas Sheraton, on the other hand, in his *Cabinet Dictionary* writes that "in ornamenting japanned furniture, no person can proceed further than to do it by lines, except he has previously been taught, or has practiced ornamental drawing himself."[28] Both give line drawings in their manuals to assist the ornamenter.

Sheraton's advice to the "practiced" ornamenter is helpful in understanding the period techniques that he describes for sketching freehand decorative patterns on japanned window cornices. After a clear varnish is applied and dried over the ground coat, the ornament is begun—though "if there be any tablet in the center, let this be painted last, that it may not be infused while the other parts are

required to dry quick; for in the case the tints will not blend into each other, if it be not effected while the colours are in some degree wet; and therefore they may be ground up in nut oil, and diluted in copal varnish, which will not set so quick, and give more opportunity to retouch the work. When the work is finished thus far, to give it effect, it should be touched with high lights,

5·34

5·35

FIGURE 5·35: *Windsor bow-back settee, 1785–1800, eastern Massachusetts; ash or white oak, pine, and hickory with painted decoration; 38 x 79 x 21³/₄ inches. The painted decoration is an early nineteenth-century addition over an original green ground. The rows of wavy black lines separated by rows of yellow dots are reminiscent of redware with slip decoration.* COLLECTION OF LAUREN AND KEITH MORGAN.

5.36

and some strong shadows laid quick on, and with colours that will set as quick as may be, to give the greater force, as these things are viewed at a good distance. Thus completed, give the work at least two coats of white hard varnish.[29]

Many fancy chairs were finished with decorative striping; Sheraton provides directions for drawing lines on chairs. He suggests using a very long camel's-hair pencil "some half inch, three-quarters, or one inch long in the hair, according to the thickness of the line to be drawn." After the pencil is primed with the color and brought "to a fine point on a marble stone," the line is drawn in by applying "the fore-finger to some straight angle of the work, and at the same time, keeping the pencil between the first finger and the thumb, drawing steadily along, and the quicker the better the line will be drawn" (figure 5.36).[30]

WINDSOR CHAIRS

The popularity of fancy chairs was embraced by Windsor chair makers, who adopted Sheraton styling and developed a new form of square-back Windsors. The most common fancy Windsors have overhanging tablet tops, spindles, U-shaped seats, and vertical tapered legs with bamboo turnings. Windsor chairs in a wide variety of forms were produced in eastern Connecticut, Boston, southern New Hampshire, Maine, and central Massachusetts (figures 5.37 and 5.38). Worcester County in south central Massachusetts developed as a major chair-making center in the 1820s. Research by the Sturbridge Village Museum identified twenty-four men who listed chair making as their occupation.[31] A three-story building served as a shop and warerooms for cabinetmaker Mark Elwell (1777–1857) in Dudley, Massachusetts. His son, Charles B. Elwell (b. 1810), practiced there until 1850 (figure 5.40).

A rich vocabulary of ornamentation is represented by the early fancy chairs and Windsor chairs. While the ornamental painter might bring to a commission the skills of a fine artist, ornamental painting on furniture was not a lucrative profession. As new routes of transportation opened up by the 1820s, the great demand for fancy chairs resulted in marketing and production innovations. With this increased demand, it is easy to see how stenciled patterns superseded the more exacting and time-consuming freehand decoration. Even Thomas Sheraton acknowledged that "stenciling is the cheapest and most expeditious method of decorating."[32]

STENCILING

Stencils began to appear soon after 1815 and gained immediate success for the decoration of Windsor chairs, as they allowed nearly anyone to produce a well-delineated design. Schoolgirls learned to make and use stencils to create theorem paintings; walls were embellished with stencils using distemper or watercolor; painted floorcloths in imitation of

FIGURE 5.36:
One of a pair of armchairs, 1810–1830, New England; pine with freehand painted decoration on a white ground, with black striping; dimensions unknown.
PHOTOGRAPH COURTESY OF HELAINE AND BURTON FENDELMAN.

FIGURE 5.37: *Windsor side chair, 1810–1830, New England; unknown wood; dimensions unknown. Marked "WARRENTED." This is one of a set of six surviving side chairs with grain-painted plank seats and carved and painted eagle crest rails.*
PHOTOGRAPH COURTESY OF MILLY MCGEHEE.

5.37

5.38

FIGURE 5.38: *Set of six step-down Windsor side chairs, circa 1820, Farmington, Maine; made by Daniel Stewart; probably basswood; 35³/₄ x 16¹/₄ x 15³/₄ inches. One chair bears the label "DANIEL STEWART, Chairmaker & Painter, Farmington, ME." The bamboo-turned tapering legs are accented with painted incised lines.*
PHOTOGRAPH COURTESY OF HELAINE AND BURTON FENDELMAN.

FIGURE 5.39: *Detail of a dresser, circa 1830, Massachusetts; wood unknown, painted and stenciled with gilded highlights; 47 x 42¹/₂ x 19³/₄ inches. This dresser is sophisticated in its construction with superbly executed stenciling highlighted with imaginative gold stenciling in an alternating pattern of stars and leaves border.*
PRIVATE COLLECTION, COURTESY OF ROBERT E. KINNAMAN & BRIAN A. RAMAEKERS, INC.

COUNTRY FURNITURE

Brussels carpets were embellished with repeated patterns with the use of stencils; and both high-style and vernacular furniture incorporated stenciling into a variety of ornamentation. Stencils permitted a more rapid decoration of running borders and other repetitive designs. Central motifs could be stenciled, and only the details needed to be hand-painted. Stencils were also used to simulate the ormolu mounts and gold striping of Empire furniture.

The introduction of bronze powders and different-colored varnishes as well as other

5.39

powdered metals such as brass, zinc, aluminum, silver, and gold created a whole new aesthetic for ornamental painters (figure 5.39). Stenciled furniture involved a base coat of paint overlaid with a coat of binder such as varnish and turpentine. When dried to the tacky stage, a stencil was laid flat on this surface. Metallic powders were then brushed onto the stencil using small velvet or leather pads. Several stencils might be used to achieve a single design, each adding different details to the overall design (figure 5.41).

Nathaniel Whittock advised that the "usual way of proceeding is to procure an elegant pattern, containing about four colours, or more if required. The stenciller must be careful to trace upon tracing paper all the outline of the subject that is in middle tint; he will on another piece of tracing paper, draw the out-

5.40

line of the first shade; and on a third paper draw the darkest shade; and on the fourth the strongest lights." To ensure that the stencils fit exactly, Whittock suggested that each stencil be secured by "making four points upon the first pattern on the tracing paper, and making the other patterns correspond with it."[33] After each stencil was applied and the paint dried, details and shading were added; when dry, the whole was given a final coat of varnish. As the century progressed, fewer stencils were used at a time, and the intricate shading and hand-painted details were dropped, giving stencils a flatter, more static appearance.

Both Nathaniel Whittock and Rufus Porter give instructions for making paper stencils. Whittock suggests using pasteboard for pat-

FIGURE 5.40: *Mark Elwell's furniture warerooms, 1831, Dudley, Massachusetts; by William S. Elwell; oil on birch panel; 11 x 17³/₄ inches. Inscribed "1831" on the back in a later hand.* COLLECTION OF OLD STURBRIDGE VILLAGE, STURBRIDGE, MASSACHUSETTS. PHOTOGRAPH BY THOMAS NEILL.

FIGURE 5.41: *Pine box containing stencils, circa 1860, belonging to William P. Eaton, Westminster, Massachusetts; 7¹/₂ x 18 x 13¹/₂ inches.* COLLECTION OF THE MUSEUM OF AMERICAN FOLK ART, NEW YORK. PHOTOGRAPH COURTESY OF SOTHEBY'S.

5.41

FIGURE 5.42: *White family stencils.* LOCATION UNKNOWN.
FIGURE 5.43: *Side chair, 1830, New England; unknown wood, stenciled decoration, rush seat.*
PHOTOGRAPH COURTESY OF AMERICA HURRAH ARCHIVES.

terns, painted over with two coats of oil color and thoroughly dried before use. Porter recommends treating paper stencils with shellac to give them a strong water-resistant effect. Several sets of nineteenth-century stencils survive in museum collections (figure 5.41), including many examples gathered by the Historical Society of Early American Decoration, which are now at the Museum of American Folk Art in New York. In addition to the original stencils in the museum's collection, over a thousand patterns were reproduced from period decorated wares and furniture.[34]

Surviving stencils that belonged to members of the White family of Boston reveal another method of transferring a pattern onto a chair. The stencils in figure 5.42 display a series of pinpricks along the lines drawn on the paper. Rufus Porter outlines this technique in a section titled "Best Method of Tracing or Copying a Picture." He writes that once the outline is perforated with some pointed instrument, so that being laid on the other ground that are to receive the copies, and

5.43

brushed over with a little fine dry whiting, or red ochre . . . the whiting or ochre will penetrate the perforated lines of the pattern and thus mark the ground on which it is laid." The ornamenter then outlines the pattern following the small dots and proceeds with the freehand ornamentation.[35] Chairs fashioned in this way reveal a delicate patterning characteristic of the chairs made by members of the White family of ornamental chair painters.

HITCHCOCK CHAIRS

The best-known stenciled furniture manufacturer was the Hitchcock Chair Company, founded by Lambert Hitchcock (1795–1852), whose marketing savvy spanned the fad for bronze stenciled chairs and settees during the second quarter of the nineteenth century (figure 5.44). Combining elements of both the fancy chair and the Windsor chair, Hitchcock produced roll-top decorated chairs and settees that sold for $1.50 each in 1829, less than half the cost of most fancy chairs. Available in a limited variety of shapes with six designs for the backs and with rush, cane, or plank seats,

5.42

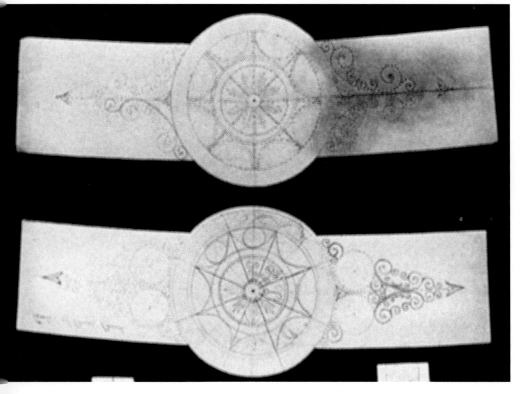

5.44

5.45

these inexpensive chairs had a stylish appeal. In a brilliant marketing move, Hitchcock labeled his chairs.[36]

While specialization in the manufacturing of fancy chairs is documented in the trade card of William Buttre of New York as early as the first decade of the nineteenth century, the Hitchcock factory applied mass-production methods to cabinetmaking. Using interchangeable furniture parts, with wood cut by the harnessing of water power for sawing lumber, Hitchcock created a specialized workforce. Each step in the chair-making process was done in repetition by a specialist. Children were employed to apply the ground coat; the stenciling was done by women. Hitchcock produced fifty chairs a day, all but eliminating the apprenticed ornamenter. Hitchcock's many Connecticut imitators included William Moore Jr. of Barkhamsted, John L. Hull of Kingworth, Seymour Watrous of Hartford, and Holmes and Roberts of Robertsville; these men also used stencils to increase production and marketed their furniture by signing their chairs. Hitchcock-style chairs were produced throughout New England, remaining a mainstay of rural households well into the twentieth century (figure 5.43).

VICTORIAN SIDE CHAIRS
The tablet tops of Windsor chairs slowly became rounded with a decidedly turned scroll by the 1840s. The ornamental painter's art was revived with metallic leaf, metallic powders, and polychrome decoration on petite chairs like the one in figure 5.45. Victorian chairs display a different vocabulary of motifs —scrolls, arabesques, drips, and flowers, particularly roses and fuchsia. Leaves were often formed with a precise half-and-half shading in dark and light green, beautifully executed by expert artisans. Seats on much of this furniture were caned, and occasionally oval backs were caned as well. Furniture was distinctly feminine and used for occasional chairs in parlors and ladies' bedrooms.

PLAIN PAINTED FURNITURE
Thoreau does not mention whether he gave any of his handmade furniture a coat of paint,

FIGURE 5.44:
Side chair, 1832–1843, Connecticut; maple with rosewood graining, shaded gilt stenciling, gilded with yellow striping, and cane seat; 34 x 15$^1/_2$ x 15$^1/_2$ inches. Stenciled "Hitchcock, Alford & Co., Hitchcockville, Conn., Warranted."
PHOTOGRAPH COURTESY OF PETER HILL, INC.
FIGURE 5.45: Victorian side chair, 1840–1870, eastern United States; poplar with painted and gilt decoration, cane seat; 32$^3/_4$ x 16$^1/_2$ x 15$^1/_2$ inches. Fancy chairs evolved into cottage furniture, typified by the Elizabethan Revival form and the stylized gilt decoration.
GIFT OF THOMAS F. CADWALLADER JR. TO THE MARYLAND HISTORICAL SOCIETY, 78.31.1.

5.46

FIGURE 5.46: *Cupboard, 1840–1860, Madawaska, Maine; white pine with blue and orange paint; 84 x 46¹/₈ x 21⁷/₈ inches. This cupboard was in the Hector Bourgoin family and was acquired in Madawaska. It has a vivid blue exterior paint with a visible pattern of wear around the doors.* COLLECTION OF MAINE STATE MUSEUM, AUGUSTA, MAINE, MSM 82.112.1.

FIGURE 5.47: *Apothecary cupboard, 1790–1800, Connecticut; pine and original red overpainted robin's egg blue; 73 x 46 x 17 inches.* PHOTOGRAPH COURTESY OF JOHN KEITH RUSSELL.

5·47

5.48

COUNTRY FURNITURE

but nearly every piece of furniture was finished in some way. Since paint needed to be ground from pigments and mixed in oil in specific proportions in a time-consuming daily process, giving a coat of paint to furniture was not a household task; it was done by a cabinet-maker or ornamental painter. Surviving day-books belonging to artisans of the first half of the nineteenth century attest to a wide variety of furniture forms that received painted finishes: sleighs, chaises, blinds, wagons, bedposts, landscapes, and window cornices.

Hezekiah Reynolds gives directions to "the Cabinet and Chair Maker, the Wheelwright, the House and Ship Joiner, and to others whose Trades are connected with building, as well as to those whose taste and genius qualify for, and invite to the practice of this useful and ornamental Art."[37] He offers the following directions for the production of several commonly used nineteenth-century colors:

For Pearl Color: To one pint of white Lead add one teaspoonful Rosin; one teaspoonful of Prussian blue; and one teaspoonful of Spruce Yellow, or in that proportion.

For Sea Green: To one pint of white Lead, add one tablespoonful of Verdigris; one [tablespoonful] of Spruce Yellow. Mix and grind them well together; and if upon experiment it should be too light, add more of the concocting ingredients at discretion.

For Prussian Blue color: To five pounds of white Lead, add one ounce of Prussian blue "best Quality"; if the quality be inferior the quantity must be increased. In laying this paint, use a half worn brush; and press the brush harder than in laying other colors.

For Red Color: May be made with either, 1. Vermilion; 2. Red Lead; 3. Rose Pink; 4. Pink,

ground in oil. Venetian red, Spanish brown and red ochre are coarser paints.

For Chocolate Color: Is made with Spanish brown and Lampblack, and may be varied at discretion.[38]

Reynolds gave directions for producing the paint, once the pigments were ground. Six or eight pounds of dry paint at a time were put in an iron kettle with an iron ball on a chain to serve as a paint mill or grinder. Oil was added "untill the ball will move easy and free." The other ingredients were added and mixed thoroughly with the ball to a consistency that "should not be so thick as to adhere to, or clog the brush; nor so thin as to run." For painting, he recommended that "new brushes may be used for priming, or the first coats; but for finishing, use only brushes about half worn." Reynolds further advised that "it is important that the hand of the painter, and the handles of the brush be kept clean, and free from oil and paint; and that the brush be held while painting, firm by the handle . . . and be laid strait and true, corresponding with the grain of the wood."[39]

Understanding of the process of producing and laying on of paint makes clear the importance of preserving the painted surfaces of nineteenth-century furniture (figures 5.46 to 5.49). Hand-ground pigments suspended in oil produced paints that catch and diffuse the light in different ways from modern paints. The recipes using a combination of pigments create a deeper and richer effect. The visible pattern of wear on nearly all plain painted furniture adds to the beauty and history of the piece. Well-used painted furniture resonates its past.

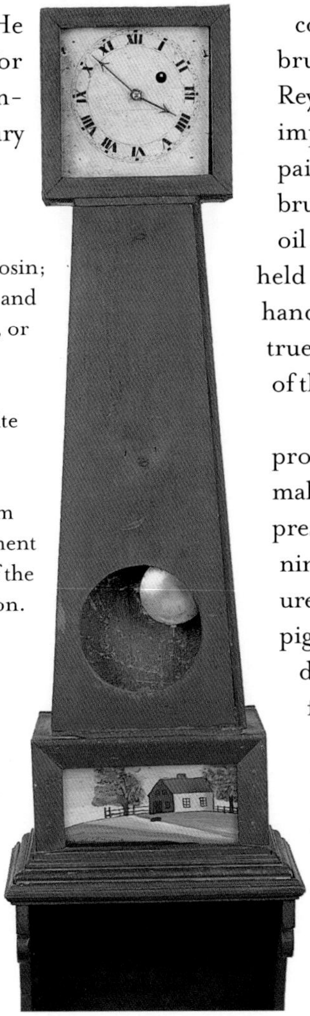

5·49

FIGURE 5.48: *Shaker sewing desk, 1860, Alfred, Maine; pine with birch stiles, butternut door and drawer fronts, and original coral red paint.* PHOTOGRAPH COURTESY OF SUZANNE COURCIER AND ROBERT W. WILKINS.

FIGURE 5.49: *Dwarf tall-case clock, circa 1834, Portsmouth, New Hampshire; works by George G. Brewster; case painted by Thomas Gerrish Furber, Newington, New Hampshire; painted pine with reverse-painted glass panel; 36 x 11½ inches. Engraved in script behind the large and small front wheels on the brass plate, "G. C. Brewster, Portsmouth, N.H. 1834." Inscribed in pencil on the wood behind the central sliding panel, "Made and warranted by T. G. Furber Newington, NH. Clocks."* COLLECTION OF SHERI AND NED GROSSMAN.

OVERLEAF, LEFT

FIGURE 6.1: *Portrait of a man, circa 1840, Ithaca, New York; attributed to Henry Walton; watercolor on paper; 7½ x 5¾ inches.* PRIVATE COLLECTION.

OVERLEAF, RIGHT

FIGURE 6.2: *Bucket bench cupboard, circa 1820, Pennsylvania; maple and pine with paint decoration that creates an abstract optical configuration, grained all over in black on a salmon ground; 72 x 44 x 15½ inches.* PRIVATE COLLECTION. PHOTOGRAPH COURTESY OF DAVID A. SCHORSCH.

6.1

THE MIDDLE

ATLANTIC STATES

THE HOME, A REFUGE FROM the outside world, was a special place in nineteenth-century America. People sought ways to create a pleasing environment in which families gathered. Whether in a large home or a one-room cabin, color and design warmed the interior and provided a feeling of comfort. Improved transportation during the second quarter of the nineteenth century eased the exchange of goods and services, allowing popular urban styles to infiltrate country towns. Because most rural Americans could not afford expensive furniture, wallpaper, and rugs, they utilized paint on the walls, floors, and furniture as a creative alternative.

Descriptions of nineteenth-century rural farmhouses occasionally appeared in journals. In 1822, when Jonas Heinrich Gudehus arrived in Berks County, Pennsylvania, from Germany, to teach in a Lutheran school, he kept a diary in which he described the beauty of the farmhouses. He was impressed by the beautifully painted kitchen walls and the life-size portraits of family members that graced the main rooms. Overwhelmed by the size of the stone or brick homes belonging to wealthy farmers, Gudehus wrote that they were equal to "princely palaces": "Their beauty from outside as well as their neatness inside and the comfortable arrangement of the same not seldom brought me to wonder and amazement."[1]

Gudehus notes particularly the creative use of paint to enhance everything. Colorful painted designs on walls and floors substituted for the expensive wallpaper and rugs seen in urban homes. The York, Pennsylvania, portrait

COUNTRY FURNITURE

6.4

of a family grouped in their parlor (figure 6.3) demonstrates how a creative combination of pattern and color accented a room. Walls hand-painted with squiggles and dots and stenciled with floral borders complement a gaily striped rug and plain painted furniture. Early nineteenth-century rural homes in New York State also boasted interior walls painted with color and designs. The stenciled wall from a Columbus, New York, home (figure 6.4) shows the attractive, warm effect of painted interior surfaces.

Just as rural people created a stylish look through the use of paint on walls and floors, rural furniture makers used

6.5

paint to achieve the effect of expensive inlay embellishments on furniture. The two drawers of the New York table in figure 6.5 demonstrate the way paint created the effect of wavy inlay. Equally impressive were the paint and gilded stencil designs that graced many Hitchcock-type chairs. Figure 6.6 displays a portrait of Mrs. Eunice Eggleston Darrow Spafford from Holley, New York, seated in a Hitchcock-type chair bearing a stencil design accented with gold powder. The stencil designs of the country artisan emulated the stenciled, carved, and gilded details on the formal furniture being made in the cities.

Throughout the nineteenth century, inexpensive painted and gilded chairs were pro-

6.6

FIGURE **6.3**: *Portrait of a York, Pennsylvania, family with Negro servant, circa 1828; unsigned; oil on wood panel; 15³/₄ x 11³/₄ inches.*
COLLECTION OF THE SAINT LOUIS ART MUSEUM (MODERN ART), BEQUEST OF EDGAR WILLIAM AND BERNICE CHRYSLER GARBISCH, 24,1981.

FIGURE **6.4**: *Stenciled walls in a parlor, 1804, Columbus, New York. During the nineteenth century, stenciled walls became popular as an alternative to expensive wallpaper.*
COLLECTION OF THE SHELBURNE MUSEUM, SHELBURNE, VERMONT, 4.19. PHOTOGRAPH BY KEN BURRIS.

FIGURE **6.5**: *Table, circa 1800, New York State; maker unknown; painted white pine; height, 29¹/₂ inches. A whimsical quality results from the unsophisticated attempt to create the Queen Anne style using cabriole legs and hoof feet. The decoration on this piece, which depicts vine and leaf borders on the top and around the drawer, is reminiscent of needlework.*
COLLECTION OF THE METROPOLITAN MUSEUM OF ART, PURCHASE, VIRGINIA GROOMES GIFT IN MEMORY OF MARY W. GROOMES, AND FUNDS FROM VARIOUS DONORS (1976), 1976.175.

FIGURE **6.6**: *Portrait of Eunice Eggleston Darrow Spafford, 1834, Holley, New York; Noah North; oil on canvas; 27¹/₂ x 23³/₈ inches. This artist is known to incorporate a portion of a stencil-decorated Hitchcock-type chair into his portraits, suggesting that he was familiar with the art of furniture-making. The chair boasts a grain-painted background with stenciled leaves and floral motifs embellished with gold powder.*
COLLECTION OF THE SHELBURNE MUSEUM, SHELBURNE, VERMONT, 27.1.1-13. PHOTOGRAPH BY KEN BURRIS.

duced throughout Pennsylvania, New York, and New Jersey by an increasing number of furniture manufacturers, large and small. Middle Atlantic craftsmen developed an extensive design vocabulary consisting of many motifs, including flowers, fruits, animals, birds, landscapes, and neoclassical elements. They combined these motifs with a variety of paint techniques on dower chests, corner cupboards, tables, and chairs as well as on small accessories such as boxes, all of which reflected the rural tastes of the craftsmen and their customers.

PENNSYLVANIA

In the late seventeenth century, large numbers of Germans from the Rhenish Palatinate, Alsace-Lorraine, Württemburg, Hesse, and German-speaking cantons of Switzerland emigrated to America in search of a better way of life, religious freedom, and vast agricultural opportunities. Most practiced the Protestant faith in Lutheran and Reform churches. A smaller number of Mennonites, Amish, Schwenkfelders, Moravians, and Dunkards also came to America before the nineteenth century, and many settled in Pennsylvania.

6.7

6.8

6.9

6.10

FIGURE 6.7: *Chest, 1803, Berks County, Pennsylvania; maker unknown; painted pine; 31 x 51 1/2 x 21 1/2 inches. This chest displays a red-orange ground faded to tan. Brown mottling or graining decorates this piece in addition to corner fans created by a putty roll.* COLLECTION OF THE PHILADELPHIA MUSEUM OF ART, GIFT OF ARTHUR SUSSEL, 45-12-1.

FIGURE 6.8: *Lift-top storage box, circa 1820–1840; southeast Pennsylvania; maker unknown; wood with polychrome decoration consisting of pots of flowers and swags in shades of red, green, and yellow; 10 1/2 x 17 3/4 x 11 inches.* COLLECTION OF PEGGY LANCASTER. PHOTOGRAPH COURTESY OF OLDE HOPE ANTIQUES, INC.

FIGURE 6.9: *Child's blanket chest, 1854, McConnellsburg, Fulton County, Pennsylvania; attributed to Joel Palmer; poplar with polychrome red base and freehand decoration; 19 1/8 x 31 3/4 x 14 1/4 inches.* COLLECTION OF MR. AND MRS. JOSEPH BRIGGS. PHOTOGRAPH COURTESY OF SOTHEBY'S.

FIGURE 6.10: *Lift-top blanket chest, circa 1810, Centre County, Pennsylvania; maker unknown; case painted white with scribed geometric patterns painted in red and dark cobalt blue within divided panels; 31 x 50 1/2 x 22 1/2 inches.* PRIVATE COLLECTION. PHOTOGRAPH COURTESY OF OLDE HOPE ANTIQUES, INC.

From 1683 to 1820, approximately 75,000 German-speaking Europeans resided in Pennsylvania.[2] Although most were farmers and tradesmen, many were artisans skilled in making furniture and ornamenting it with paint. Recalling from memory European furniture, textiles, and pottery, many first-generation immigrant craftsmen re-created these designs in the eighteenth and nineteenth centuries. French Huguenots who settled in Berks, Lehigh, and Northumberland Counties painted surfaces to imitate grained woods,

continuing the European tradition. Likewise, Berks County dower chests (figure 6.7) demonstrate the influence of the migrated tradition, as in the prancing horse design seen woven into European fabrics and on Swiss furniture and pottery.[3] Craftsmen were trained through an apprenticeship system in Europe and America in order to learn the art of furniture making and decorating. By the second decade of the nineteenth century, artisans keen on sharpening their skill referred to readily available paint-decorating manuals. In

COUNTRY FURNITURE

6.11

6.12

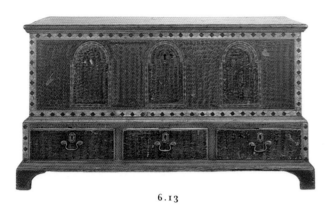

6.13

6.14

FIGURE 6.11: *Chest, nineteenth century, Centre County, Pennsylvania; maker unknown; wood painted a background color of reddish salmon with freehand decoration; 26³/₄ x 49 x 21 inches. The source for the design of the playful lions on the front of this chest is a fraktur by the Flat Tulip artist, Heinrich Otto.* PRIVATE COLLECTION. PHOTOGRAPH COURTESY OF CHEW & CO.

FIGURE 6.12: *Chest, 1796, Jonestown, Lebanon County, Pennsylvania; signed Christian Seltzer; white pine and paint; 23⁵/₈ x 52¹/₈ x 22¹/₈ inches.* COURTESY OF THE WINTERTHUR MUSEUM, GARDENS & LIBRARY, 59.2803.

FIGURE 6.13: *Lift-top blanket chest, 1780–1790, probably Centre County, Pennsylvania; maker unknown; pine painted in salmon with brown sponging, bands of diamonds, with three tombstone cartouches outlined with a yellow stripe containing blue diamonds; 27¹/₂ x 50 x 21¹/₂ inches.* PRIVATE COLLECTION. PHOTOGRAPH COURTESY OF OLDE HOPE ANTIQUES, INC.

FIGURE 6.14: *Miniature chest, 1861, Soap Hollow Valley, Pennsylvania; made by Peter K. Thomas; poplar, paint, and gilt stencil decoration; 24³/₄ x 15¹/₄ x 10³/₈ inches.* COLLECTION OF MR. AND MRS. ANTHONY P. PICADIO.

addition, the vast forests of Pennsylvania provided a bountiful supply of poplar and pine.

REGIONAL CRAFTSMEN AND THEIR PAINTED DESIGNS

Nineteenth-century artisans creatively decorated furniture with a variety of designs and paint surfaces. Cultural and religious traditions, geographic location, and shared taste for certain design motifs and techniques led to the formation of four distinct regional style centers in southeastern Pennsylvania. In Lebanon County, the Jonestown area was known for dower chests painted with floral bouquets in jugs. The Schwaben Creek valley area employed on furniture stylized motifs of the tree of life, birds, stars, angels, and praying children. By the middle of the century, Mennonites from Soap Hollow in Somerset County incorporated stenciling into their paint-decorated furniture and included designs of stars, hearts, horses, and birds. Unlike these craftsmen, the Amish of Lancaster and Mifflin Counties conformed to strict religious rules of simplicity that forbade fancy painted furniture.

At the end of the eighteenth century and the beginning of the nineteenth, the Jonestown school of decoration in Lebanon County demonstrated how a small group of craftsmen could share similar designs and furniture construction techniques. Researchers have identified at least four decorators from two families who worked in or near Jonestown. Each of these signed his furniture with decorative floral motifs on a background painted in a mottled, sponged effect. John Seltzer (1774–1845) was the son of Christian Seltzer, or Selzer (1749–1831), and John (1763–1828) and Peter Ranck (1770–1851) were brothers. Christian Seltzer, a joiner, constructed and decorated his chests with symmetrically designed panels of floral patterns, signing and dating each piece. A gifted artist, Seltzer drew graceful floral arrangements freehand in German-style jugs. Figure 6.12 shows three panels with floral arrangements in jugs. These are painted on the front of the chest, while the central panel portrays a woman in an elaborate headdress sprouting from a jug. After the drawing was inscribed into the wood with a sharp instrument such as a knife or compass point, the designs were painted.[4] The vase on the right bears the inscription "Chris/tian Seltzer/ his work/1796."

In an essay on Pennsylvania German furniture, Benno Forman states that "the central panel of the Christian Seltzer chest portrays the last gasp of the mannerist European high style in eighteenth-century America. The explicitly rendered female figure, emerging like a good-natured, wasp-waisted genie from a two-handled jug, is an echo of caryatids carved on European furniture in the sixteenth century, as are the asymmetrical leaves above the flowers in the upper quadrants of the panel."[5] Forman also describes the metamorphosis of tulips into pomegranates, a symbol in the Middle Ages of hope, fertility, and fruitfulness.[6] Seltzer was by far the leader of the Jonestown school.

Peter Ranck, another craftsman associated with this school, also made and decorated chests. From his account book, we are able to document that he made various types of furniture, including two painted chests.[7]

As in Jonestown, craftsmen from Schwaben Creek valley in southeastern Pennsylvania developed a reputation for producing distinct furniture. Originally, this furniture was called Mahantango Valley; however, after careful research, Frederick S. Weiser and Mary Hammond Sullivan renamed this group because it more accurately represented the Schwaben Creek region of Schuylkill and Northumberland Counties.[8]

Two groups of furniture emerged from this isolated German community of Lutheran and Reformed church members. One group consists of blanket chests, or dower chests, known

6.15

6.16

as *Kisten,* which were made for both adolescent women and men and were used to store objects in anticipation of marriage. Approximately ten are known, dating from 1798 to 1828. Each was constructed using a joined panel-and-frame technique, with two panels painted on the front, one bearing the owner's name, the other inscribed with the date. The chests' similar construction indicates that one craftsman may have made and decorated all of them.[9] Some of these chests were painted first with a reddish brown base coat and then decorated with a rag or instrument to create a swirling pattern. Others were simply painted a single color. Between the owner's name and the date, craftsmen painted pots of flowers similar to those grown locally—tulips, bleeding hearts, pinks, and daisies—or to the designs found in embroidery and on frakturs (illuminated texts with hand-drawn decoration, which include writing samplers (*Vorschriften*), decorated baptismal certificates (*Taufscheine*), house blessings (*Haussegen*), and other secular and religious items.[10]

The second group of furniture consisted of chests of drawers, desks, kitchen cupboards, and hanging cupboards made from 1827 to 1838. These pieces made greater use of color and playful designs of birds, flowers, animals, angels, praying children, and geometric forms. The Weiser and Sullivan study discovered twelve different decorators and three ornamenters who used a similar style. This study also revealed significant printed sources for a large percentage of the motifs found on this furniture.[11] Figure 6.17 shows a chest of drawers in the popular English style of that period, with two small drawers over three graduated drawers and turned feet. Painted on the reddish brown chest is a skillfully arranged composition of birds, vases of flowers and leaves, six-petal rosettes, rays, and stars.

The rosettes and corner rays frequently used to decorate this second group of furniture were influenced by the stenciled designs on American Empire furniture and the neoclassical paterae in marquetry on veneered

6.17

Adam-style furniture. Other motifs were the tree of life, a significant aspect of Medieval European vocabulary, and birds with foliage, a pattern from the mannerist style of sixteenth-century northern Europe.[12] The praying children motif seen on the lift-top chests in figures 6.15 and 6.16 is another popular design found on furniture of the Schwaben Creek valley. The front panel of the chest in figure 6.15 has hand-stamped rosettes against a dark green painted background framing the front, a tree of life motif, and two birds facing each other. The birds and the rosettes originated in manuscript and frakturs printed by publishers such as G. S. Peters of Harrisburg, while the stars and compasslike devices are from manuscript frakturs.[13] Stars decorated Pennsylvania German barns, butter molds, and tombstones, while angels frequently decorated baptismal certificates (*Taufscheine*). Weiser and Sullivan also traced the angel motif to a painting by Sir Joshua Reynolds entitled *The Infant Samuel.*[14]

FIGURE 6.17: *Chest, circa 1830, Mahantango Valley, Pennsylvania; maker unknown; painted pine; 48 x 42 1/2 x 22 inches. The rosettes and corner rays frequently used to decorate the furniture from this region were influenced by the designs seen on formal American Empire furniture and by the neoclassical paterae seen on veneered furniture in the Adam style.*
PRIVATE COLLECTION.
PHOTOGRAPH COURTESY OF SOTHEBY'S.

Another region known for painted furniture was Somerset County, specifically the Mennonite community of Soap Hollow. Recent research has identified eight cabinetmakers who signed their furniture and worked in a small, remote community within Conemaugh Township, Somerset County.[15] From the middle of the nineteenth century through the early twentieth century, these craftsmen produced paint-decorated furniture in a Germanic cabinetmaking tradition. They used a variety of decorative treatments, including freehand striping to imitate graining, freehand floral designs, and stenciled designs. The discovery of wood templates suggests a standardization of parts for this school of furniture.[16] Equally significant is the influence of neoclassical form and design on Soap Hollow furniture. Diamond escutcheons, reeding, turned columns, and urns of flowers became part of their neoclassical furniture vocabulary.[17]

Born and raised in Somerset County, in southwestern Pennsylvania, the progenitor of this school of furniture, John Sala Sr. (1819–1882), was listed in the official records not only as a carpenter and a farmer but also as a coffin maker and undertaker. Scott T. Swank, the director of Canterbury Shaker Village in Canterbury, New Hampshire, described Sala as "the change agent who synthesized and established the visual vocabulary of form and decoration that we recognize as Soap Hollow furniture."[18] Sala's apprentices carried on a distinctive tradition of furniture making and paint decoration, both of which were popular in his community. Makers stenciled their names or initials prominently on the front of case pieces with the phrase "manufactured by" or its abbreviation. This practice was a distinct characteristic of Soap Hollow furniture.

Another hallmark of Soap Hollow furniture is the use of silver and gilt stenciled inscriptions, dates, and decorations on plain, sponged, or grained backgrounds. The pine and poplar chest in figure 6.18 displays a red background with faux graining and freehand black diagonal stripes imitating rosewood. Silver and gold stenciled horses enhance the piece. Because it is believed that John Sala used horse stencils and hearts on his chests, this piece is attributed to him. In this case, stencils were laid on a wet varnish, after which gold and silver powders were placed on the still wet surface. Like other Pennsylvania German craftsmen, those of Soap Hollow worked with strong color and design. Red or maroon was most commonly used on the

FIGURE 6.18: *Chest, 1854, with initials "BKM"; Conemaugh Township in Soap Hollow valley; attributed to John Sala; pine and poplar with paint, silver, and gilt stencils. The background of this chest is painted red with black diagonal striping to simulate rosewood graining.*

6.18

cases, and black accented the moldings, feet, and side panels.

Soap Hollow furniture was not the only type of decorated furniture made in Somerset County. In the mid-nineteenth century, Jacob (1796–1883) and Elias (1832–1910) Knagy, father and son, made faux-grained furniture with gilt stencil designs using pine, poplar, and cherry. The case pieces had fine dovetail work similar to that of a quarter century earlier.[19] The Knagys, like many artisans of this period, used buttermilk paint. They used various shades of red, from salmon to vermilion to brown-maroon, with stencil designs of morning glories, eight-pointed stars, and baskets of flowers. The table and wardrobe in figures 6.19 and 6.20 serve as excellent examples of the fine stencil work and graining executed by the Knagys. Although Jacob Knagy initialed many of his pieces, no piece bears the signature of Elias, leading experts to believe that he merely assisted his father.

Amish craftsmen were responsible for another distinctive category of furniture. In the early 1700s they emigrated from Germany, the Alsace, and Switzerland and settled in Lancaster and Mifflin Counties, where they set to work as farmers.[20] The artisans among

6.20

6.19

them made and decorated their own furniture, which conformed to rules forbidding fancy painted furniture. In accordance with their belief in simplicity, humility, and modesty, the Amish restricted the use of decorations or "proud" expressions of any kind.[21] As a result, craftsmen in Lancaster and Mifflin Counties painted surfaces with a red or light blue background, occasionally using subdued black decorations or faux graining in shades of brown. In Somerset County, stenciled paint-decorated chests were popular with the Amish as well as the Mennonites. Decals, another decorative feature, were popular at the end of the century.

Until commercial lead-based paint became available in the 1860s, the Amish used milk-based paint. Although several recipes for milk

FIGURE 6.19: *Table, 1866, Somerset County, Pennsylvania; made by Jacob Knagy; wood painted to simulate graining, with gilded stenciling and the name "Nancy Kretchman" stenciled on the drawer.*
PRIVATE COLLECTION. PHOTOGRAPH COURTESY OF CHARLES MULLER.

FIGURE 6.20: *Wardrobe, 1852, Somerset County, Pennsylvania; made by Jacob Knagy; pine with poplar, painted red with turkey-feather graining and gilded stenciling; 76 x 54 x 21 3/4 inches.*
COLLECTION OF MR. AND MRS. ANTHONY P. PICADIO.

6.22

FIGURE 6.21:
Drawing of a desk and saltbox, Pennsylvania; by Henry Lapp; watercolor and ink; 4 1/2 x 8 inches.
COURTESY OF THE PHILADELPHIA MUSEUM OF ART, TITUS C. GEESEY COLLECTION, 58.110-31.

FIGURE 6.22: *Sewing box, 1885–1895, Pennsylvania; attributed to Henry Lapp; painted pine; 7 1/2 x 4 1/4 x 6 1/8 inches.*
COLLECTION OF THE PEOPLE'S PLACE, INTERCOURSE, PENNSYLVANIA.

6.21

paint existed, nineteenth-century Americans seemed to prefer a formula similar to the one used by the French. The recipe combined skimmed milk, fresh lime, oil of caraway, or nut or linseed oil, and Spanish white (calcium carbonate pigment).[22] Amish craftsmen grained furniture in a manner similar to that done by other regional craftsmen. After applying a base coat, the artisan applied a top coat and, while it was still wet, used combs, rags, sponges, or even crumpled paper to create a grained pattern.

Some Amish craftsmen decorated their own furniture with the help of family members. Henry Lapp (1862–1904), a well-known Amish craftsman, made simple, elegantly restrained furniture as well as paintings and watercolors. The 1890 Lancaster County directory listed Lapp as a carpenter; by 1896, however, he had opened a cabinet-making business.[23] Lapp's sister, Lizzy, occasionally assisted him by painting and graining the various pieces.[24] Figure 6.22 shows a small sewing box by Lapp, painted red with a yellow-grained drawer. Lapp, born deaf and partially mute, created a handbook that included pencil drawings and watercolors of his furniture and assisted him in selling furniture. The watercolor drawing of a desk and saltbox in figure 6.21 came from this handbook, in which he illustrated his designs. Lapp's sketchbook, now in the Philadelphia Museum of Art, indicates his skill and taste but also represents the material culture of the Amish people. The exact prototypes made from the furniture drawings have not yet been discovered.

These four regions of Pennsylvania were inhabited by Germans with varying backgrounds, philosophies, and design concepts; all produced extremely creative yet practical furniture. Craftsmen developed a visual vocabulary that expressed a love of color and design, incorporating creative pictorial scenes, flowers, animals, birds, and stars. Furniture-making techniques developed from region to region and included influences brought to America from Europe by immigrants. From the study of their furniture, an understanding of their material culture and philosophy emerges.

desk 25

desk.

salt box.

PENNSYLVANIA COUNTRY CHAIRS AND SETTEES

Throughout the nineteenth century, painted furniture continued to be an important part of most rural homes in Pennsylvania. Country craftsmen decorated chairs with various techniques including faux graining, smoke decoration, freehand decoration, and stencil work. The crest rails and tablet tops of these chairs proved to be ideal places for designs and surface treatments. The chairs in figure 6.23 display a technique called smoke decoration. To achieve this effect, artisans would first apply a light-colored base coat, then a varnish. Before the varnish dried completely, they would pass a lighted candle over the surface, achieving a pattern created by the soot which adhered to the varnish. The crest rails on the chairs in figure 6.23 flaunt a smoky green, marblelike surface design with a trio of freehand painted roses. Another compelling

plank-bottom chairs and settees were produced in central Pennsylvania. Made and decorated in small shops and placed primarily in the kitchen or parlor, they were colorful, sturdy, and inexpensive. They derived their strength from thick, bulbous legs and spindles and served the utilitarian needs of their rural owners. Fiddle, spindle, arrow, and balloon backs were the most popular forms. Craftsmen stenciled the tablet top and applied freehand striping to the plank seat and other areas of the chairs. Certain motifs, including pomegranates, grapes, apples, and pears, were popular in some counties and reflected the taste of the ornamenter. Apples, pears, and pomegranates were seen on chairs from Union County, for example, while grapes were used extensively in Snyder, Mifflin, and Juniata Counties.[25]

In the early part of the nineteenth century, Pennsylvania German craftsmen created exu-

6.23

example of rural decorated furniture is the settee in figure 6.24 from the manufactory of Robert Buehler of Pottstown, Pennsylvania. The ornamenter first painted the settee brown and then applied a varnish. Separate stencils were arranged to make a pattern on the tacky varnish. While the varnish was still wet, bronze powders were applied with a velvet pounce or brush against the curved edge of each stencil. Smaller details were applied with a small brush called a pencil.

During the second half of the nineteenth century, a wide variety of painted and gilded

berant, colorful designs that left a distinct mark on Pennsylvania painted furniture. The chest was an especially popular form that displayed designs incorporating faux graining, compass-made designs, real and imagined animals, and floral designs, plus motifs such as the heart and the star. In the second half of the nineteenth century, however, furniture became more sedate, reflecting the Victorian influence. Sturdy plank-bottom chairs and settees were painted with dark and quiet colors such as brown, black, and tan with stenciling colored with bronze or silver powders.

FIGURE 6.23: *Six chairs, 1820–1849, Bucks or Lancaster County, Pennsylvania; maker unknown; mixed hardwoods painted with smoke decoration; $33^3/_4$ x $18^3/_4$ x $18^1/_2$ inches.*
COLLECTION OF THE PHILADELPHIA MUSEUM OF ART, GIFT OF SUSANNE STRASSBURGER ANDERSON, VALERIE ANDERSON READMAN, AND VERONICA ANDERSON MACDONALD FROM THE ESTATE OF MAE BOURNE AND RALPH BEAVER STRASSBURGER, 1994-20-36-41.

Throughout the century the tradition of paint-decorated furniture flourished.

NEW YORK STATE

The promise of rich, fertile farmland and a location along the Hudson River led to several migrations of German settlers to New York State during the eighteenth century. By the mid-nineteenth century a wave of New Englanders had settled in northern New York State, increasing the number of towns oped even further when the railroad presented another means of transportation in New York State. Territorial expansion in the regions of northern New York State that bordered the Hudson River led to an increase in the number of towns as well as in the manufacture of furniture.

DECORATED FURNITURE

German-speaking immigrants are usually associated with Pennsylvania; however,

6.24

along the Hudson and in the outermost rural areas. Trade and commerce grew and prospered with the introduction of turnpikes and the appearance of the steamboat. In 1813, Albany listed three hundred mercantile firms, making it a commercial center.[26] The Erie Canal linked the Great Lakes with the Hudson River in 1825, and Albany's population doubled within a few years. Changes in transportation led to the expansion of commerce and faster movement of raw materials and products to cities and towns along the routes. Production of wheat, flour, and lumber and the manufacture of cotton increased as water power became readily available. Trade devel-

Palatines migrated to New York, Maryland, Virginia, and Ohio, and brought with them their tradition of paint-decorated furniture. As early as 1710, German-speaking immigrants arrived in the upper Hudson Valley. During the nineteenth century another wave of German immigrants settled in the Mohawk and Schoharie Valleys and nearby Albany County. Artisans from the area painted beguiling wreaths, swags of bellflowers, and bouquets with cabbage roses. The motifs were in sharp contrast to the hearts, stars, birds, and tulips that graced many of the pieces of Pennsylvania German and Virginia furniture.

As with the Pennsylvania Germans, the

chest was an important piece of furniture in many New York homes. Proof of this lies in the inventories that prominently list furniture. In fact, many nineteenth-century pieces from the northern part of New York State are painted chests composed of six pine boards, most of which have simple bracket bases.[27]

One design associated with painted furniture from New York State was the floral bouquet with cabbage roses set in urns. Originally seen on furniture, paintings, and engravings from the German-speaking regions of Austria, Germany, and Switzerland, these distinctive designs appeared on furniture made by German immigrants.[28] Blanket chests painted with flowers but made in Virginia and Pennsylvania do not exhibit the distinctive cabbage rose associated with New York examples. The colorful floral bouquets on chests from Albany and Schoharie Counties have distinctive designs of red and white cabbage roses arranged in an urn. Figure 6.25 shows a chest with a classically inspired two-handled urn filled with red and white cabbage roses and other flowers. A leafy vined border painted freehand frames this floral composition. Another interpretation is the miniature chest (figure 6.26) painted to simulate mahogany, which demonstrates changes that occurred within this school of design. The classical urn has been transformed into a squat bowl, and a mixture of flowers with the distinctive cabbage rose is framed by a stenciled border of vines and flowers.

During the nineteenth century, German-speaking immigrants fashioned distinctive painted furniture in northern New York, and

6.25

by the third decade, small shops and factories produced paint-decorated furniture. These artisans built a reputation for understanding the styles of the time as well as the needs of their customers. In many cases, the same person painted the walls in houses, the portraits of the farmers and their families, and the furniture as well.

COUNTRY FURNITURE CRAFTSMEN
In the nineteenth century, artisans who painted furniture often needed other ways to supplement their income. Business directories, census records, and newspaper advertisements list ornamental painters who decorated chairs, window shades, fire buckets,

FIGURE 6.25: *Chest, circa 1830, Schoharie County, New York; maker unknown; pine and poplar.*
PRIVATE COLLECTION.

FIGURE 6.26: *Miniature chest, 1830–1850, probably Albany County; pine painted to simulate mahogany with freehand and stencil decoration; maker unknown.*
COLLECTION OF SIDNEY GECKER, AMERICAN FOLK ART.

FIGURE 6.27: *Miniature blanket chest, circa 1830, Schoharie County; maker unknown; pine with freehand decoration.*
COURTESY OF ROBERT E. KINNAMAN & BRIAN A. RAMAEKERS, INC.

6.26

6.27

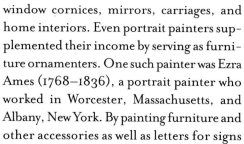

6.28

window cornices, mirrors, carriages, and home interiors. Even portrait painters supplemented their income by serving as furniture ornamenters. One such painter was Ezra Ames (1768–1836), a portrait painter who worked in Worcester, Massachusetts, and Albany, New York. By painting furniture and other accessories as well as letters for signs and interior walls, Ames was able to augment his income.[29] Another portrait painter from upstate New York, Noah North (1809–1880), painted portraits of adults and children, including Eunice Eggleston Darrow Spafford (figure 6.6). North is also thought to have painted furniture, because several of his portraits, including the one of Mrs. Spafford, feature a grain-painted and stenciled Hitchcock-type chair. The chair in this particular painting has a tablet top decorated with a stencil design, and actual gold powder is used to accent the floral designs. An 1850 directory of western New York State lists North as having a partner; they called their operation "Painters—House, Sign, and Fancy."[30]

Before opening their own shops, most rural decorators apprenticed in other shops or factories, where they learned the art of ornamental decoration. Allen Holcomb (1782–1860) probably learned his trade while serving just such an apprenticeship. Prior to opening his own business, Holcomb worked for Simon Smith, a chair maker in Troy, New York.[31] From 1809 to about 1835, Holcomb's account books show the range of furniture he made. Chairs, either plain-painted or ornamented with various techniques, were his most popular items.[32] A picture of the typical country cabinetmaker emerges from the pages of his account books. He created furniture for his local customers and painted fireboards, pails, tin trays, and picture frames. In addition, he repaired furniture, especially chairs, and was known to grind pigments and mix his own paints, as other ornamenters did. Figure 6.28 shows a Hitchcock-type chair made by Holcomb and featuring imitation rosewood, a very popular wood of the time. He used stencils and bronze powders on the crest rail, middle slat, and side posts. By varying the amount of bronze powder in each motif when rubbing

6.29

COUNTRY FURNITURE

it along the edge of the stencil, he created a full-bodied form with shading. To create the basket of fruit and flowers on the crest rail, Holcomb used several separate stencils. The stencils in figure 6.29 were used on the crest rail of the chair in figure 6.28.

By combining his own artistic ability and creative skills with popular techniques and styles of the time, Holcomb epitomized the rural craftsman. His designs benefited from the fact that improved transportation made it possible for craftsmen to travel and share their ideas and techniques. By the 1840s many chairs produced in northern New York were similar to the fancy chairs made and decorated by Allen Holcomb. Because of the stenciled decoration and simple construction, this chair resembled the Hitchcock-type chair from Connecticut. By the second half of the nineteenth century, these popular designs strongly influenced painted furniture and eventually replaced the regional styles.

Producing furniture that was at the same time practical and stylish was another goal of the rural craftsman. The chair in figure 6.34, from Ithaca, in northern New York, merged elements from the fancy Sheraton and Hitchcock-type chairs. Its paint and gilded decoration are stylish examples of sophisticated taste. The broad tablet top reveals a scene of a mill, a waterfall, and a forest. A stenciled and bronze-powdered leafy-vine design embellishes the scroll arms and the lower back posts, and the cross slat of the lower back is ornamented with a gilded and bronzed eagle and a cornucopia filled with fruit. These designs, popular symbols seen on Federal furniture from New York and Philadelphia, invoked patriotic pride in America's strength and plenitude.

Another New York craftsman, Rufus Cole (1804–1874), worked with his father, Abraham, in the Mohawk Valley. The New York State Business Directory of 1859 lists Cole as a "painter house and sign" in Broadalbin, New York. Later, the Fulton County Census of 1870 records Cole's occupation as

6.30

FIGURE 6.28: *Chair, circa 1835, New York State; made by Allen Holcomb; wood painted to simulate rosewood, with stencil and bronze powder decoration; height, 35$\frac{1}{2}$ inches.*
COLLECTION OF THE NEW YORK STATE HISTORICAL ASSOCIATION, COOPERSTOWN.

FIGURE 6.29: *Stencils, circa 1835, New York State; made by Allen Holcomb. These stencils were probably used to decorate the posts and crest rail of the chair in figure 6.28.*
COLLECTION OF THE METROPOLITAN MUSEUM OF ART, HARRIS BRISBANE DICK FUND, 1947, 47.31.83, 47.31.1(1).

FIGURE 6.30: *Tall-case clock, circa 1825, New York State; signed "Ab. Cole and R. Cole"; clock movement made by Riley Whiting, Winchester, Connecticut; wood painted to simulate wood graining with stencil decoration and bronze powder; 83$\frac{1}{2}$ x 17$\frac{1}{4}$ x 9$\frac{3}{4}$ inches. "R. Cole" is stenciled on the bottom apron of the clock, and a penciled signature inside of the clock door states, "Made and Sold by Ab. . . . Cole of. . . ."*
COURTESY OF JOEL AND LINDA EINHORN.

"Paintor-Carriage." His father was listed in the Grantor Records in Montgomery County in 1835 as part owner of a sawmill, which suggests that the father made the clocks, and the son decorated them.[33]

Cole accented tall-case clocks with faux graining and stencil decoration in bronze powder designs. The faux graining and imaginative whirl of color in figure 6.30 simulated graining but of no particular wood. After applying a base coat of yellow ochre to the tall clock, Cole used an instrument—perhaps a rag, feather, or pounce—to apply a brownish red color in a swirling pattern. While the graining solution was wet, he created striping by removing the solution in straight lines, revealing the base coat. Cole incorporated stenciled designs of fruit, leaves, and pinecones in a diamond pattern on the throat and base and at the top of the bonnet. The inside of the throat door bears a pencil signature, "Made and Sold by Ab. . . . Cole of . . ."; "R. Cole" is stenciled on the bottom of the clock. Over a dozen clocks with similar graining and stenciling have been discovered, and many have the penciled signature of Abraham Cole on the inside of the throat. The stenciled signature of his son, Rufus, appears on the bottom of the base of other pieces.

Figure 6.32 illustrates a tall-case clock decorated with exuberant swirls in imitation of graining. This clock has a bronze powder stencil decoration on the bonnet, throat, and base with freehand feather graining in imitation of veneer. It is signed "J. D. Green." The decorative graining on Green's clock resembles Cole's, so it's possible that Green served as an apprentice to Cole.[34] The stenciled

name "J. D. Green" is positioned on the center of the apron, the same place Cole signed his clocks. The decoration also features a diamond motif with a stenciled design on the throat, yet another feature similar to Cole's work.

From chairs to clocks, New York craftsmen became masters of decorative painted furniture and accessories. Freehand designs and stenciling combined with bronze powders and gilding raised the simplest, most practical pieces to a new level of creativity. As the nineteenth century progressed, and transportation improved, craftsmen came to northern New York State and spread their ideas and designs. New Englanders migrating to northern New York introduced their styles to the region, further influencing painted decoration on furniture. Furniture decorated with stencils in the manner of Hitchcock were extremely popular throughout New England, and by 1830, these patterns were found on New York chairs.

NEW JERSEY

By the second decade of the nineteenth century the demand for painted furniture had grown to the extent that manufactories and warehouses conducted business near style centers like New York, Philadelphia, and Baltimore. Newark, New Jersey, developed as a commercial manufacturing center where the chairmaking business prospered. In 1826, seventy-nine chair makers were in business there, led by David Alling, a well-known manufacturer.[35] Alling was apprenticed to his father but most likely furthered his education by serving as a journeyman in New York around 1790. He made low- to

6.31

6.32

6.33

medium-priced fancy, Windsor, and rush-bottomed chairs, which were sold in local and regional markets and exported to Latin America. In 1803, one of Alling's first sales —170 "unfinished" chairs—was to William Palmer, a New York fancy chair maker.[36]

By 1819, Alling had shipped 144 ornamented chairs in a variety of styles to New Orleans. Some of these had a more expensive faux-rosewood graining, gilding, and bronze decoration and were priced at $50 a dozen to $27 for a yellow painted chair with plain spindles.[37] To meet the demand for his furniture,

Alling contracted work outside his shop for chair parts and decorative labor such as bronzing, gilding, and striping. Specifically, in 1816, Alling contracted Moses Lyon to bronze 434 chairs, to ornament 248, to gild 143, and to stripe 56 chairs.[38] Business at Alling's factory reached new heights between 1825 and 1835, when he shipped 17,000 chairs to Natchez, Mobile, and New Orleans.

Alling and other manufactories were responsible for introducing stylish furnishings to upper- and middle-class southerners.[39] The fancy chair with a roll-top crest in figure 6.35 may have been the typical style shipped to southern ports. Faux grained to simulate rosewood, this chair features gilt stenciling on the posts and back slat and stenciled cornucopias filled with fruit. The cornucopias of fruits resembled the designs on Empire furniture made in the style centers of New York, Boston, and Philadelphia, which had impressively carved and gilded decorative elements. By borrowing features from the sophisticated vocabulary of city cabinetmakers, New Jersey craftsmen like Alling were able to give less expensive furniture a feeling of elegance and sophistication.

The nineteenth century was an important era in the development of painted furniture in the Middle Atlantic states. Early in the century, furniture reflected the influences of Europe. In addition, geographic isolation and a shared taste for certain designs and paint techniques led to distinct schools in Pennsylvania and New York. The rapid development of the hinterlands increased the production of painted furniture, leading to the growth of manufactories. The construction of turnpikes and canals, coupled with the emergence of the steamboat and the railroads facilitated commerce and further enhanced furniture production.

6.35

FIGURE 6.34: *Chair, circa 1825, Ithaca, New York; signed "R. H. Ranney Ithaca" on back of crest rail; polychrome scene with stencil decoration, bronze powder, and gilt on wood.*
PRIVATE COLLECTION.

FIGURE 6.35: *Chair, 1825–1835, Newark, New Jersey; made by David Alling; wood painted to simulate graining with stencil decoration; height, 34½ inches. Inspired by the elegant fancy chairs made for the wealthy, this less costly fancy chair, one of a pair, was made for the middle-class market and was used in the parlor or dining room.*
COLLECTION OF THE NEWARK MUSEUM, GIFT OF MADISON ALLING (1923), 23.2467.

6.34

7.1

154

CHAPTER SEVEN

THE
SOUTH

THE RICH, FERTILE SOIL OF the South drew immigrants from Europe and settlers from the northern states into areas of Virginia, Georgia, Tennessee, and North Carolina. English, Scotch-Irish, Irish, German, Swiss, and a small number of Welsh immigrants came to this region and, by the end of the eighteenth century, were joined by German-speaking immigrants from Pennsylvania. Most of these people settled in Virginia and North Carolina, where they cultivated the land and lived as backcountry farmers. Their lives centered on farming and the church, and their simply built homes and furniture reflected their conservative taste. The furniture and interior walls of many homes, whether log cabins or two-story structures, were embellished with faux graining, pictorial scenes, and stenciling.

Cragfont was located forty miles outside of Nashville, Tennessee, and was owned by Brigadier General James Winchester, who served in the War of 1812 and later became the first Speaker of the Tennessee Assembly. Constructed of limestone and timber rather than logs, this home emulated the Georgian style of those built in Maryland and brought an aura of sophistication to a virtual wilderness. The faux graining that adorned the overmantel in the parlor (figure 7.3) and the furniture, which was either made locally or imported from Baltimore and New Orleans, attest to this sophistication.[1] Like other homes in America, southern homes were gathering places for family and friends and reflected the values of the farmers and merchants who built them.

In the late eighteenth and early nineteenth centuries, Pennsylvania Germans from Berks, Lancaster, York, Bucks, and Montgomery Counties

7·3

7·4

FIGURE 7.4: *Fireplace wall, 1836, near Wagram, Scotland County, North Carolina; painted by I. (or J.) Scott; polychromed wall with cityscape possibly of New York City. The panels below the chair rail are grain-painted to simulate a variety of woods, including bird's-eye maple, quarter-sawn oak, and mahogany. The baseboard is marbleized, as are portions of the fireplace surround. The swags around the top of the room are painted freehand. The overmantel painting shows New York City's waterfront in flames.* COLLECTION OF THE ABBY ALDRICH ROCKEFELLER FOLK ART CENTER, WILLIAMSBURG, VIRGINIA, 1956.101.1.

joined the large numbers of Europeans and settled on the rich, fertile land of the back-country of Virginia.[2] These settlers traversed the wagon road from Pennsylvania to Maryland and then to Virginia. An eighteenth-century traveler, in describing the beautiful Shenandoah Valley as "rich and fertile," wrote: "far from the bustle of the world, they live in the most delightful climate and the richest soil imaginable. They are everywhere surrounded with beautiful prospects and sylvan scenes—lofty mountains, transparent streams . . . the whole interspersed with an infinite variety of flowering shrubs, constitute the landscape surrounding them. . . . Their inexperience of the elegances of life precludes any regret that they have not the means of enjoying them; but they possess what many princes would give up half their dominions for —health, content, and tranquillity of mind."[3]

Wythe County in southwestern Virginia attracted German-speaking Swiss, Scotch-Irish, German, and English settlers. In 1792, Stophel Zimmerman and John Davis donated land to establish a county seat, Wytheville. This town boasted a population of 700, eight stores, two newspaper printing offices, one Presbyterian, one Methodist, one German Lutheran, and one Catholic church.[4] By 1800 a community of Germans and Swiss inhabited western Wythe County, the area with the most fertile farmland. Because of strong family ties, a community closely associated with the Lutheran or Reformed church, and the use of the German language, these people were culturally isolated from their Scotch-Irish neighbors.[5]

Like Virginia, Georgia, another state rich with fertile soil, experienced a noticeable increase in its population during the eigh-

7.5

teenth century. This was due in part to the migration along the wagon road of Scotch-Irish, English, and Welsh settlers from the northern states. These settlers were joined by a few second-generation Germans. At the beginning of the nineteenth century, after the Creek and Cherokee ceded their land, large numbers of northerners and farmers from South Carolina, North Carolina, and Virginia settled in Georgia as well, and their conservative lifestyle dominated the area. A few plantations existed in the "plantation belt" along the fall line in the middle of the state, down the western portion of the Central Plain, and in the tidewater counties.[6] The plantation owners, however, were absentee planters. The farmer who worked alongside the owner's slaves was the actual planter and lived on the farm, which was the most common agricultural unit.

By 1860, two-thirds of the population of North Carolina, another rural state, was composed of yeoman farmers working small, self-sufficient farms of 100 acres or less.[7] A smaller number farmed larger tracts, but all the landowners concentrated on producing crops to meet their families' needs, with just a small percentage of the crops going to market. Geographic barriers and poor transportation isolated these backcountry southerners and strengthened their community and family lives. Moving west beyond the Mississippi River, settlers from North Carolina, Virginia, and Pennsylvania

FIGURES 7.5 & 7.6:
Wall murals, 1870–1880, West Virginia; attributed to the Reverend Daniel Schroth; polychrome on wood.
THE WARNER COLLECTION OF THE GULF STATES PAPER CORPORATION, TUSCALOOSA, ALABAMA. PHOTOGRAPH COURTESY OF DEANNE LEVISON'S AMERICAN ANTIQUES.

7.6

settled in Tennessee. The farming of tobacco and cotton was their primary occupation.

Southern country furniture reflected the isolation of these communities from the more sophisticated cities and, therefore, lagged far behind in style and design. Relying on their own creative ability and talent, the country artisans produced simple, individualistic furniture reflecting the conservative lifestyle of each community. Conservative attitudes were further represented by furniture decorated in brown, black, dark red, blue, and ochre. Frequently, itinerant artists executed a variety of decorative wall treatments. I. (or J.) Scott painted the parlor walls in the home of Colonel and Mrs. Alexander Shaw of Scotland County, North Carolina (figure 7.4). Grain-painted doors, dados, and painted, swagged draperies combined with an overmantel painting of a view of the New York waterfront in flames to create a charming, dramatic background for this family. Another pictorial wall scene is part of a group of scenic wall treatments painted by the Reverend Daniel F. Schroth and once graced a log home in Randolph County, West Virginia (figures 7.5 and 7.6). Schroth painted similar scenes for each of his four daughters, and each serves as a pictorial commentary on agrarian life amid the natural beauty of the bucolic countryside.

Although southern furniture displayed surface techniques similar to those used in northern designs, including smoke decoration, grain painting, geometric designs, and some pictorial scenes and stenciling, it had an individual character and charm that set it apart from northern painted furniture. Consider a chest from Georgia made of yellow pine with a solid board top bordered with a beaded mitered molding and a case with dovetail joints and turned feet (figure 7.10). Its ochre background color has been dotted and rubbed with umber over its surface. The earth's rich colors inspired the paint, and nature's creatures influenced the designs. Carrots with their roots exposed and sun faces are whimsically painted in combination on the front.

Southern country furniture expressed homespun resourcefulness—furniture with a purpose. The basic, conservative life of farmers left little room for wastefulness. Craftsmen therefore built pieces that were attractive yet practical: blanket chests, pie safes, hunt boards, and sugar chests. The variety of wall treatments and creatively decorated utilitarian furniture found in southern homes expressed the unique individuality of the southern craftsmen and reflected their uncomplicated lifestyle.

No single type of furniture demonstrated the creativity of southern craftsmen better than the blanket chest. Whether placed in a log cabin or in a more substantial two-story frame structure, chests were practical, attractive examples of painted furniture. In fact, the distinctive culture of the German community in Wythe County, Virginia, led to the development of a school of decorated furniture. All of the identified furniture from this school can be classified into five groups, displaying variations on a design of tulips or dahlialike flowers set in an urn (figure 7.8). On each of the two or three panels a distinctive arc hovers over each tulip. Thirty or more decorated blanket chests from Wythe County have been discovered and may have been influenced by the Jonestown, Pennsylvania, school of decoration.[8] This connection results from the fact that the design layout and paint techniques are similar. In addition, all of the chests share similar construction, dimensions, and paint colors. Most chests were made of pine and have dovetailed cases with bracket feet, pegged base and foot construction with a pegged molding. Background colors range from brown to dark red, with one having a dark blue background. Sponged or mottled treatments cover the background color on some, and most have lids decorated with either two classical panels with a star or two large white circles. Using a compass or template, the craftsmen developed designs in a manner similar to that used by the Pennsylvania Germans of Jonestown. Paint was applied after the

7.7

7.8

7.9

7.10

7.11

7.12

FIGURE 7.7: *Blanket chest, circa 1800, Wythe County, Virginia; possibly from the Johannes Hudel shop; sponge and freehand decoration on poplar; 25¹/₂ x 49³/₄ x 20¹/₂ inches.* PRIVATE COLLECTION. PHOTOGRAPH COURTESY OF CHRISTIE'S.

FIGURE 7.8: *Blanket chest, circa 1800, Wythe County, Virginia; maker unknown; painted poplar; 25¹/₂ x 52 x 23 inches. More than likely, the decoration on this chest was inspired by the Pennsylvania German designs seen on furniture from Jonestown.* COLLECTION OF RODDY AND SALLY MOORE. PHOTOGRAPH BY GREG VAUGHN.

FIGURE 7.9: *Blanket chest, 1800–1820, Wythe County, Virginia; possibly from the Johannes Hudel shop; poplar; 27¹/₂ x 50⁷/₈ x 21¹/₂ inches. Four distinct groups of chests have been identified from Wythe County. This is one of the later chests displaying lunette panels.* COLLECTION OF THE MUSEUM OF EARLY SOUTHERN DECORATIVE ARTS, 4009.

FIGURE 7.10: *Chest, 1850–1870, Franklin County, Georgia; maker unknown; yellow pine with freehand decoration; 24 x 38 x 17¹/₂ inches. Inside the lid are the following inscriptions: "SAB, Susan M. Winn, Susan Burden, S M Winn her chist 1870." The surface is painted with an ochre background and then rubbed with an umber color and embellished with carrot-shaped designs and sun faces.* PRIVATE COLLECTION. PHOTOGRAPH COURTESY OF DEANNE LEVISON'S AMERICAN ANTIQUES.

FIGURE 7.11: *Blanket chest, nineteenth century, North River, Augusta County, Virginia; maker unknown; yellow pine with freehand and stencil decoration; 26¹/₂ x 54¹/₂ x 21 inches.* PRIVATE COLLECTION. PHOTOGRAPH BY GREG VAUGHN.

FIGURE 7.12: *Chest, Shenandoah County, Virginia; made by Johannes Spitler; sponge and graining with freehand decoration on wood, inscribed "DP/1796/jSP."* PRIVATE COLLECTION. PHOTOGRAPH COURTESY OF DEANNE LEVISON'S AMERICAN ANTIQUES.

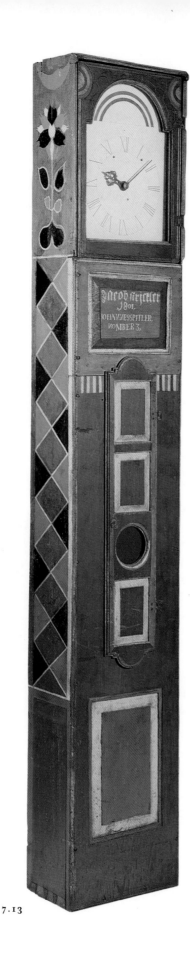

7.13

design was scratched onto the wood. Figures 7.7 and 7.8 show two variations of the Wythe County school of decoration. The floral arrangement in the middle panel of figure 7.7 differs from the others in that the halo over the central tulip is more complex. The chest in figure 7.9 has two lunette panels with a sponged background and is attributed to Johannes Hudel (1772–1839), who was possibly the decorator and joiner. Two chests similar to this one have been found and carry the signature of Johannes Hudel either scratched or painted into one of the urns.

Another area of Virginia attractive to Swiss and German settlers who came to farm the land was Shenandoah County, a rich, fertile area situated between the Massanutten Mountain ridge and the Shenandoah River. Although these people continued the Germanic tradition of cabinetmaking, their unique paint-decorated furniture reflected the area's isolation and vast creative ability. Johannes Spitler (1774–1837), a Shenandoah County artisan, crafted furniture that displayed designs of birds, hearts, flowers, geometric motifs, and architectural forms. His paint-decorated furniture has been either signed by him or attributed to his hand. Similar paint-decorated furniture has surfaced from this area, indicating that Spitler influenced other artisans from this region. His bold, idiosyncratic style can be seen in the clock (1801) signed by Spitler in figure 7.13. It was made for Mennonite preacher and fraktur artist Jacob Strickler (1770–1842), who was related to Spitler and lived on an adjacent farm.[9] The painted motifs on the clock resemble the forms incorporated into Strickler's Zierschrift, an ornate fraktur (figure 7.14). The diamond and floral designs and the upside-down heart of the fraktur appear on the side of the clock. Spitler went so far as to copy the name "Strickler" as it was written on the fraktur onto the front panel of the clock. Like other creative artists, Spitler incorporated geometric and architectural motifs into paint-decorated furniture, creating an exciting interplay of forms. The most expressive piece of furniture made and decorated by Spitler is the yellow pine blanket chest with walnut battens at either end of the lid in figure 7.19. The front of this chest exhibits geometric and architectural designs. A pair of swan's-neck pediment motifs, possibly derived from the bonnet of a tall-case clock or from a secretary bookcase, grace the central panel. The quarter-fans painted above a band of diamonds and vertical columns as well as the red and white bars indicate that neoclassical furniture influenced Spitler's work. His designs, however, were not limited to one source, as demonstrated by his use of birds, hearts, and flowers as embellishment. With the help of a compass, Spitler created a symmetrical design of hearts and tulips on the yellow pine blanket chest with dovetailed corners and bracket feet (figure 7.17). The birds were drawn freehand and then painted. With great success, Virginia craftsmen produced individually designed painted furniture that incorporated sponging and faux graining with various designs of birds, hearts, flowers, and geometrical forms.

During the first half of the nineteenth century, Georgian painted furniture reflected the region's rural lifestyle. Fanny Kemble recorded her thoughts and experiences as the wife of a Georgia plantation owner. In describing the furniture as lacking in any sophisticated details, she wrote that "the wash stands, clothes-presses, sofas, tables, etc., with

FIGURE 7.14: *Zierschrift, 1794, Shenandoah County, Virginia; signed by Jacob Strickler; watercolor and ink on paper; 12 1/8 x 15 1/8 inches.* COURTESY OF THE WINTERTHUR MUSEUM, GARDENS & LIBRARY.

7.14

7.15

7.16

7.17

7.18

FIGURE 7.15: *Chest, 1829, possibly from Greene County, Tennessee; painted tulip poplar and yellow pine, tinplate, and iron; 27¹¹/₁₆ x 48³/₄ x 22¹/₄ inches.*
COLLECTION OF THE ABBY ALDRICH ROCKEFELLER FOLK ART CENTER, WILLIAMSBURG, VIRGINIA, 85.2000.1.

FIGURE 7.16: *Blanket chest, 1801, Chatham or Randolph County, North Carolina; maker unknown; yellow pine painted with freehand decoration; 29 x 48 x 18 inches. The brushwork of the eagle and the border on this chest is reminiscent of the single-stroke brushwork of decorated tinware known as tole.*
COLLECTION OF THE MUSEUM OF EARLY SOUTHERN DECORATIVE ARTS, 2528.

FIGURE 7.17: *Blanket chest, 1795–1810, Shenandoah County, Virginia; attributed to Johannes Spitler; yellow pine with polychrome decoration; 28 x 49¹/₂ x 22³/₈ inches.*
COLLECTION OF THE MUSEUM OF EARLY SOUTHERN DECORATIVE ARTS, 3806.

FIGURE 7.18: *Blanket chest, circa 1830, Madison County, North Carolina; maker unknown; polychromed southern yellow pine; 20³/₄ x 37¹/₄ x 18³/₈ inches. The chest is paneled with applied moldings reminiscent of early Jacobean furniture. The panels of varying sizes create an interesting design.*
COLLECTION OF THE HIGH MUSEUM OF ART, ATLANTA, PURCHASED WITH FUNDS FROM THE DECORATIVE ARTS ACQUISITION TRUST AND AN ANONYMOUS GIFT, 1979.1000.30.

7.19

FIGURE 7.19: *Detail of blanket chest, circa 1800, Shenandoah County; attributed to Johannes Spitler; yellow pine with paint decoration.*
PRIVATE COLLECTION.

7.20

Many of the decorative features found on furniture from Virginia and Georgia, like faux graining, freehand decoration, and architectural designs, were replicated on painted furniture from North Carolina. The pine chest from Madison County, North Carolina (figure 7.18), displays applied molding reminiscent of early Jacobean furniture. The chest is painted green with black moldings and base and has panels of varying sizes that create an interesting geometric design, which adds to the unusual quality of the piece. The scalloped apron appears on both the front and the back in different arrangements of arches. Another yellow pine chest with bracket feet, this one from Randolph County, has an eagle, an important American symbol that was rarely seen on southern furniture (figure 7.16). In addition, this chest bears brushwork on the eagle and border design that is similar to the brush strokes seen on tole, or decorated tinware.

Homespun resourcefulness and conservative taste combined to produce practical furniture throughout the South. Whether safes, sugar chests, or hunt boards, these representative pieces found a useful place in homes. From the middle of the nineteenth century, elaborately designed punched-tin safes were made in and around Wythe County, Virginia.[11] These safes stored food and were ventilated by panels of punched tin. The designs consisted of the urn-and-grape pattern with

which our house is furnished . . . are very neat pieces of workmanship, neither veneered or polished indeed, nor of costly materials."[10] Most southerners rejected the newer, more popular styles of furniture, and craftsmen from Georgia were equally unwilling to embrace the sophisticated designs that permeated the market in the cities. Plain furniture was frequently painted in shades of brick red, brown, green, black, dark blue, and ochre. Some pieces showed a sponged or grained surface treatment that also was painted in these colors.

7.21

7.22

FIGURE 7.20: *Food safe, 1835–1850, Taylor County, Georgia; maker unknown; yellow pine with paint; 82⅝ x 43½ x 19¾ inches. This safe has a sponged and dotted surface decorated in blue, rust, and green.*
PRIVATE COLLECTION. PHOTOGRAPH COURTESY OF THE ATLANTA HISTORICAL SOCIETY.

FIGURE 7.21: *Slab or hunt board, 1800–1830, Spartanburg, South Carolina; maker unknown; yellow pine.*
PRIVATE COLLECTION. PHOTOGRAPH COURTESY OF DEANNE LEVISON'S AMERICAN ANTIQUES.

FIGURE 7.22: *Sugar chest, 1820–1830, with paint, 1850–1860, Maury County, Tennessee; maker unknown; cherry and tulip poplar; 37½ x 30½ x 29¼ inches. The graining on this chest resembles oak and is also reminiscent of the swirling pattern seen on redware plates.*
COLLECTION OF THE TENNESSEE STATE MUSEUM, NASHVILLE.

7·23

FIGURE **7·23**: *Food safe, 1830–1880, Wythe County, Virginia; attributed to the Fleming K. Rich shop; poplar and punched tin with paint; 53½ x 53½ x 18 inches. The punched-tin panels display the urn-grape and diamond pattern.* PRIVATE COLLECTION. PHOTOGRAPH COURTESY OF *THE MAGAZINE* ANTIQUES.

FIGURE **7·24**: *Food safe, 1870, probably Wythe County, Virginia; polychromed punched tin and walnut, dated and initialed "RDH"; 54½ x 43 x 18 inches.* PRIVATE COLLECTION. PHOTOGRAPH COURTESY OF MILLIE MCGEHEE.

COUNTRY FURNITURE

7.24

7.25

they were dovetailed. Doors and cases had mortise-and-tenon joints held together with brass or iron hinges. The short legs were either tapered or turned. Five distinct decorative patterns were attributed to Wythe County designs. One was an urn with grapes and tulips and a star, sunflower, diamond, or tulips at the top of the central stalk. Other patterns included a diamond, a fylfot, an urn, and a double urn over double urns. More than likely, the craftsman used a template to lay the design on a piece of tin. Many of the punched-tin panels appeared on painted furniture. The food safe in figure 7.23, made in the shop of Fleming K. Rich, displays a punched-tin pattern of clusters of grapes on either side of the main stalk. Rich and his family made furniture and safes between 1830 and 1880 and were known to have as many as forty apprentices and cabinetmakers associated with their shop. Surviving letters, daybooks, bills of sale, and contracts document the existence of this shop and its apprentices. The punched-tin safes and paint-decorated blanket chests of Wythe County attest to the creative artistry of the German culture in Virginia.

Even though most southerners lived a simple rural life, they enjoyed entertaining and were known for their hospitality. Furniture therefore served a practical purpose in storing and serving food. The painted Georgian food safe in figure 7.20 does not have punched tin, but it is made of yellow pine with a painted sponged treatment on the drawers, lower doors, and sides. The slab, or hunt board (figure 7.21), the sugar chest (figure 7.22), and the cellarette, or liquor stand, are all practical southern pieces. Craftsmen

a sunflower, diamond, star, or tulip at the top of the central stalk. Artisans produced a variation on this design on the urns and in the corners of the tin panels. Made of walnut, cherry, or poplar with punched-tin panels, Wythe County food safes were larger than some found elsewhere and served as a practical means of ventilating the food as well as decorative additions to the home. The pattern of the punched-tin panels on these safes made them different from the safes being made elsewhere. The Wythe County safes boasted four ten-by-fourteen-inch panels or two twenty-by-fourteen-inch panels crimped together. When drawers were incorporated into the safe,

COUNTRY FURNITURE

elevated them on tall legs so that air could circulate around the food; furthermore, tall furniture accented high-ceilinged rooms, which were standard architecture in substantial southern homes.[12] Figure 7.21 represents an excellent example of a tall sideboard known as a slab and possessing a shallow case. The long legs were either turned or squarely tapered. This particular slab boasts unusual openwork on the apron below the case. Weddings and festive parties, where an elaborate array of food was usually displayed, served as ideal occasions for using a slab. An account of the wedding of Wil-liam Benson Jefferson Norman to Julia Ann Maxwell on July 9, 1871, describes a typical menu:

> The wedding supper consisted of three famous Southern meats, ham, steak, and chicken; the three famous Southern indispensables, bread, butter, and gravy; the three famous Southern pies, potato, apple, and egg custard, and topped off with boiled custard and cake. . . . There were not as many guests as were at the wedding and sometimes the guests were seated for the infare dinner. But usually they stood at a high table decorated with fancy food similar to the wedding table.[13]

While conservative and traditional, country furniture from Georgia met the needs of rural families.

The wide variety of decorated furniture from Virginia, North Carolina, and Georgia represented the southern craftsmen's creative resourcefulness. Blanket chests ornamented with a broad spectrum of designs indicative of the artisans' individual talents and cultural backgrounds constituted the most extensively used pieces of furniture. Completing the genre were other southern furniture pieces, including slabs and sugar chests. Local woods such as tulip poplar, white and yellow pine, and cherry were frequently utilized to fashion furniture that was eventually placed anywhere from a one-room log cabin to a plantation house. Craftsmen painted and decorated these pieces with expressive brush strokes that created pictorial scenes, faux graining, and abstract designs. The country furniture from the South represented the idiosyncratic, vibrant nature of the region.

7.26

FIGURE 7.26: *Door, circa 1820, from the Edwards-Franklin House, Surry County, North Carolina; wood painted to imitate graining.*
PHOTOGRAPH BY GARY CLARK AS SEEN IN *SOUTHERN ACCENTS.*

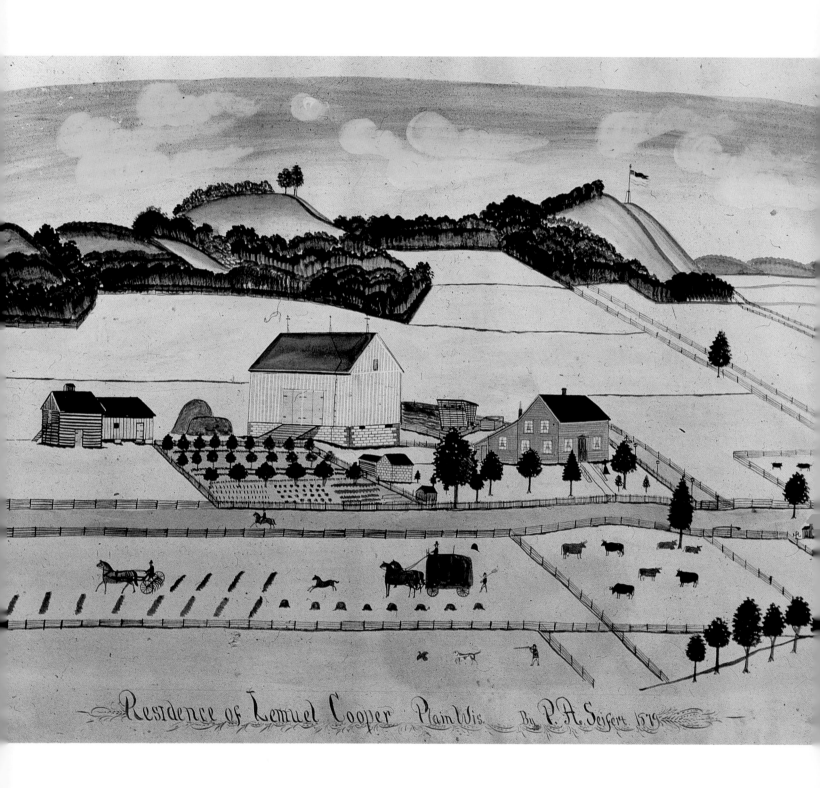

Residence of Lemuel Cooper Plain Wis. By P. A. Seifert 1879

CHAPTER EIGHT

THE WESTERN

FRONTIER

I N HIS FIRST INAUGURAL ADDRESS in 1801, Thomas Jefferson described America as a "chosen country, with room enough for our descendants to the hundredth and thousandth generation." Two years later he purchased the Louisiana Territory from France, doubling the size of the nation. In 1804, Meriwether Lewis and William Clark led a carefully selected group up the Missouri, across the Great Divide, and into the valley of the Columbia River, returning the following year. In their wake, other explorers, fur traders and trappers, naturalists, documentary artists, mapmakers, and surveyors ventured into Arkansas, Oklahoma, Texas, the upper Mississippi Valley, the Colorado region, Santa Fe, and the upper reaches of the Rio Grande. For Americans this vast stretch of land meant opportunity, a place to build a new life, find religious freedom, seek fortune, and escape industrialization and a new social order. Thus begun America's great western migration.

Following the War of 1812, large numbers of migrants from the original thirteen colonies began to move over the Appalachian Mountains into the Mississippi River valley and across the Great Plains. Ralph Waldo Emerson spoke of America as "a country of beginnings, of projects, of designs, of expectations,"[1] a land that could accommodate the new settlers of the western frontier. Restless and optimistic New Englanders left their farms, and whole families from soil-depleted southern plantations traveled along the trails and roads of the early explorers to seek out new lives. At the same time, immigrants from Europe crossed the Atlantic to the coastal cities of America, then pushed on to Ohio and beyond. Alexis de Tocqueville described "this double emigration" to the West as a "gradual and continuous progress of the European race towards the Rocky Mountains."[2] Thus is it not surprising that western frontier furniture reflects many traditions. Native Americans, New Englanders, French, Germans, Swedes, English, Swiss, Norwegians, Spaniards, and Mexicans each brought distinctive decoration to the furniture built for their frontier homes.

The sharp physical realities of the westward journey and frontier life often clouded the mythic sweep of the vast landscape and the great promise of a second chance. The problems of the frontier called for ingenious solutions; making do with what was at hand was part of every task. Vernacular furniture of the West was built from native wood, using the tools at hand, and decorated to suit the taste of the owner. A few pieces of furniture made the trip west and were copied. Most furniture, however, was constructed on arrival in a joinery tradition similar to that used by the settlers before they journey west. Decoration drew from folk traditions and from prevailing furniture styles. In many frontier towns grainpainting was considered the height of style and fashion.

THE NORTHWEST TERRITORY
Established in 1787, the Northwest Territory comprised Michigan, Ohio, Illinois, Wisconsin, and Indiana. Immigration to this area was slow until after the 1795 signing of the Treaty of Greenville with Native American tribes. Thereafter, settlers from the East Coast, England, Wales, and Germany traveled along the canals and turnpikes, establishing homesteads and forming communities (figure 8.1). From 1810 to 1840 the population of these five states grew tenfold, from 276,424 to 2,893,783.[3] After attaining statehood in 1803, Ohio became the gateway to the Northwest Territory, a crossroads of American and European culture. Marietta, the first settlement in the state, was established by the Ohio Company, a speculative land grant enterprise composed of New Englanders; Cincinnati was founded by John Cleves Symmes and associates from New Jersey. Settlers from Virginia clustered in Adams and Ross Counties, near the Virginia border; and the northeastern section of Ohio was settled by people from Connecticut. New England Shakers established settlements near Lebanon, and another communal group, the Society of Separatists of Zoar, left Germany and, with the assistance of Philadelphia Quakers, founded the village of Zoar in 1817. Other Germanic groups like the Amish and the Mennonites first settled in Pennsylvania, then migrated and formed new communities in northern Ohio. Swiss, French, Scottish, English, and Dutch settlers arrived as well and clustered together in communities throughout the fertile farmland and along the rivers.

The furniture produced in Ohio reflected not only the background of the makers but also something of the prevailing Federal and Empire styles of the East Coast design centers. Ohio furniture is made of local woods—black walnut, cherry, maple, and poplar—and is characterized by "generally heavy construction, and the use of bold turnings."[4] Common forms included freestanding corner cupboards, one- and two-drawer stands, punched-tin pie safes, turned-leg drop-leaf tables, wardrobes, wall cupboards, six-board blanket chests, and a variety of Windsor and fancy chair forms. Federal and Empire styling prevailed, the latter well into the 1880s in some regions of the state. The broad flat surfaces of much of this furniture provided a ready surface for grain painting and freehand ornamentation, often characterized by sophisticated and well-developed graining techniques. Surviving examples of Ohio paint-decorated furniture give evidence of the variety of cultures and the genius of individual craftsmen.

Like the furniture of Pennsylvania, many of the boldly painted surviving Ohio blanket chests reflect the vocabulary of German

PAGE 172
FIGURE 8.1: *Residence of Lemuel Cooper, 1879, Plain, Wisconsin; painted by Paul A. Seifert (1840–1921); watercolor, oil, and tempera on paper; 21⅞ x 28 inches.*
COLLECTION OF THE MUSEUM OF AMERICAN FOLK ART, NEW YORK, MUSEUM OF AMERICAN FOLK ART PURCHASE.
PAGE 173
FIGURE 8.2: *Side chair, one of a pair, 1820–1830, Ohio; pine with painted decoration; dimensions unknown.*
PRIVATE COLLECTION. PHOTOGRAPH COURTESY OF ROBERT E. KINNAMAN & BRIAN A. RAMAEKERS, INC.

vernacular furniture. Amish Mennonites moved from Pennsylvania into Ohio between 1820 and 1860, settling in the north-central part of the state. The carpenter and cabinet-maker Moses Troyer (1838–1923), a member of the Amish Mennonite church, made a chest as a wedding gift for his wife, Nancy Sommers. The painted central reserve displays his initials and Nancy's, which flank a vase and bouquet of flowers. This asymmetrical arrangement of roses, vines, and native wildflowers is a variation on the more traditional symmetrical arrangements of Pennsylvania German flowers, which usually feature stylized tulips and lilies. The overall ground of the chest is grain-painted; the four corners ending in ring-turned feet are stained a darker shade to create columnlike corners. Another Ohio chest with an urn and wheat motif on the central panel of the front, attributed to Valentine S. Yoder (1831–1912) of Sugarcreek, Tuscarawas County, features a decoration motif, which is reminiscent of the decorative designs on the furniture of Schoharie Valley in New York, another area settled by Germans.

Two other Tuscarawas County blanket chests reflect the popularity of light-colored woods among mid-century Ohioans. The unique foxtail decoration, with its flowing edges, on the front of the chest in figure 8.3 is framed by the sponge-painted top, bracket feet, and trim. A single feather runs diagonally across each side of the chest. This skillfully rendered motif was executed in a spon-

taneous, graceful manner by an unknown ornamenter. The blanket chest in figure 8.4, dating from about 1870, was also found in Tuscarawas or Wayne County. The yellow ground with brown glaze was manipulated in a rhythmic pattern on the front, top, and sides of the chest in a carefully wrought pattern that resembles a woven coverlet.

The painted furniture of the communal society of Zoar, Ohio, had its roots in German folk art, represented in the small-scale cupboard in figure 8.5. This is one of the earliest known dated examples of furniture made by the Separatists who bought a 5,500-acre tract of land along the Tuscarawas River. The blue-painted base with scalloped top is inscribed in white paint. Translated, the inscription on the top door reads: "Love God not his gifts if you want [to have] Him for a friend" and, on the bottom drawer, "Grant that I be toward you and all people Meek [in] Heart, Plain in Words, Humble [in] Works."[5] The wardrobe in figure 8.6 reflects the revival of the fine-grained furniture characteristic of northern Ohio furniture throughout the second half of the nineteenth century. The carefully planned and executed flame graining is trimmed with green paint, which has oxidized to black. The distinctive "cat eyes" created by the graining also appear on a companion piece, a blanket chest, which bears the stenciled inscription "Barbara Geiger 1847" on the front.

The surviving furniture made and deco-

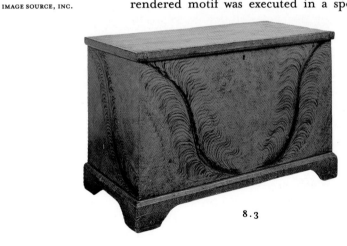

8.3

8.4

8.5

8.6

FIGURE 8.5: *Cupboard, 1823, Zoar, Tuscarawas County, Ohio; painted and decorated walnut and poplar; 67¹/₄ x 40 x 16³/₈ inches.* COLLECTION OF JACK AND PAT ADAMSON. PHOTOGRAPH COURTESY OF *THE MAGAZINE ANTIQUES.*

FIGURE 8.6: *Wardrobe, 1856, Pandora, Putnam County, Ohio; mixed woods, grain-painted and decorated; 85 x 66¹/₂ x 18¹/₂ inches. This Mennonite piece displays wood graining highlighted by the vertically grained "cat eyes" in the central panels.* COLLECTION OF GALE FREDERICK AND DANIEL OVERMEYER. PHOTOGRAPH BY IMAGE SOURCE, INC.

rated by Jacob Werrey (1838–1893) of German Township in Fulton County represents some of the most masterful of all Ohio painted furniture. Seventeen specimens of Werrey's furniture-making, including twelve blanket chests, are signed by him on the bottom in a fancy scrolled script. The blanket chest in figure 8.7, which echoes the lingering Germanic form in its bold turned legs, is a superb example of Werrey's late work. The rhythmic, glistening wood grainings with imaginative veneered borders on the front and sides of the chest are strong, bold, and ingenious. A yellow stenciled vase with flowers and wheat harks back to earlier Empire-style stencil gilding. The graining on another Werrey chest dated 1863, in figure 8.8, is thought to be one of his earliest chests. A typical early-nineteenth-century jack-of-all-trades, Jacob Werrey is listed in census records as a farmer; he must have spent his idle winter days making and presumably decorating furniture. The earliest examples of his furniture date to the 1860s, and his patterning remains similar for the twenty-year span of these examples.[6]

Communal societies from Sweden and French immigrants from New Orleans founded communities and prospered throughout the Northwest Territory. Members of the Rappite Society settled in New Harmony, Indiana, and Swedish Jansenists settled at Bishop Hill, forty-five miles east of the Mississippi River in western Illinois. The Swedish-born decorative painter Olaf Krans (1838–1916) grew up in this community. Krans made a living painting houses, barns, signs, coffins, flagpoles, fire plugs, and duck decoys.

French architecture and decorative arts prevailed throughout the eighteenth century along the lower Mississippi River in and around New Orleans. With the founding of Saint Louis at the juncture of the Mississippi and Missouri Rivers in 1764, the French influence made itself felt in parts of Indiana and Missouri. It can still be seen in the surviving furniture. The buffet, a French-style cupboard or sideboard, shown in figure 8.9 is painted a decorative red. The shaped skirt and short cabriole legs of this rare surviving specimen are characteristic of French Provincial furniture well adapted to the

8.7

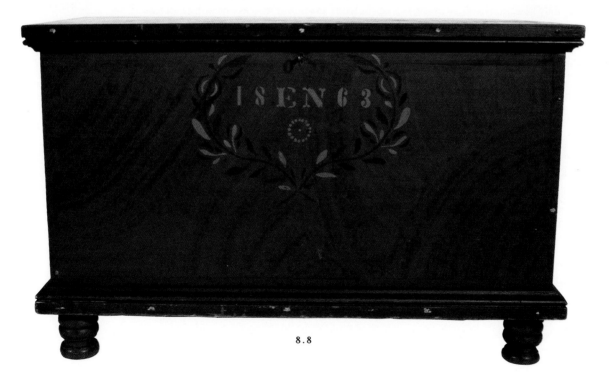

8.8

COUNTRY FURNITURE

delicate rectilinear style of the Federal-era furniture of the urban centers.

Windsor and fancy chair makers were among the early migrants to the Northwest Territory. In 1825, the *Indiana Farmer* advertised that H. H. Morgan and R. Charles "have established a Paint Shop in Salem, where they intend carrying on the Painting Business in its different branches, as follows:—Sign, House and Ornamental Painting,—Glazing, Mahoganizing doors and Marbling Stair cases. —Windsor chair painting and ornamenting. Canvass painting.—Constant supply of putty on hand. Furniture cleansed and Varnished."[7] Furniture cleaning is seldom mentioned in early newspaper advertisements, though it is noted in woodworkers' account books and refers to the refinishing of oil or shellac surfaces. This advertisement is a good summary of the many offerings of well-established chair manufactories.

Fancy chair maker William Coles (1804–1862) of New York City settled in Springfield, Ohio, where he continued to produce stylish plank-seat and fancy chairs. Several versions of Coles's chairs include stenciled and hand-painted patterns with Empire motifs of urns, acanthus leaves, and rosettes reminiscent of high-style versions from Baltimore, New York, and the Hitchcock Chair Company of Connecticut. Coles's chairs are stenciled on the back of the seat, "Made by: W. Coles. Springfield, Ohio."

The fancy settee in figure 8.10 is also identified by its maker: "J. Huey/Zanesville" is stenciled on the bottom of the seat. Huey (b. 1805) advertised in the *Ohio Republican* on May 2, 1829, that he intended to keep "on hand a general assortment of Grecian, Windsor, Fancy, and Common chairs made in the latest and most approved fashions."[8] According to the 1850 *United States Census Industry Schedule for Ohio*, Huey's chair factory had steam-powered machinery, employed twenty men for $440.00 a month, and produced furniture with an annual value of $8,000.[9]

THE PLAINS STATES

By the middle of the nineteenth century the Northwest Territory was no longer the American frontier. Cincinnati was a prosperous center for cabinetmaking, and grand houses were built throughout Ohio's towns and cities. The states west of the Mississippi River—Minnesota, Iowa, Missouri, North and South Dakota, and Nebraska—with their rich farmland and rolling plains, attracted settlers not only from back east but also from Norway, Denmark, and Sweden. From 1836 to 1876, nearly 200,000 Norwegians settled in the undeveloped prairie land of Illinois, Iowa, Wisconsin, the Dakotas, and Minnesota.[10]

Most of the early furniture constructed by the Norwegians lacked the rose-painting, or rosemaling, that decorated the boxes they had brought with them to this country. Only isolated individuals appear to have continued this tradition (figure 8.11), which enjoyed a revival during the last quarter of the nineteenth century after Norway gained its independence from Sweden.[11] By the time the settlers began arriving in America, tastes in rural Norway were changing. Rosemaling had given way to plain painted surfaces and grain-painting in imitation of wood.

The cupboard held a prestigious place as a symbol of material wealth in the Norwegian home. Paint-decorated examples in the collection of Vesterheim: The Norwegian-

8.9

FIGURE 8.7: *Blanket chest, 1872, German Township, Fulton County, Ohio; made by Jacob Werrey; painted and grained poplar with stenciled decoration; 28 x 48 x 23 inches. This chest is signed on the bottom in blue paint, "German Township, Fulton co./Febrary [sic] 11, 1880/Made by Jacob Werrey."*
COLLECTION OF GALE FREDERICK AND DANIEL OVERMEYER.

FIGURE 8.8: *Blanket chest, 1863, Fulton County, Ohio; made by Jacob Werrey; painted, grained, and stencil decoration on poplar; 22 x 38 x 19 inches. Signed on the bottom "March the 6th, 1863 No. 4: Jacob Werrey." This chest was made for Elias Nofsinger.*
COLLECTION OF GALE FREDERICK AND DANIEL OVERMEYER.

FIGURE 8.9: *Buffet, circa 1800, Vincennes, Indiana; painted yellow poplar and curly maple; 46 1/2 x 48 x 24 1/4 inches.*
COLLECTION OF THE MUSEUM OF FINE ARTS, BOSTON, GIFT OF DANIEL AND JESSIE FARBER AND FRANK B. BEMIS FUND, 1989.50.

American Museum, in Decorah, Iowa (figures 8.12 and 8.13), represent different forms of the traditional cupboard form and decoration.

THE SANTA FE TRAIL

In 1851, New York newspaperman Horace Greeley repeated his famous advice: "Go to the West; there your capacities are sure to be appreciated and your industry and energy rewarded."[12] That year marked the beginning of the largest migration of Americans to the West. Indeed, by the mid-1800s the roughest stages of exploration were over. There were 9,000 miles of railroad tracks, and more than a thousand steamboats plied the waters of the Mississippi, its tributaries, and 3,200 miles of canals. In the spring of each year mile-long caravans of wagons set out on America's historic highways—the Oregon Trail and the Santa Fe Trail, the latter extending some 800 miles from Independence, Missouri, to Santa Fe.

The vast Mexican province of Texas, which had been largely colonized by emigrants from the United States, declared its independence on March 2, 1836. By December 1845, Texas had drafted a constitution and was admitted to the Union as a state. Homesteaders to the vast lands of Texas built log cabins like the one shown in the idyllic setting in figure 8.16, the farm of Julius Meyenberg at Bluff-Williams Creek in Fayette County.

Texas frontier furniture was large, bold, and utilitarian. Among the most remarkable surviving pieces is the wardrobe shown in figure 8.14, which had a history of ownership in another Fayette County family, the Tiemanns of Warrenton. The Germanic influence is evident in the form, but the large-scale cross section of an exotic tree spanning the center of the cupboard's two front doors is pure Texas. Superbly executed graining techniques exhibited by this piece include stippling, sponging, and grain-painting on the skirt and drawer fronts and along the bold cornice.

THE HISPANIC TRADITION IN NEW MEXICO

Some of the most boldly painted furniture in the West came from Hispanic cabinetmakers who were introduced to new tools and a new aesthetic following the Anglo-American occupation of New Mexico in 1846. Most New Mexican houses were sparsely furnished with movable furniture, supplementing built-in adobe benches, beds, shelves, and tables. As a result, the New Mexican *carpinteros* made a limited variety of furniture forms. The interior of the home of a well-to-do New Mexican was described in 1848 by W. H. Emory:

> The town of Bernalillo is small, but one of the best built in the territory. We were led into an oblong room, furnished like that of every Mexican in comfortable circumstances. A banquette runs around the room, leaving only a space for the couch. It is covered with cushions, carpets, and pillows; upon which the visitor sits or reclines. The first floor is usually covered a third or a half with common looking carpet. On the uncovered part is the table, freighted with grapes, sponge cake, and the wine of the country. The walls are hung with miserable pictures of the saints, crosses innumerable, and Yankee mirrors without number. These last are suspended entirely out of reach; and if one wishes to shave or adjust his toilet, he must do so without the aid of a mirror, be there ever so many in the chamber.[13]

The portable furniture forms made by Hispanic cabinetmakers were almost totally flat and rectilinear, with shallow or applied carving. Most commonly they consisted of chairs, benches, chests, and wardrobes. Ponderosa pine, which covered the mountain slopes and high mesas of the Rio Grande valley, is a soft wood, easily worked in tongue-and-groove construction. The cabinetmakers decorated furniture with distemper, a water-based paint, in strong reds, greens, blues, and yellows—the palette of textiles, rugs, and architectural elements of the same period. Unfortunately,

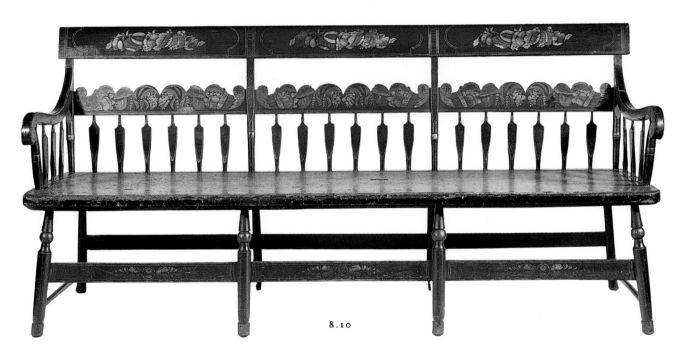

8.10

FIGURE 8.10: *Settee, 1830–1840, Zanesville, Muskingum County, Ohio; made by James Huey; maple and pine, painted and stenciled; 35^1/$_2$ x 72^1/$_2$ x 22^1/$_2$ inches. The unique scalloped shape of the center rail combines with the stenciled paired cornucopias and bunches of grapes in a pleasing rhythmic pattern.* PRIVATE COLLECTION. PHOTOGRAPH COURTESY OF *THE MAGAZINE ANTIQUES*.

8.11   8.12   8.13

since water-based paints do not have the permanence of oil-based paints, years of wear have removed much of the painted surfaces of nineteenth-century New Mexican furniture. The red ground of the cupboard in figure 8.15 has faded to reveal the natural wood graining. The ground is believed to be a house paint, the turquoise accents a water-soluble paint. Typically, this cupboard, or *alacena*, would have been made to fit into the wall of a house as part of the stationary furniture.

THE MENNONITE TRADITION

The Mennonites who settled in Pennsylvania during the late eighteenth and early nineteenth centuries had their roots in southern Germany and Switzerland. In the 1870s and 1880s a second migration of Mennonites arrived from Poland, Russia, and Prussia and settled in central Kansas, the Dakotas, and Nebraska, usually bringing only a dowry chest, which served as a trunk. Skilled Mennonite cabinetmakers and carpenters immediately

went to work to create large, sturdy furniture constructed of native ash or pine. They brought a strong tradition of grain painting, staining, and hand-painted decoration to the furniture they produced. Using light-colored woods, Mennonite ornamenters painted the surfaces of their furniture with delicate floral patterns. The result was a combination of Slavic folk traditions and Dutch architectural elements. Characteristic Mennonite forms included resting benches (figure 8.17), large wardrobes (figures 8.18 and 8.20), tables (figure 8.23), and dowry chests.

The floral embellishment on the wardrobe in figure 8.18 is similar to that on embroidered textiles and drawings, which were derived from contemporary prints and watercolors (figure 8.19). The very fine paint graining over pine imitates two different woods; columns of faux black marble graining adorn the front, sides, and skirt of the wardrobe. The superb graining techniques of Mennonite furniture were used on fur-

8.14

8.15

niture and on interior doors and moldings, a rich tradition brought to this country with the settlers.

The fifteen-page notebook of Jacob Adrian with recipes for paints, stains, and polishes, probably copied from an eighteenth-century printed book, is among the holdings of the Kauffman Museum, Bethel College, North Newton, Kansas. The book contains elaborate directions for producing red, yellow, black, scarlet, green, and blue stains, a reminder of the skills needed to embellish furniture. The least complicated stain, yellow, called for saffron to be mixed in a mortar with "about l *Quentchen* [dram] to one penny's worth of dye, and then pour strong pure rye whiskey or *spiritus* wine on it and let it evaporate for 12 hours." The manual suggests applying several coats of the fine yellow extract and then lacquering it with amber for long-lasting results.

Also included are recipes for mahogany stains similar to those in other American journals. A recipe for an ebony stain calls for Brazil nut wood shavings, which are cooked in hot water; when the water boils, alum is added. After simmering for a few minutes the stain is applied when still warm with a brush until the desired color is attained. To remove the resulting foam, a brush dipped in vinegar is used to smooth the surface.[14]

Polishing furniture must have been left to women, according to Adrian's advice on polishing furniture: "Mama usually got her own wax, sometimes with a lot of effort. She took half of a coarse wool cloth and put a glob of wax on it that had been worked to soft stage. Put it on the furniture keeping it all even. For the last part, melt 3 lots of wax in hot water. Then 1 lot *Sal Tartari* and keep stirring until it is right for polishing. This will make it bright and

FIGURE **8.14**: *Wardrobe, 1860–1870, Fayette County, Texas; cedar with grain-painted decoration; 76 1/2 x 61 x 23 inches. The wardrobe is marked "C. W." on the back in chalk.*
COURTESY OF THE DALLAS MUSEUM OF ART, THE FAITH P. AND CHARLES L. BYBEE COLLECTION, GIFT OF FAITH P. BYBEE.

FIGURE **8.15**: *Hispanic-style cupboard, circa 1850, New Mexico; 191 x 72.5 x 45 centimeters. This cupboard was found north of San Juan Pueblo at a ranch near Alcalde.*
COLLECTION OF SHIRLEY AND WARD ALAN MINGE, CORRALES, NEW MEXICO. PHOTOGRAPH BY MARY PECK.

JULIUS MEYENBER

reek: Settelment by *La Grange* Fa

Louis Hoppe fecit.

'S, FARM, Bluff · Willia
ette County, State of TEXAS

shiny. It will last year after year and it will make the furniture last longer."[15]

THE OREGON TRAIL

Between 1840 and 1870, a quarter of a million Americans crossed the continent to Oregon and California following the Oregon Trail. The trail began at Independence, Missouri, then ran northwest to the Platte River and followed its north fork into southern Wyoming. From there it made an easy crossing of the Rockies at South Pass and followed the Snake River to a cutoff that led to the Columbia River, which it followed to the Willamette Valley. In *The Emigrant's Guide to California,* Joseph E. Ware told travelers how to outfit a wagon for the journey.[16] No furniture was included on his list of supplies, but undoubtedly a few treasured pieces began the journey with the family. A chest might be the only piece of furniture to survive the journey and it would be used for many purposes—as storage, for example, or as a table for serving a meal. Some pioneers did not go all the way to Oregon, stopping instead in Nebraska, Utah, or Wyoming. They lived in dirt caves, constructed sod houses from the rye grasses that grew on the plains, or built log cabins using the straight, tall trees—red pine, juniper, quaking

aspen, and cottonwood—that grew at the foot of the mountains. In *O Pioneers!,* her great novel of life on the prairies of Nebraska, Willa Cather describes a little cave house:

> He had but one room, neatly plastered and whitewashed, and there was a wooden floor. There was a kitchen stove, a table covered with oilcloth, two chairs, a clock, a calendar, a few books on the window-shelf; nothing more. But the place was as clean as a cupboard.
>
> "But where do you sleep, Ivar?" Emil asked, looking about.
>
> Ivar unslung a hammock from a hook on the wall; in it was rolled a buffalo robe. "There, my son. A hammock is a good bed, and in winter I wrap up in this skin. Where I go to work, the beds are not half so easy as this."[17]

At first, the settlers fashioned basic furniture for their own use from available timber, using few tools. However, among those traveling west were cabinetmakers and furniture dealers who started new businesses, advertising furniture in exchange for lumber. The Utah carpenter H. W. Naisbett advertised in 1857, "I am prepared to supply Flour Boxes made of good seasoned lumber at reasonable prices. For those who supply their own material, I will make up Boxes for a low figure." Prairie fur-

PRECEDING PAGES
FIGURE 8.16: *Julius Meyenberg's Farm, circa 1864, Texas; painted by Louis Hoppe; opaque and transparent watercolor and ink on paper; 8¼ x 11¼ inches.* COURTESY OF THE WITTE MUSEUM, SAN ANTONIO, TEXAS.
FIGURE 8.17: *Resting bench, 1885–1895, Nebraska; made by Heinrich Rempel; grain-painted and stenciled pine with flower decals; 34 x 24 x 78¼ inches. The Russian émigré Heinrich Rempel was a full-time cabinetmaker who grain-painted both furniture and woodwork. He is known to have worked behind a curtain while graining, so that his graining techniques could not be copied.* PRIVATE COLLECTION. PHOTOGRAPH COURTESY OF KAUFFMAN MUSEUM/GOOD BOOKS.

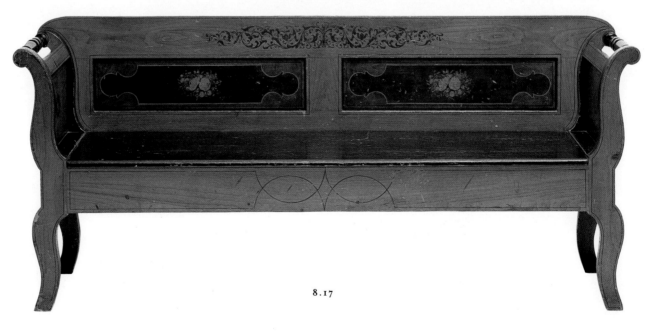

8.17

niture had plank or rawhide seats in place of upholstery, but furniture in the Empire, fancy, or Windsor styles was soon being manufactured and ornamented. In September of 1864 the *Desert News* carried a revised list of prices for furniture: common bedstead, $14; Windsor chair, $3; rush-bottom chair, $2; large rocking chair, $9; scrolled double lounge, $16; center table $3^{1}/_{2}$ feet in diameter, $26; washstand with drawer, $10.[18]

Many of these furniture forms were ornamented with wood graining for beauty and protection by western cabinetmakers. Native pines were grained with metal combs, feathers, and brushes to simulate oak, mahogany, and bird's-eye maple. If the basic ingredients for mixing paint were not readily available, stains were made or milk paints were substituted, for pigments did not become available until mid-century. At that same time an approved price list was circulated among craftsmen, giving prices for graining: for graining oak, mahogany, and rosewood, $3.00 a yard; for marbling a mantelpiece, $4.00 to $6.00. Blue paint cost $1.25 a pound; greens and yellow, $1.50; vermilion and red cost more. Flax was grown so that the seeds could be used for linseed oil, which was used as the vehicle for paint pigments.[19]

WOOD-GRAINED MORMON FURNITURE

The first members of the Church of Jesus Christ of Latter-Day Saints, the Mormons, arrived in the Utah Territory in 1847. Their leader, Brigham Young, was himself a cabinetmaker who immediately directed a furniture manufactory called the Public Works in Salt Lake City. The Mormons accepted converts from every religion; among new arrivals in Salt Lake City were cabinetmakers from Scandinavia, England, Ireland, and New England. Common to all these traditions was Empire-style furniture. The many forms of this style of furniture were immediately constructed, painted, and grained to resemble both rosewood and local softwoods.

8.18

FIGURE **8.18**: *Wardrobe, 1882, Kansas; made by Franz Adrian; grained and painted pine; $86^{1}/_{2}$ x 48 x 19 inches. The roses and bird motif may have been added around 1900 to the superb graining, which imitates light and dark wood.*
PHOTOGRAPH COURTESY OF KAUFFMAN MUSEUM/GOOD BOOKS.

FIGURE **8.19**: *Page from an arithmetic book, 1797, Montau, West Prussia; Gerhard Nichel; 8 x $6^{1}/_{2}$ inches. The bow-tied roses are similar to those used to decorate painted furniture in the 1870s in America.*
MENNONITE LIBRARY & ARCHIVES, BETHEL COLLEGE, NORTH NEWTON, KANSAS. PHOTOGRAPH COURTESY OF KAUFFMAN MUSEUM/GOOD BOOKS.

By the winter of 1847–1848 a total of 1,681 people had migrated to the valley of the Great Salt Lake. By 1852 the population had swelled to 20,000.[20] The homes built for these settlers were constructed by sheer determination from native woods and were filled with furniture made by skilled carpenters. During the next two decades cabinetmakers created Windsor chairs, fancy chairs, klismos chairs, beds, pedestal tables, and chests of drawers reflecting the styles of the period and the traditions of their homelands. Some cabinetmakers, such as William Bell and fellow Englishman Ralph Ramsay, fashioned many unique and skillfully painted furniture pieces, like the octagonal desk in figure 8.21. The masterful rendering of the green-and-black faux marble is matched by the ingenuity of construction— the table rotates, and the desk

8.19

8.20

FIGURE 8.20: *Wardrobe, 1888, Kansas; made by Heinrich Rempel; pine grain–painted to simulate inlay and marble;*
91½ x 51 x 19. PRIVATE COLLECTION. PHOTOGRAPH COURTESY OF KAUFFMAN MUSEUM/GOOD BOOKS.
FIGURE 8.21: *Octagonal desk, circa 1850, Salt Lake City; made by William Bell; pine, painting and graining attributed to Brigham*
Young; diameter, 82 inches. COLLECTION OF THE MUSEUM OF CHURCH HISTORY AND ART.

FIGURE 8.22: *Side
chair, 1856, Salt Lake City;
Public Works; grain-painted
softwood; 44.5 x 43
centimeters. In another
version of the Empire klismos-
form chair, this is thought to be
a "French" chair listed on the
1864* Cabinetmaker's
List of Prices *for $5.*
COLLECTION OF THE MUSEUM
OF CHURCH HISTORY AND ART.

FIGURE 8.23: *Parlor
table, 1898, Kansas;
unknown wood, grained, with
painted decoration; 28 x
28½ inches. The painted
tabletop displays an open book
in which is written
"Christlicher Haussegen,
1898" (Christian Belling for
the Home).*
PRIVATE COLLECTION.
PHOTOGRAPH COURTESY OF
KAUFFMAN MUSEUM/GOOD
BOOKS.

FIGURE 8.24: *Desk,
circa 1860, made by Edward
McGregor Patterson; grained
pine; 90 x 31½ x
26 inches.*
COLLECTION OF THE MUSEUM
OF CHURCH HISTORY AND ART.

tilts. The desk was used in Brigham Young's office and in the church tithing office.[21]

Another cabinetmaker, Edward McGregor Patterson of Northumberland, England, produced the bookcase with scrolled pediment and the tightly grained desk shown in figure 8.24, ingeniously combining cabinetmaking and wood-graining. In 1869, when the transcontinental railroad joined Utah to two coasts, the twenty-three cabinetmakers of Utah were up against competition from the major furniture-making centers of Cincinnati, San Francisco, and New York. Nonetheless, the Mormon furniture-making tradition continued as skilled cabinetmakers were sent to colonize new communities throughout the West.

Immigrants from Scandinavia, Germany, France, Spain, England, Mexico, and the East Coast who settled in close-knit communities during the nineteenth century brought with them a myriad of furniture-making and decorating traditions. On arrival, they made furniture of native woods, constructed quickly and efficiently with a minimum of tools, and finished with stains and paints for protection. Skilled cabinetmakers, they also maintained traditions of decoration. Much of their furniture was grain-painted to simulate mixed woods and to satisfy a need for beauty, pattern, and color in the home. The desire to create beauty meant that some furniture was highly decorative and exuberantly grain-painted. The golden age of grain painting that had prevailed on the East Coast during the first three decades of the nineteenth century was reborn and reinterpreted in the West during the last half of the century. Here faux-grained furniture was regarded as high style; two-, three-, and even four- and five-color painted surfaces prevailed. This distinctive furniture accented and brightened the adobe and log houses and cabins and became an integral part of frontier life. Ingenuity came quickly to the settlers of the frontier, and the painted and grained furniture of their own making speaks loudly of the tenacious will of the frontier settlers.

8.23

COUNTRY FURNITURE

8.24

PAINT

FIGURE A.1: *"We Go for the Union," 1840–1850, artist unknown; oil on canvas; 18³/₁₆ x 24³/₁₆ inches. This rare look into a mid-nineteenth-century painter's shop depicts the grinding of pigments by the apprentice, and the tools of the house painter and the ornamental painter.*
COLLECTION OF THE NATIONAL GALLERY, GIFT OF EDGAR WILLIAM
AND BERNICE CHRYLSER GARBISCH, 1956.13.13 (1468).

UNTIL THE YEARS following the Civil War, paint was not available in cans ready for use. It had to be laboriously handmade using dry pigments, or colors, which were ground and mixed with oil in a time-consuming process passed down from master to apprentice. A nineteenth-century manual defined pigments as "solid bodies as required to be mixed with some fluid before they can be spread on, or made to adhere, to any surface that is to be painted."[1] Paint is a liquid mixture consisting of a pigment, which provides color when dispersed in a liquid vehicle consisting of a binding medium and a thinner. When the mixture of pigment, binder, and thinner is applied to a surface, the thinner evaporates, leaving the binding medium, which dries into a semisolid form that holds the pigment in place.[2]

A rare look into a mid-nineteenth-century ornamental painter's shop is seen in figure A.1. Here an apprentice grinds the pigment, combining it with oil to the right consistency. The most commonly used oil was linseed; walnut oil and fish oil were less expensive alternatives. Two stones were used to grind small quantities of pigment. The first stone, called a muller, was a handheld conical tool that was worked against the second stone, a slab—a flat, hard surface 18 to 24 inches square. To produce a desired color, different pigments were combined in varying proportions. These recipes were kept secret by the guilds. The longer the pigment was ground with the oil, the finer the particles became and the richer the paint. To make watercolors or distemper, the painter mixed the pigment with a water-based binder instead of oil. The pigments intended

for varnishes and japanning were ground in either oil, turpentine, or alcohol.[3]

In 1753, John Smith described the grinding of colors in detail:

> Let your grinding stone be placed about the height of your middle; . . . then take a small quantity of the colour you wish to grind (2 spoonfuls is enough), for the less you grind at a time the easier and finer your colour will be ground; . . . put a little of your linseed oil to it, then with your muller mix it together . . . and grind it till it come to the consistence of an ointment; . . . when you find you have ground it fine enough by the continual motion of your muller about the stone, holding it down as hard as your strength will permit, . . . then cleanse it off the stones into a galley pot.[4]

To test the fineness of the paint once the ingredients were combined, the painter laid a smear across a sheet of glass and held it up to the sun. If it looked too coarse, he would continue grinding the pigment; if it was satisfactory, he would use a palette knife to scrape it off the slab and into a bucket. As only small amounts of pigment were ground at a time, each consecutive batch needed to be mixed with the preceding batch to produce a consistent color. Should the texture of the paint need correcting, the craftsman would add oil to make it more viscous; to thin it, he added spirits of turpentine. The greater the proportion of turpentine to pigment, the less sheen the paint would have when it dried. When the grinding was complete, the painter cleaned the slab and muller with a soft cloth, often using stale bread crumbs to absorb any remaining paint. New paint had to be mixed

for each day's work because if paint sat too long, the binders would form a scum on top and the pigment would settle to the bottom and form a solid cake, rendering the paint unusable.

Pigments and other paint materials needed to be handled with care, as many were poisonous. Ornamental painters in the nineteenth century often reported suffering from painter's colic, a painful and debilitating condition.[5] Fire was another ever-present hazard. Varnishes needed to be placed on a "gentle fire" for long periods of time, and manuals warned that "great care must be taken in making varnish, so as not to set the house on fire."[6] Even turpentine vapors could catch fire in high heat.

An assortment of brushes and "pencils" was used to apply paint. Brushes for painting on walls, like those held by the house painter in figure A.1, were round, unlike the flat sash brushes used today. Illustrations in painters' and varnishers' manuals depict the range of brushes available to the nineteenth-century painter. One such guide recommended that brushes "possess elasticity combined with softness, and that the hairs are sufficiently fixed, so that taking hold of one hair, it will not pull out or separate from the rest."[7] Large brushes were made from bristles that had grown on the backs of hogs and wild boars; the bristles were tied together and affixed to wooden handles. The small brushes called pencils, used for fine details and decorative striping, were made of soft sable or camel's hair that could hold a point. They were available in a range of sizes for producing lines of different widths. Some pencils were produced by binding hair together and inserting the tied bundle into the end of a goose quill. The tube of the quill was then softened in water. As it dried, it contracted and held the bristles securely in place. Other pencils were tied to long wooden handles "so that a large sweep may be taken when required."[8]

This method of processing, grinding, and mixing paints remained basically the same through much of the first half of the nineteenth century, but industrialization did begin to change the production and marketing of pigments, paints, varnishes, oils, and turpentine. Imported pigments became available starting in the eighteenth century and were sold by the "colourman" in whole, half, and quarter casks. The American pigment-making industry was established in Philadelphia in 1804–1805, and New York, Boston, and Pittsburgh soon followed. Within a decade, commercial turpentine distilleries opened in North Carolina

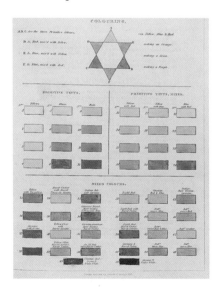

and New York. Linseed oil, expressed from flaxseed, was produced locally throughout the country. Patented, hand-cranked paint mills were advertised in New York newspapers as early as 1803, replacing mullers and slabs.

By mid-century nearly every town had a colorman or merchant who supplied painters with quality pigments. The Civil War diverted attention away from much industry, but the first ready-mixed paints appeared soon after the conclusion of the war. Although these paints were revolutionary in concept, many artisans and artists continued to grind their own colors well into the twentieth century to guarantee the quality.[9]

Common nineteenth-century colors included Tucson red, vermilion, burnt umber, lampblack, carmine, ultramarine, king's yellow, Spanish brown, Prussian blue, and verdigris. As Nathaniel Whittock wrote in 1827, despite their period names "colours may be classed under the following heads:—White, Black, Red, Blue, Yellow, Green, Orange, Purple, and Brown; from these every tint that can be required in any kind of painting, may be obtained by mixing one colour with another" (figure A.2).[10]

Pigments were composed of minerals, clays, woods, resins, or vegetables. White, for example, was derived from lead, chalk, and zinc oxide; black came from lampblack, the soot that collected from the smoke of burning pine and fir wood. Bone black and ivory black were made from charred animal remains or ivory, while browns were derived from mineral deposits mined from soil.

Yellow ochre and raw sienna were produced from clay containing iron oxide and were used by furniture ornamenters as the ground coat for

imitation grained woods. Chrome yellow, which had come into commercial use by the 1820s, was made by treating lead salt with an alkali. The resulting bright yellow was used as a base coat for fancy furniture and as imitation gold for highlights and details. Two very popular colors, Spanish brown and Venetian red, also known as red ochre or iron oxide, were made from earth that contained ferric oxide. Vermilion, or cinnabar, was a red made from liquid mercury and fused sulfur. This expensive pigment was nearly always used as an accent rather than on its own. Ultramarine was considered the finest and dearest of the blues. Prussian blue, a strong blue that could be produced at a reasonable cost, was the principal blue used in the nineteenth century. It was made of hydrochloric acid, dried blood, potash, alum, and green vitriol according to a formula that had been discovered by accident. Indigo, a ground plant from the genus and species *Indigofera tinctoria,* of Indian origin, was a fugitive blue—that is, one that faded over time. Smalt, crushed blue glass, produced a fine bright blue-purple but was very hard to work into oil. Ultramarine, derived from lapis lazuli, a semiprecious stone, was also extremely expensive. Indeed, until the invention of an artificial ultramarine in 1828, blue was a sign of wealth and was rarely used on furniture. Verdigris, a blue-green made by treating copper with vinegar, was also expensive and difficult to grind into oil. A more effective green came from mixing yellow ochre with Prussian blue, but this produced a dull green color. In the 1820s chrome green, made with chrome yellow and Prussian blue, became a bright, affordable option.[11]

Paints that were mixed by hand show their age. They rarely became smooth before drying, and because they were applied with bristle brushes, the painted surface is often ropy—that is, it has pronounced ridges. Random streaks of pure pigment are sometimes visible as well. Because of the relative inconsistency of particles in early hand-ground pigments, each grain of color reflects light differently. For example, while the pigment of modern green reflects green light, early greens reflect both blue and yellow light because the pigments were not thoroughly combined. As a result, later repainting is often visible when the object is moved in and out of different light. The properties of the paint itself could be manipulated to coordinate with a desired decorative scheme. Linseed-oil paint dried into a very glossy finish. If neoclassical coloration was desired, in imitation of the frescoed walls of Pompeii and Herculaneum, a flatter finish was called for, so spirit of turpentine was added to reduce the sheen. The fluidity of paint, its variety of colors, and a host of application techniques combine to create the incalculable combinations of surface treatments and decorative details that enhance both high-style and vernacular furniture throughout the nineteenth century.

PAINTERS' MANUALS

In addition to the familiar cabinetmaking manuals by Thomas Chippendale, Thomas Sheraton, and George Hepplewhite, a number of books were published for painters, stainers, and gilders. The original guidebook of the painters', stainers', and varnishers' guild of York, England, titled *The Olde and Annciente*

Ordinances Articles and Customes or Mistery, or Occupation of the Painters . . . , for example, was published in 1515. The volume most often cited, however, is the pivotal work by George Stalker and John Parker, *A Treatise on Japaning and Varnishing,* published in Oxford in 1688. This book is particularly important for its lengthy description of japanning in imitation of Oriental lacquerwork. The *Diderot Encyclopedia,* printed in England, and J. F. Watin's *L'Art du Peintre, Doreur, Vernisseur (The Art of the Painter, Gilder, Varnisher),* printed in Paris beginning in 1769, followed. Jacques André Roubo's *L'Art du Menuisier (The Art of the Woodworker),* a three-volume work published in Paris (1769–1774), is considered the seminal source for information on cabinetmaking and includes a section on furniture finishing, which served as the source of information for later manuals. Thomas Sheraton's *Cabinet Dictionary,* published in 1803, defines common period colors and painting techniques and includes eight chapters on the techniques of common and domestic furniture-finishing, including a chapter on the painting of furniture.

A plethora of nineteenth-century English tradesmen's guidebooks revealed to countless professionals and amateurs the trade secrets of the dissolving guild system. In an era before plagiarism was legally proscribed, each new edition drew heavily on the paint formulas and directions provided by earlier treatises. Consequently, discovering the original source for painting techniques and formulas is difficult. *The Handmaid of the Arts* (1758, 1764, and 1796), by Robert Dossie, owes much to John Smith's *Art of Painting in Oyl.* The *Laws of Harmonious Colouring* (1828), a manual on color

theory by the house painter and author David Ramsay Hay of Edinburgh, is another often plagiarized manual. *The Painter's and Varnisher's Guide* by P. F. Tingry (Geneva, 1803) was reissued in 1830 as *The Painter's and Colourman's Complete Guide.* It appeared again in 1837 as *The Cabinetmaker's Guide, Or Rules . . .* with authorship ascribed to G. A. Siddons. Many of these English publications were available in America, including Nathaniel Whittock's *Decorative Painters' and Glaziers' Guide* (1828) (figure A.3), and W. and T. J. Tower's *Every Man His Own Painter* (1830).

As training and apprenticeships were shortened, enterprising Americans could learn the secrets and skills of the cabinetmaker and painter-stainer in the jack-of-all-trades economy of the opening decades of the nineteenth century. To meet the demand for this sort of information, experienced tradesmen published manuals revealing the trade secrets of the guilds. Although *Dobson's*

FIGURE A.3: *Page from Nathaniel Whittock's* Decorative Painters' and Glaziers' Guide. *For those seeking to paint landscapes Whittock provided these six scenes to be copied.* COLLECTION OF THE SMITHSONIAN LIBRARIES, COOPER-HEWITT, NATIONAL DESIGN MUSEUM.

Encyclopaedia; or a Dictionary of Arts, Sciences . . . , published in Philadelphia in 1798, included information on the production of varnishes, stains, and resins, the first American publication of this sort is believed to be the pamphlet by Hezekiah Reynolds titled *Directions for House and Ship Painting; Shewing in a plain and concise manner, the Best Method of Preparing, Mixing and Laying the Various Colours Now in use, Designed for the Use of Learners* (New Haven, 1812). This work was directed at "the Cabinet and Chair Maker, the Wheelwright, the House and Ship Joiner; and to others whose Trades are connected with building," and in it Reynolds revealed the secrets of his thirty years' experience. This pamphlet served as the Rosetta stone for today's paint conservators, giving the exact proportions of pigments for mixing interior and exterior colors. *The Cabinet-Maker's Guide,* printed by Jacob B. Moore (Concord, N.H., 1827), is considered the first American furniture finisher's manual. It includes directions for japanning, silvering, bronzing, gilding, and lacquering wood as well as recipes for making varnishes. Its appendix is meant to assist cabinetmakers with mathematical calculations. *The Cabinet-Maker and Upholsterer's Companion* by J. Stokes (Philadelphia, 1852), available in numerous reprints under different titles, is another manual that draws heavily on *The Cabinet-Maker's Guide.*

Rufus Porter, an inventor, mural painter, and founder of the magazine *Scientific American,* printed his own manual, *A Select Collection of Valuable and Curious Arts,* in several editions beginning in 1825. This pamphlet, which combines scientific know-how and Yankee ingenuity, is noteworthy for its explanations of gilding, painting on interior walls, making stencils, and tracing and copying pictures.

As the printing process and transportation improved during the second half of the nineteenth century, published guides to painting and other decorative treatments became more numerous and widely available. *The Painter, Gilder, and Varnisher's Companion,* for instance, ran to sixteen editions between 1869 and 1873. John W. Masury, founder of a large Brooklyn paint and varnish firm, printed several booklets, including *House-Painting: Plain and Decorative* in 1868 and *The American Grainer's Hand-Book* in 1872. Primarily meant to be marketing tools for his own products, Masury's booklets went through several printings and provide invaluable clues to paint production in the last quarter of the century. Other ready-mixed paint factories, like E. W. Devoe & Company in New York and Sherwin-Williams produced color-sample cards that today record the color trends of the late nineteenth century. *The Gilder's Manual; A Complete Practical Guide to Gilding in All Its Branches* (New York, 1876) remains today a superb handbook for a wide range of gilding techniques.[12] In their many incarnations, these manuals provide a valuable resource for historians, furniture restorers, and conservators.

THE CONSERVATION OF PAINTED SURFACES

Thanks to modern technology and science, the surfaces of painted furniture are now being preserved and cared for in a manner similar to panel painting. Furniture conservation has benefited from the alternative cleaning systems and ultraviolet light cross-section analysis first developed for the treatment of easel painting. This technology enables conservators to identify the range of pigments used to produce the original colors and to develop appropriate conservation treatments. Tiny paint samples are taken from the crevices of furniture and examined in cross section under high magnification to determine the original pigment and binder, the priming layers, and the buildup of wax and oil on the surface. With this information in hand, the surface can then be cleaned down to the original paint. If necessary, early pigments can be duplicated and inpainted to restore any paint loss. Once restoration is complete the object again reveals the original intent of the ornamenter.

Of course the most highly prized specimens of painted furniture are those that retain their original surface paint. For some, "a patina of age" and a visible pattern of wear are highly desirable qualities to be preserved rather than cleaned and restored. Others choose to clean old varnishes and stabilize any flaking paint to reveal the original intent of the piece. Other furniture is conserved like an easel painting when the details and the skills of the gilder or painter are the overriding artistic intent of the piece. In this case, conservators often duplicate the original colors or gilding using techniques practiced in the nineteenth century to re-create the original surface treatments. All conservation seeks ways to stabilize the original surface, and all conservation efforts can be reversed should scientific advances result in new methods of conservation.[13] The preservation and restoration of decorative and protective furniture finishes are changing and evolving at an exciting rate.

PAINT

GILDING

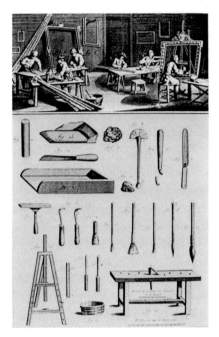

FIGURE B.1: *This illustration shows the varied tools of a gilder. From* Diderot Encyclopedia: The Complete Illustrations, 1762–1777, *vol. 1, Harry N. Abrams, Inc. (New York), p. 690.*

In nineteenth-century America, urban and rural craftsmen, appreciating the radiant, dramatic effect gained through the use of gold leaf and bronze gilding (gold or silver reduced to a powdered form), practiced the popular technique of gilding on surface areas of furniture.[1] Some artisans occasionally gilded entire pieces of furniture; at other times the gilder's brush touched only selected areas. Initially, gold leaf was imported. However, by the beginning of the nineteenth century, goldbeaters in New York, Boston, and Philadelphia sold gold leaf to the gilders who responded to listings in local directories. Marcus Bull placed such a listing in the *Philadelphia Directory and Stranger's Guide 1833*.[2]

Producing gold leaf required special tools and materials. After being cast in a mold and rolled into a thin sheet, it was then cut into small pieces and placed between the gold-

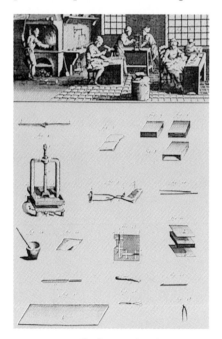

FIGURE B.2: *This illustration shows the varied tools of a goldbeater. From* Diderot Encyclopedia: The Complete Illustrations, 1762–1777, *vol. 1, Harry N. Abrams, Inc. (New York), p. 294.*

beater's skin to prevent sticking. The goldbeater then placed them on the hard surface of the workman's bench or stool for beating with a mallet or hammer. After the first beating, the gold was rewrapped and beaten several times more until the craftsman achieved the desired consistency and thinness. At this point, the gold was cut into thin sheets about three inches square and placed into small books of twenty-five gold leaves, each one $1/_{282,000}$ of an inch thick.[3]

Water gilding and oil gilding were the two methods used in applying gold leaf to wood surfaces. Water gilding is applied by wetting a specially prepared surface of gesso ground (whiting calcium carbonate) topped with a colored bole (gilder's clay) layer. Following the gold application the surface is either left matte or burnished to a high sheen. Water gilding, also known as burnish gilding, was used on architectural details and carved or reeded areas of furniture, with the greatest beauty achieved by the interplay of matte and burnished areas.

Oil gilding was more versatile, for it could be applied without elaborate surface preparation and had the ability to withstand the outdoors. It can be adhered with a varnish size on a gesso ground or directly on finished wood. Although oil gilding cannot be burnished, this application, if done well, can approach the brilliant luster of a burnished water-gilded surface.[4]

Detailed descriptions of the necessary materials and recipes for the gilding process existed for several centuries in English and European manuals. By the first quarter of the nineteenth century, American manuals designed for a broad audience of urban and rural craftsmen were

published and revealed gilding techniques.

Specific tools were recommended to gilders for use with gold leaf. The following glossary describes the items frequently found in a gilder's work area:

Gilder's cushion. An oblong piece of wood covered in calfskin with a parchment border capable of keeping the leaves from being blown about when removed from the book.

Gilder's knife. A knife with a straight, smooth edge.

Camel's-hair pencils. Thin brushes that were available in several sizes.

Tip. A special brush made of very fine squirrel or badger hair, used to take the gold from the cushion after the leaf is cut to size.

Burnisher. A crooked piece of agate or wolf's tooth with a wooden handle.

The Cabinet-Maker's Guide of 1827 contains a detailed description of the preparation of the wood for gilding and the actual gilding process, using most of the above items. It was recommended that a white ground consisting of extremely hot size combined with a mixture of size and whiting be used on the wood surface. The exact recipe for size is given in *The Cabinet-Maker's Guide*: "Take half a pound of parchment shavings, or cuttings of white leather; add three quarts of water, and boil it in a proper vessel till it is reduced to nearly half the quantity; take it off the fire and strain it through a sieve." This guide then advised the craftsman to go over the wood with boiling hot size, which was allowed to dry. Whiting and size was then mixed to the consistency of heavy cream and several coats were carefully applied until the surface was approximately one-sixteenth of an inch.[5] At this point, the gilder polished the area with a damp, fine cloth, making sure the entire surface was smooth.

The next step in the process was to make the gold size. A combination of ingredients including ground "boll-ammoniac" (bole ammoniac or gilder's clay), beef suet, parchment size, and water were mixed with a knife. After heating the bole mixture, two or three coats were brushed on the surface. When it was completely dry, the surface was polished with a stiff brush to remove any residue.[6] Now completely smooth, the surface was ready for laying on the gold.

For this process, *The Cabinet-Maker's Guide* suggests the following procedure:

> Place your work before you, nearly horizontal, and with a long-haired camel-hair pencil, dipped in water (some use a small quantity of brandy in the water), go over as much of your work as you intend the piece of gold to cover; then take up your gold from your cushion by means of your tip; by drawing it over your forehead or cheek, it will damp it sufficiently to adhere to the gold. . . . [G]ently breathing on it, it will be found to adhere; but you must mind that the part you apply it to is sufficiently wet; indeed it must be floating, or you will find the gold apt to crack. . . . [I]f you find any flaws or cracks appear, take a corresponding piece of gold, and apply it immediately.[7]

If a gilder had difficulty getting the gold to properly adhere, it was suggested that he use a pencil to release water so it would run under the gold.

After the gold had dried for eight or ten hours, the gilder, using a smooth agate stone in quick, gentle strokes, polished the areas that were intended to have a burnished appear-ance. Other areas were left unburnished or matted, resulting in a visual contrast between the burnish and matte. *The Cabinet-Maker's Guide* describes applying a pigmented toning coat over the gold: "Grind some vermillion, or yellow ochre, very fine, and mix a very small portion, either with parchment size, or with the white of an egg, and with a very soft brush lay it even and smooth on the parts intended to look dull; if well done, it will add greatly to the beauty of the work."[8]

Metallic powders, also known as bronze powders, consisted of finely ground gold, silver, or copper. Generally, they were a cheap substitute for more expensive gold leaf and were often used on furniture to create dramatic, richly colored details and shading. The cornucopia brackets and parts of the dolphin bodies on the Philadelphia pier table in figure 2.22, display a metallic powder, probably gold, over verdigris. During the early nineteenth century, metallic powder was applied freehand; however, around 1815–1820, it was used in conjunction with stencils. Indeed, stencils accelerated the decorating process on furniture and rapidly increased production.

Shading was achieved by varying the amount of bronze powder applied across a design. Rufus Porter, in his manual *A Select Collection of Valuable and Curious Arts,* states that in order to use bronze gilding, the ground had to be varnished with an equal mixture of copal varnish and old linseed oil. The manual further instructed the ornamenter to place a stencil on a surface only slightly sticky or tacky and "take a piece of soft glove-leather, moisten it a little by breathing on it, dip it in some dry bronze, and apply it to the figures, beginning at the edges—tap the figure gently with the leather and the bronze will stick to the varnish according to the pattern. Thus, any figure may be produced in a variety of shades by applying the bronze more freely to some parts of the work than to others."[9]

After the application of gold leaf or metallic powder, craftsmen applied a coat of varnish to protect the gilded surface. Some artisans recommended using copal, while others suggested vermille. Vermille was made by grinding vermilion, gamboge, a mixture of a gum and a resin, and red lead, very fine, with oil of turpentine.[10]

Gilding added a special dimension to painted furniture of the nineteenth century. Whether the gold was applied as leaf or powder, whether it covered the entire surface of a piece or just a specific area, gilding enhanced the beauty of furniture, creating the special works of art seen throughout the text.

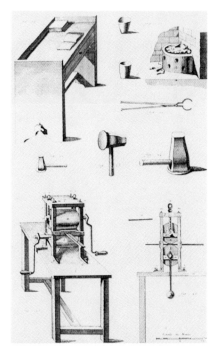

FIGURE B.3: *This illustration shows the varied tools of a goldbeater. From* Diderot Encyclopedia: The Complete Illustrations, 1762–1777, *vol. 1, Harry N. Abrams, Inc. (New York), p. 295.*

DIRECTORY OF PAINTED AND GILDED FURNITURE

SOURCES, SUPPLIES, *AND* RESTORATION SERVICES

THIS DIRECTORY IS PROVIDED AS A SERVICE. THE INFORMATION HEREIN WAS ACCURATE AT THE TIME OF PUBLICATION.

CONNECTICUT

David Dunton Antiques
Weekeepeemee Rd.
Woodbury, CT 06798
(203) 263-5355

Joel Einhorn Antiques
P.O. Box 432
Woodbury, CT 06798-0432
(203) 266-9090

Fred & Kathryn Giampietro
153 ½ Bradely St.
New Haven, CT 06511
(203) 787-3851
See also New York

Alan Katz
175 Ansonia Rd.
Woodbridge, CT 06525
(203) 397-8144

Marguerite Riordan
8 Pearl St.
Stonington, CT 06378
(203) 535-2511

Peter & Jeffrey Tillou
P.O. Box 145
Litchfield, CT 06759
(203) 567-5706

GEORGIA

Levison/Cullen Gallery
2300 Peachtree Rd.
Atlanta, GA 30309
(401) 351-3435

ILLINOIS

Frank & Barbara Pollack
1214 Green Bay Rd.
Highland Park, IL 60035
(708) 433-2213

LOUISIANA

Didier, Inc.
3439 Magazine St.
New Orleans, LA 70115
(504) 899-7749

MARYLAND

Stiles T. Colwill
Halcyon Farm
11245 Greenspring Ave.
Lutherville, MD 21093
(410) 828-7805

Millie McGehee
P.O. Box 666
Riderwood, MD 21139
(410) 653-3977

Aileen Minor
Somerset House
30550 Washington St.
P.O. Box 40
Princess Anne, MD 21853
(410) 651-0075

MASSACHUSETTS

Crafts Manufacturing Company
72 Massachusetts Ave.
Lunenberg, MA 01462
(508) 342-1717

Robert Mussey Associates, Inc. (*restoration*)
1415 Hyde Park Ave.
Boston, MA 02136
(617) 364-4054

Stephen Score, Inc.
73 Chestnut St.
Boston, MA 02108
(617) 227-9192

Elliott & Grace Snyder
Box 598
South Egremont, MA 01258
(413) 528-3581

Walters-Benisek
One Amber Lane
Northampton, MA 01060
(413) 586-3909

NEW HAMPSHIRE

Peter Hill, Inc.
Box 187
East Lempster, NH 03605
1 (800) 927-1001

Hoitt and Wentworth Arts and Crafts
    Catalog
559 Central Ave.
Dover, NH 03820
(413) 749-6406

NEW MEXICO

W. E. Channing & Co.
53 Old Santa Fe Trail
Santa Fe, NM 87501
(505) 988-1078

Morning Star Gallery
513 Canyon Rd.
Santa Fe, NM 87501
(505) 982-8187

NEW YORK

American Hurrah, Joel & Kate Kopp
766 Madison Ave.
New York, NY 10021
(212) 535-1930

Marna Anderson
2 Wawarsing Rd.
New Paltz, NY 12561
(914) 225-1132

Art Essential of New York, Ltd.
3 Cross St.
Suffren, NY 10901
(914) 368-1100

BCA: Bob Corey Associates (*bronze powders*)
P.O. Box 22
Malverne, NY 11565
(516) 485-5544

Deborah Bigelow (*restoration*)
177 Grand St.
Newburgh, NY 12550
(914) 838-3928

Carswell Rush Berlin
140 Riverside Drive
New York, NY 10024
(212) 721-0330

Suzanne Courcier—Robert W. Wilkins
Route 22
Austerlitz, NY 12017
(518) 392-5754

Sidney Gecker
226 West 21st St.
New York, NY 10011
(212) 929-8769

Fred & Kathryn Giampietro
25 East 73rd St.
New York, NY 10021
(212) 861-8571

Samuel Herrup Antiques
12 East 86th St.
New York, NY 10028
(212) 737-9051

Hirschl & Adler Galleries, Inc.
21 East 70th St.
New York, NY 10021
(212) 535-8810

Margot Johnson
18 East 68th St.
New York, NY 10021
(212) 794-2225

Leigh Keno
980 Madison Ave.
New York, NY 10021
(212) 734-2381

Robert E. Kinnaman & Brian A.
   Ramaekers, Inc.
P.O. Box 1140
Wainscott, NY 11975
(516) 537-0779

Bernard & S. Dean Levy, Inc.
24 East 84th St.
New York, NY 10028
(212) 628-7088

Kelter Malce
74 Jane St.
New York, NY 10014
(212) 675-7380

Mohawk Finishing Products (*shellac*)
Route 30 North
Amsterdam, NY 12010
(518) 843-1380

John Keith Russell
Spring St.
South Salem, NY 10590
(914) 763-8144

Israel Sack, Inc.
730 Fifth Ave.
New York, NY 10019
(212) 399-6562

David A. Schorsch, Inc.
30 East 76th St.
New York, NY 10021
(212) 439-6100

Sepp Leaf Products (*gold, gold size, and
   bronze powder*)
381 Park Ave. South
Suite 1312
New York, NY 10016
(212) 683-2840

James Allen Smith (*decorative painting*)
83 Halsey Lane
Water Mill, NY 11976
(516) 726-5401

Sotheby's Restoration
P.O. Box 657 Maple Ave.
Clanerack, NY 12513
(518) 851-2544
or
1425 York Ave.
New York, NY 10021
(212) 860-5446

Thos. K. Woodard
American Antiques & Quilts
506 East 74th St.
New York, NY 10021
(212) 794-9404

NORTH CAROLINA
Laura A. W. Phillips, Architectural
   Historian
637 Spring St.
Winston-Salem, NC 27101
(910) 727-1968

OHIO
Gale Frederick & Dan Overmeyer
1959 Richmond Rd.
Toledo, OH 43607
(419) 535-5606

PENNSYLVANIA
James & Nancy Glazer
1308 Mt. Pleasant Rd.
Villanova, PA 19085
(610) 525-5658

Hayes Antiques
R.D. 1, P.O. Box 134
Belleville, PA 17004
(717) 935-5125

Chris Machmer Antiques
146 West Main St.
Annville, PA 17003
(717) 867-4244

Olde Hope Antiques, Inc.
6465 Route 202
New Hope, PA 18938
(215) 862-5055

Donald Sack
P.O. Box 132
Buck Hills, PA 18323

RHODE ISLAND
Carson & Ellis, Inc.
1153 Warwick Ave., Box 971
Warwick, RI 02888
(401) 781-7010

SOUTH CAROLINA
Robert M. Hicklin Jr.
509 East Saint John St.
Spartanburg, SC 29302
(803) 583-9847

VIRGINIA
Sumpter Priddy III
601 South Washington St.
Alexandria, VA 22314
(703) 299-0800

WYOMING
Fighting Bear Antiques
P.O. Box 3812
Jackson, WY 83001
(307) 733-2669

MUSEUMS *AND* HISTORIC HOUSES

CONNECTICUT
Lyman Allyn Art Museum
625 Williams St.
New London, CT 06320
(203) 443-2545

Hitchcock Chair Museum
1 Robertsville Rd.
Riverton, CT 06065
(203) 738-4950

Yale University Art Gallery
1111 Chapel St.
P.O. Box 2006 Yale Station
New Haven, CT 06520
(203) 432-0600

DELAWARE
Winterthur Museum, Gardens & Library
Route 52
Winterthur, DE 19735
(302) 888-4600

GEORGIA
High Museum of Art
1280 Peachtree St., NE
Atlanta, GA 30309
(404) 892-3600

IOWA
Vesterheim: The Norwegian-American
    Museum
502 West Water St.
Decorah, IA 52101
(319) 382-9681

KANSAS
Kauffman Museum
Bethel College
North Newton, KS 67117-9989
(316) 283-1612

MAINE
Maine State Museum
State House Station #83
Augusta, ME 04333
(207) 287-2301

MARYLAND
The Baltimore Museum of Art
Art Museum Drive
Baltimore, MD 21218
(410) 396-7100

Hampton National Historic Site
535 Hampton Lane
Towson, MD 21286-1397
(410) 962-0688

The Maryland Historical Society
201 West Monument St.
Baltimore, MD 21201
(301) 685-3750

MASSACHUSETTS
Concord Museum
200 Lexington Rd., P.O. Box 146
Concord, MA 01742
(508) 936-9609

Hancock Shaker Village
Albany Rd., Route 20, P.O. Box 898
Pittsfield, MA 01202
(413) 443-0188

Heritage Plantation of Sandwich
Pine and Grove Sts.
Sandwich, MA 02560
(508) 888-3300

Historic Deerfield, Inc.
The Street, P.O. Box 321
Deerfield, MA 01342
(413) 774-5881

Historical Society of Old Newbury
Cushing House Museum
98 Hight St.
Newburyport, MA 01950
(508) 462-2681

The Homes of the Society for the
    Preservation of New England
    Antiquities
Harrison Gray Otis House
141 Cambridge St.
Boston, MA 02114
(617) 227-3956

Museum of Fine Arts, Boston
465 Huntington Ave.
Boston, MA 02115
(617) 267-9300

Old Sturbridge Village
1 Old Sturbridge Village Rd.
Sturbridge, MA 01566
(508) 347-3362

Peabody Essex Museum
East India Sq.
Salem, MA 01970-3783
(508) 745-1876

MICHIGAN
Henry Ford Museum & Greenfield
    Village
20900 Oakland Blvd.
Dearborn, MI 48121
(313) 271-1620

MISSOURI
The Saint Louis Art Museum
1 Fine Arts Dr.
St. Louis, MO 63110-1380
(314) 721-0072

NEW HAMPSHIRE
Currier Gallery of Art
192 Orange St.
Manchester, NH 03104
(603) 669-6144

Rundlet-May House
364 Middle St.
Portsmouth, NH 03801
(603) 436-3205

Strawbery Banke Museum
Marcy St., P.O. Box 300
Portsmouth, NH 03801
(603) 433-1100

NEW JERSEY
The Newark Museum
49 Washington St.
P.O. Box 540
Newark, NJ 07101-0540
(201) 596-6550

NEW YORK
Abigail Adams Smith House
421 East 61st St.
New York, NY 10021
(212) 838-6878

Albany Institute of History & Art
125 Washington Ave.
Albany, NY 12210
(518) 563-4478

Boscobel Restoration, Inc.
R 2 P.O. Box 24
Rt. 9D
Garrison-on-Hudson, NY 10524
(914) 265-4405

The Brooklyn Museum
200 Eastern Pkwy.
Brooklyn, NY 11238
(718) 638-5000

The Farmers Museum
New York Historical Association
Fennimore House
Lake Rd., P.O. Box 800
Cooperstown, NY 13326
(607) 547-1400

The Metropolitan Museum of Art
American Wing
82nd St. and Fifth Ave.
New York, NY 10028
(212) 535-7710

Morris-Jumel Mansion
65 Jumel Terrace
New York, NY 10032
(212) 923-8008

Munson-Williams-Proctor Institute
Fountain Elms
310 Genesee St.
Utica, NY 13502
(315) 797-0000

Museum of American Folk Art
2 Lincoln Sq.
New York, NY 10023
(212) 977-7170

Museum of the City of New York
103rd St. and Fifth Ave.
New York, NY 10128
(212) 534-1672

Shaker Museum
Shaker Museum Rd.
Old Chatham, NY 12136
(518) 794-9105

Southampton Historical Museum
Meeting House Lane
Southampton, NY 11968
(516) 283-2494

NORTH CAROLINA
Museum of Early Southern Decorative
    Arts
P.O. Box 10310
924 South Main St.
Winston-Salem, NC 27108-0310
(910) 721-7360

OHIO
Historic Southwest Ohio
Sharon Woods Village
John Hauck House
P.O. Box 62475
Cincinnati, OH 45262
(513) 563-9484

Ohio Historical Center
1982 Velma Ave.
Columbus, OH 43211
(614) 297-2300

PENNSYLVANIA
Philadelphia Museum of Art
Benjamin Franklin Pkwy.
Box 7646
Philadelphia, PA 19101
(215) 763-8100

TENNESSEE
The Tennessee State Museum
Polk Cultural Center
505 Deaderick St.
Nashville, TN 37243-1120
(615) 741-2692

TEXAS
The Bayou Bend Collection
Museum of Fine Arts, Houston
1 Westcott St., Box 13157
Houston, TX 77019
(713) 529-8773

The Witte Museum
3801 Broadway
San Antonio, TX 78209
(210) 820-2111

UTAH
Museum of Church History and Art
45 North West Temple St.
Salt Lake City, UT 84150
(801) 240-2299

VERMONT
The Bennington Museum
West Main St.
Bennington, VT 05201
(802) 447-1571

Shelburne Museum
Rt. 7
Shelburne, VT 05482
(802) 985-3346

VIRGINIA
Abby Aldrich Rockefeller Folk Art Center
307 South England St.
P.O. Box 1776
Williamsburg, VA 23187-1776
(804) 229-1000

The Colonial Williamsburg Foundation
P.O. Box 1776
Williamsburg, VA 23187-1776
(804) 229-1000

Prestwould Foundation
P.O. Box 872
Clarksville, VA 23927
(804) 374-8672

Virginia Museum
2800 Grove Avenue
Richmond, VA 23221
(804) 367-0147

GLOSSARY

Anthemion. A flower motif borrowed from the ancient Greeks by neoclassical craftsmen.

Bole. A thick, creamy mixture of finely ground earth pigment combined with a fixed proportion of rabbit-skin glue and water. Bole provides a smooth, pliant surface for the application of gold and other metal leaf. Bole comes in three basic colors—red, black, and yellow—with a range of intermediate hues.

Bronzing or metal powder. Powdered gold, silver, aluminum, brass, or bronze used to decorate furniture. Metallic powders were applied by free-hand or with stencils atop gilder's oil size or mixed in a medium to create a metallic paint. To prevent tarnishing, metal powder decoration was covered with a protective varnish. In some instances the varnish was tinted with pigments or dyes to create a brighter, richer color.

Bronzing, bronzing in gold or copper, patina antiqua. Nineteenth-century terms for what today is commonly called verd antique. By employing combinations of painting and gilding techniques, verd antique results in making wood, plaster, and metal appear bronzed. The ultimate appearance was intended to imitate naturally patinated or corroded bronze sculpture or furniture by employing greens, browns, and gold leaf or gold powder.

Carmine. A pigment which Sheraton says produces a "very beautiful red colour, a fine bright crimson."

Caryatid. A decorative support in the form of a female figure derived from ancient Greek architecture. Caryatids were used in Empire furniture, primarily to support tabletops and stands.

Copal. A hard resin used as the basis of varnish until 1840 when synthetic resins were invented. Copal varnishes made a fine transparent varnish used as furniture finish.

Distemper. A water-based paint or glaze with an animal glue medium that did not require the craftsmanship of oil painting but was not as durable a paint. Distemper was less expensive than oil paint; however, some favored distemper for graining for its ease of correction.

Dragon's blood. A dark red resin used to tint varnishes.

Ebonizing. The exotic dark hardwood, ebony, was often imitated by ebonizing, or staining and polishing, light woods to a jet-black color. Sheraton recommended staining "a few washes of a hot decoction of galls, and when dry, adding writing ink, polishing it with a stiff brush, and a little hot wax."

Églomisé or verre églomisé. A pictorial or decorative design gilded and painted on the reverse side of glass panels and sometimes protected with a varnish on mirrors and furniture. The decoration is applied from details to background, opposite of that employed by painting on canvas, from background to details. It is also referred to as reverse-painted glass. Sheraton referred to this method of applying paint to glass as back-painting.

Fauteuil. A gilded or painted French upholstered armchair form with open sides, a molded top rail, and turned legs.

Flake white. A white-lead pigment widely used in painting.

Freehand bronze. A method of applying metal powders to a varnish painted on the surface in a pattern without the use of a stencil or theorem. Gold, silver, copper, bronze, or brass in powdered form was applied with a small pad in a painterly technique, called stumpwork, onto a tacky composition of pigment and varnish or gold size within an outlined shape.

Freehand gilding. Gold leaf applied to an oil size painted in a pattern on a smooth japanned or varnished surface. Fine lines are painted with a brush or etched with a stylus on the gold leaf pattern. This creates a three-dimensional pictorial resembling French ormolu mounts.

Gesso. A white ground prepared from calcium carbonate and parchment-size or rabbit-skin glue, which varies in viscosity from a thick cream to a putty. Gesso is applied to furniture to create a smooth surface for gilding or painting.

Gilder's liquor. A mixture of alcohol and water used in water gilding.

Gilding. The application of a thin metal leaf to a surface to create the effect of solid metal. *Oil gilding* can be done on either a gesso ground or directly on wood. Beginning in the nineteenth century it was adhered with a varnish size containing a drying oil component. It cannot be burnished and therefore does not achieve the high gloss possible with water gilding. In *water gilding* the leaf is applied with a water-based mordant to a highly prepared surface of gesso and bole. The color of the bole layers can be manipulated for different aesthetic effects. This type of gilding produces a matte surface, but it can also be pressed or polished with an agate burnisher to a high sheen.

Gum. A viscous secretion of some trees and shrubs that hardens on drying. Unlike resin, gum is water-soluble and is used in glue.

Indigo. A dark blue vegetable dye used for coloring fabrics. In powdered form it is used as a paint pigment. Derived principally from *Indigofera tinctoria,* a plant of Indian origin, in the nineteenth century.

Ivory black. A pigment prepared by finely grinding ivory or burned bones, which results, according to Sheraton, in "a beautiful black, but does not cover so well."

Japanning. The European adaptation of Asian lacquering, which in the nineteenth century Sheraton defined as a "kind of painting." In America the term describes a decorative painting method of employing dyes or pigments mixed with shellac varnish as a medium. Multiple ground coats of japan varnishes sealed the wood and provided a smooth, colorful base for decorative painting and gilding. Exact methods and materials used in japanning varied over time and from one country to another.

King's yellow. A pigment prepared from the mineral arsenic trisulfide. Because it was highly poisonous and destroyed the color of other pigments, it fell into disuse.

Klismos-form chair. An ancient Greek chair form seen on Greek vases and widely adopted by neoclassical artisans. This chair has a gently curved back and saber legs that are slightly splayed to the front and to the rear. Above the seat frame, at the back, two curving stiles continued the lines of the rear legs, and a central splat supported a curved tablet top at shoulder height. Roman klismos-form chairs had turned front legs.

Lacquer. An Asian varnish in use as early as the first century to decorate furniture and small objects. Made from the sap of the *Rhus vernicifera,* a plant found only in the Far East, lacquer was used in japanning by applying many layers, each polished to a high gloss.

Lake. A transparent or translucent pigment used in distemper painting and for varnish glazes. Dyestuff are the source of lake pigments. Lake is also a crimson pigment generally prepared from scarlet rags, cochineal, and brazilwood.

Lampblack. Soot collected from the smoke of burned resinous pine and fir trees, used to tint paint. Not true black, lampblack was slightly bluish in color.

Linseed oil. A natural drying oil expressed from flaxseed. The most common basis of oil paints and oil-based varnishes in the nineteenth century.

Meglip. "A vehicle made of oil of turpentine and pale drying oil in equal proportions. These ingredients gelatinize and, when mixed with oil colors, give them a certain body and a pulpy transparency." William Dwight Whitney, *The Century Dictionary,* vol. 4 (New York: The Century Company, c. 1890), p. 3572.

Milk-based paint. A combination of skim milk, fresh lime, oil of caraway or nut or linseed oil, and Spanish white to which pigments could be added.

Mordant. An adhesive compound for affixing gold leaf.

Muller and stone. Implements traditionally used for grinding paint pigments. The stone—sometimes called a grindstone or grinding slab—was a rectangular slab of flat-topped granite or marble, usually eighteen inches square. The muller was most often an egg-shaped piece of granite about three inches in diameter and five inches long with a large round end that was rubbed against the grindstone to pulverize pigments into a uniform consistency.

Ochre. A natural earth pigment consisting of silica, clay, and iron oxides that produces different colors, including red, yellow, and, less commonly, brown, blue, and green.

Ormolu mounts. Small figures cast in bronze and finished with a thin layer of gold leaf or a golden tint, used to decorate the surfaces of French, English, and some American eighteenth- and nineteenth-century furniture.

Parcel gilding. Selective gilding used to highlight details of a wood or painted surface.

Patent yellow. A bright and permanent yellow pigment widely used from 1790 to 1830 because it was not as dangerous as king's yellow.

Patera (plural: paterae). A classical Greek ornament or motif in the shape of a circle or ovoid that was carved, inlaid, or painted on neoclassical furniture.

Patina antiqua. See *bronzing.*

Pier. The section of wall between two windows, where during the nineteenth century it was a convention in formal parlors to place a *pier table* above which was a long, rectangular *pier glass*.

Pigment. The coloring agent that is mixed with a vehicle to make paint. Pigments were derived from both organic and inorganic sources.

Plumbago. Black lead or natural graphite used in tracing patterns onto a wood surface.

Poppyseed oil. A natural light drying oil derived from the seeds of the opium poppy. Used as a paint medium and with some varnishes when extreme clarity and lightness of colors were required.

Prussian blue. The first modern synthetic pigment of a deep blue color.

Rosin. A resin derived from raw sap of pine or spruce trees.

Sandarac. A translucent reddish varnish used as a substitute for Asian lacquer.

Shellac. A type of lacquer made from the secretion of the lac insect *Coccus lacca*. Shellac was used in the nineteenth century to impart a shiny finished surface to furniture.

Sienna. An earth pigment similar to ochres, used in oil paint and watercolors. Raw sienna is brownish yellow. When heated it becomes burnt sienna, a warmer, reddish brown.

Size. A very thin, watered-down mixture of glue or resinous substance, used as an initial sealer coat on wood surfaces before gilding or painting to reduce surface porosity, preventing further coats of finish from soaking in too much. See *mordant*.

Smoke graining. Two-toned graining that has a marbled or smoked finish, applied by drawing a candle over a painted ground covered by a size. When the size is almost dry, soot from the lighted candle will adhere to it. When

the pattern is complete and thoroughly dry, it is varnished.

Spanish brown. An inexpensive and easily ground earth pigment in an earthy red-brown color, often referred to as barn red in America.

Spirits of wine. Ethyl alcohol, derived by distilling wine or another alcoholic beverage, which was often redistilled for making varnish.

Staining. The process of coloring wood using a liquid dye on the surface of a completed piece of furniture. The dye was applied with a brush or rag, and then the excess wiped off.

Stencil. A thin sheet of metal or prepared paper in which designs are cut to facilitate the application of images to furniture, walls, floorcloths, and textiles.

Trompe l'oeil. From the French for "fool the eye." The use of paint to create an illusionary effect, most often of landscapes, still-lifes, or another medium altogether, such as marble or wood.

Turpentine. When the sap of certain conifers, particularly pine and spruce, is distilled, it yields "spirit of turpentine," which is used as a paint thinner.

Umber. A natural brown earth pigment similar to but darker than ochre and sienna but containing iron and manganese dioxide. Raw umber, a rather cold brown, when heated forms burnt umber, a warmer reddish brown color.

Varnish. A coating for wood, which Sheraton defined as "a clear limpid fluid, capable of hardening without losing its transparency." Nineteenth-century varnishes included copal varnish, white spirit varnish, mastic varnish, linseed oil varnish, amber varnish, and turpentine varnish. They were used to highlight the wood grain

and give additional luster and protection to the surface.

Verd antique. Describes an early-nineteenth-century method of imitating patinated or corroded bronze surfaces found on ancient sculpture. Many methods were employed in creating this decorative effect, which on furniture is referred to as bronzing, bronzing in gold, and patina antiqua in printed sources of the period. See *bronzing*.

Verdigris. A blue-green pigment, the product of the corrosion of copper, brass, or bronze, used in paint to simulate corroded bronze. It results in a lighter tone than that produced by the bronzing or verd antique.

Vermilion (vermillion, cinnabar). A red pigment of mercuric sulfide found in nature in the mineral cinnabar.

Vinegar painting. A two-toned graining method created by applying a darker glaze mixed with vinegar over a lighter colored ground and using a roll of putty as a tool to work patterns onto the darker layer. The linseed oil in the putty causes the glaze to separate, creating a seaweedlike effect.

Whiting or gilder's whiting. Ground calcium carbonate or chalk prepared by slaking plaster of Paris, which when mixed with a glue preparation becomes gesso.

Yellow. A pigment that went by many names in the nineteenth century, including Dutch pink, English pink, king's yellow, patent yellow, Naples yellow, and yellow ochre.

The authors thank Deborah Bigelow of Deborah Bigelow Associates, furniture and gilded decorative arts conservator, for her assistance in writing this glossary.

NOTES

HIGH-STYLE FURNI-
TURE INTRODUCTION

1. M. A. DeWolfe Hose, ed., *The Articulate Sisters* (Cambridge, Mass., 1946), p. 34, as quoted in Jane Nylander, "Henry Sargent's *Dinner Party* and *Tea Party*," *The Magazine Antiques* 121, no. 5 (May 1982): 1179.

1. BOSTON AND SALEM

1. Walter Muir Whitehill, *Boston: A Topographical History* (Cambridge, Mass.: Harvard University Press, 1968), p. 47.

2. Charles A. Place, *Charles Bulfinch, Architect and Citizen* (Boston: Houghton Mifflin, 1925), p. 6.

3. Ibid., p. 8.

4. Julian Boyd et al., eds., *The Papers of Thomas Jefferson*, vol. 8, Thomas Jefferson to James Madison, 20 September 1785 (Princeton: Princeton University Press, 1950), pp. 534–35.

5. Thomas Pemberton, "Topographical and Historical Description of Boston," *Collections of the Massachusetts Historical Society* 3 (1794): 255–256, quoted in *Paul Revere's Boston: 1735–1818*, exhibition catalog (Boston: Museum of Fine Arts, 1975), p. 157.

6. Page Talbott, "Seating Furniture in Boston, 1810–1835," *The Magazine Antiques* 139, no. 5 (May 1991): 958.

7. George Hepplewhite, *The Cabinet-Maker and Upholsterer's Guide*, 3d ed. (1794; reprint, New York: Dover Publications, 1969), p. 2.

8. Nathaniel Whittock, *Decorative Painters' and Glaziers' Guide* (London: Isaac Taylor Hinton, 1828), p. 66.

9. Thomas Sheraton, *The Cabinet Dictionary*, 1803; reprint, with introduction by Wilford P. Cole and Charles F. Montgomery (New York: Praeger, 1970), vol. 2, p. 258.

10. Robert Dossie, *The Handmaid to the Arts*, vol. I (London: J. Nourse, 1764), p. 478.

11. Hepplewhite, p. 2.

12. Thomas Sheraton, *The Cabinet-Maker and Upholsterer's Drawing-Book* (1793; reprint, New York: Dover Publications, 1972), p. 211.

13. Hepplewhite, p. 2.

14. J. Michael Flanigan, *American Furniture from the Kaufman Collection* (Washington: National Gallery of Art, 1968), pp. 110–12. Large numbers of these chairs were copied by descendants of the Derby family in later years of the nineteenth century, and caution should be taken in dating these chairs.

15. Sheraton, *The Cabinet Dictionary*, vol. II, pp. 435–40.

16. Rita Susswein Gottesman, *The Arts and Crafts in New York, 1777–1799* (New York: New-York Historical Society, 1954), p. 113.

17. Hepplewhite, p. 2. See also Sumpter Priddy, "Fancy, Acceptance of an Attitude, Emergence of a Style," master's thesis, University of Delaware, Winterthur Program in Early American Culture, 1981, p. 59. Also, Ulysses G. Dietz writes that the term "fancy" referred "not to the degree of elaboration of the ornament on a piece, but to the fanciful nature of the decoration"—*Century of Revivals: Nineteenth-Century American Furniture from the Collection of the Newark Museum* (Newark, N.J.: Newark Museum, 1983), p. 8. Charles F. Montgomery refers to painted furniture as "the *dernier cri*" in English taste, a fashion that "American fancy-furniture makers quickly followed"—*American Furniture: The Federal Period in the Henry Francis du Pont Museum* (New York: Viking, 1966), p. 446.

18. Hepplewhite, p. 2.

19. Sheraton, *The Cabinet Dictionary*, vol. 2, pp. 422–23.

20. Hepplewhite, p. 21.

21. Joseph Downs, "Derby and McIntire," *Metropolitan Museum of Art Bulletin* 6, no. 2 (1947): 78. Also see Edwin J. Hipkiss, *Three McIntire Rooms from Peabody, Massachusetts* (Boston: Museum of Fine Arts, 1931), pp. 39, 41, 43, 67, 71.

22. Philip Zea and Robert C. Cheney, *Clock Making in New England, 1725–1825* (Sturbridge, Mass.: Old Sturbridge Village, 1992), p. 29.

23. John Stalker and George Parker, *A Treatise on Japanning and Varnishing, Being a Compleat Discovery of Those Arts* (Oxford: Stalker and Parker, 1688), pp. 73–75. The authors thank Nonnie Frelinghuysen for bringing to their attention the use of mezzotints for painting on glass described in her thesis [Alice Knotts Bossert Cooney] *Ornamental Painting in Boston, 1790–1830*, master's thesis, University of Delaware, Winterthur Program, 1978, p. 26.

24. Rufus Porter, *A Select Collection of Valuable and Curious Arts* (Concord, N.H.: Rufus Porter, 1825), p. 32.

25. Ibid., pp. 13–14.

26. George Smith, *A Collection of Designs for Household Furniture and Interior Decoration* (London: J. Taylor, 1808), p. 25.

27. *The Diary of William Bentley, D.D., Pastor of the East Church, Salem, Massachusetts*, vol. 2 (Salem, 1905–1914), p. 400.

28. Hipkiss, *Three Rooms*, pp. 22–24.

29. Mabel M. Swan, "The Man Who Made Simon Willard's Clock Cases: John Doggett of 'Roxbury,'" *The Magazine Antiques* 15, no. 3 (1929): 196–97.

30. Carol Damon Andrews, "John Ritto Penniman (1782–1841), an Ingenious New England Artist," *The Magazine Antiques* 120, no. 1 (July 1981): 166, 165.

31. Ibid., pp. 147–70. See also Carol Damon Andrews, "The Penniman Coat of Arms Painted by John Ritto Penniman," unpublished paper, 1992. The authors thank Peter Hill for providing a copy of this paper.

32. Andrews, "John Ritto Penniman," pp. 147, 149. Among the items disposed of by John Penniman in a public sale of his painting equipment are listed "a large number of Choice Prints and Engravings, suitable for artists and amateurs"—*Columbian Centinel*, April 19, 1827.

33. Other work credited to Penniman by Carol Damon Andrews includes the name board decoration on a pianoforte made by Benjamin Crehore of Boston and on a piano by Babcock, Appleton and Babcock, also of Boston; Andrews, "John Ritto Penniman," p. 166.

34. Stacy J. Glass, "The Holden Chairs at Israel Sack, Inc.," unpublished paper, Sotheby's Educational Studies American Arts Course, 1994, pp. 1–16. The authors thank Deanne Levison for bringing this research to their attention, and Stacy Glass Goldstone for her assistance with this inquiry.

35. Quoted in Wendell Garrett, ed., "Clues

and Footnotes," *The Magazine Antiques* 107, no. 5 (May 1975): 939.

36. Archibald Robertson, *Elements of the Graphic Arts*, vol. 1 (New York, 1802), p. 16.

37. Ibid., p. 8. See also Nina Fletcher Little, "Artists' Boxes of the Early Nineteenth Century," *The American Art Journal* (Spring 1980): 28–39.

38. Porter, p. 24.

39. John Hill, *A Series of Progressive Lessons Intended to Elucidate the Art of Flower Painting in Water Colours* (Philadelphia: M. Thomas, 1818).

40. Andrew Jackson Downing, *The Architecture of Country Houses* (1850; reprint, New York: Dover Publications, 1969), p. 415.

41. Alice Knotts Bossert Cooney, "Ornamental Painting in Boston, 1790–1830," unpublished master's thesis, University of Delaware, Winterthur Program, 1978, pp. 150–75.

2. PHILADELPHIA

1. Russell F. Weigley, ed., *Philadelphia: A 300-Year History* (New York: Norton, 1982), p. 178.

2. Ibid., p. 177.

3. Alfred Coxe Prime, *The Arts and Crafts in Philadelphia, Maryland, and South Carolina, 1721–1785*, vol. 2 (Topsfield, Mass.: Walpole Society, Wayside Press, 1932), p. 304.

4. Theodore Zuk Penn, "Decorative and Protective Finishes, 1750–1850: Materials, Process and Craft," master's thesis, University of Delaware, 1966, p. 73. The information about pigments in this chapter is from this study.

5. Wendell Garrett, *Classic America: The Federal Style and Beyond* (New York: Rizzoli, 1992), p. 121.

6. Beatrice B. Garvan, *Federal Philadelphia: 1785–1825, The Athens of the Western World* (Philadelphia: Philadelphia Museum of Art, 1987), p. 56.

7. Ibid., pp. 57, 59.

8. The authors thank Jack Lindsey for bringing this information to their attention.

9. Marie Kimball, "Thomas Jefferson's French Furniture," *The Magazine Antiques* 15, no. 2 (February 1929): 124.

10. Garvan, p. 57.

11. Deborah Ducoff-Barone, "Philadelphia Furniture Makers, 1800–1815," *The Magazine Antiques* 119, no. 5 (May 1991): 982.

12. Garvan, p. 66.

13. Ducoff-Barone, p. 985.

14. Marie Kimball, "The Original Furnishings of the White House," part 1, *The Magazine Antiques* 15, no. 5 (June 1929): 485.

15. In addition to this chair and one other in the collection of the Winterthur Museum, other chairs are known. The Bayou Bend Collection of the Museum of Fine Arts, Houston, owns one, another chair is in the collection of the Yale University Art Gallery and one other is in the collection of the Kaufman Americana Foundation. Two are in a private collection.

16. *Philadelphia, Three Centuries of American Art, Selections from the Bicentennial Exhibition Held at the Philadelphia Museum of Art* (Philadelphia: Philadelphia Museum of Art, 1976), p. 206.

17. Marilynn Johnson, *Baltimore Federal Furniture* (New York: Metropolitan Museum of Art, 1972).

18. Garvan, p. 67.

19. Jack L. Lindsey, "An Early Labtrobe Furniture Commission," *The Magazine Antiques*, 139, no. 1 (January 1991): 212.

20. Wendy A. Cooper, *Classical Taste in America: 1800–1840* (New York: Abbeville Press, 1993), p. 116.

21. Lindsey, p. 214.

22. Garvan, p. 92.

23. Lindsey, p. 214.

24. Kathleen M. Catalano, "Cabinetmaking in Philadelphia 1820–1840: Transition from Craft to Industry," *Winterthur Portfolio* 13 (1979): 81.

25. David H. Conradsen, "The Stock-in-Trade of John Hancock & Company," in Luke Beckerdite, ed., *American Furniture* (Hanover, N.H.: University Press of New England, 1993), pp. 39, 42.

26. Robert D. Mussey Jr., ed., *The First American Furniture Finisher's Manual: A Reprint of "The Cabinet-Maker's Guide" of 1827* (New York: Dover Publications, 1987), pp. 45–46.

27. Wendy Wick, "Stephen Girard: A Patron of the Philadelphia Trade," master's thesis, University of Delaware, June 1977.

28. Robert C. Smith, "The Furniture of Anthony G. Quervelle, Part 1: The Pier Tables," in John J. Snyder Jr., ed., *Philadelphia Furniture and Its Makers* (New York: Universe Books, 1975), p. 105.

29. Donald L. Fennimore, "Gilding Practices and Processes in Nineteenth-Century American Furniture," in Deborah Bigelow et al., eds., *Gilded Wood: Conservation and History* (Madison, Conn.: Sound View Press, 1991), p. 144.

30. Cooper, p. 142.

31. We thank Robert D. Mussey Jr. for the definition of verd antique.

32. Rufus Porter, *A Select Collection of Valuable and Curious Arts* (Concord, N.H., 1825), p. 81.

33. Fennimore, p. 151, n. 6.

34. Page Talbott, "Allen and Brother, Philadelphia Furniture Makers," *The Magazine Antiques* 149, no. 5 (May 1996): 716.

35. Ibid., p. 721.

36. Nancy Goyne Evans says that "Windsor" is "a name applied to a type of stick-and-socket-framed furniture utilizing a wooden seat plank as the principal unit of construction. The name derives from the castle town of Windsor in England. Because of the number of visitors to the site, the castle grounds were furnished with rustic seating of stick-and-socket construction by the early eighteenth century." Evans, *American Windsor Chairs* (New York: Hudson Hills Press, 1996), p. 724.

37. Nancy Goyne Evans, "Unsophisticated Furniture Made and Used in Philadelphia and Environs, ca. 1750–1840," in John D. Morse, ed., *Country Cabinetwork and Simple City Furniture* (Charlottesville: University Press of Virginia, 1970), pp. 167, 169.

38. Charles Santore, *The Windsor Style in America* (Philadelphia: Running Press, 1992), p. 43.

39. Nancy Goyne Evans, "American Painted Seating Furniture: Marketing the Product, 1750–1840," in Gerald W. R. Ward, ed., *Perspectives on American Furniture* (New York: Norton, 1988), p. 162.

40. Santore, p. 48.

3. BALTIMORE

1. Lynne Dakin Hastings, *Hampton National Historic Site* (Towson, Md.: Historic Hampton, 1986), p. 12.

2. Ibid., p. 48.

3. Hamilton Owens, *Baltimore on the Chesapeake* (New York: Doubleday Doran, 1941), pp. 138, 149.

4. Ibid., pp. 228–29.

5. Mary Ellen Hayward, "The Mercantile Community of Baltimore, from Town to City," *Classical Maryland 1815–1845* (Baltimore: Maryland Historical Society, 1993), p. 6.

6. Bayard Tuckerman, ed., *The Diary of Philip Hone, 1828–1851*, vol. 1 (New York: Dodd, Mead, 1889), p. 144.

7. Gregory R. Weidman, *Furniture in Maryland, 1740–1940* (Baltimore: Maryland Historical Society, 1984), p. 77.

8. Ibid., p. 75.

9. Gregory R. Weidman et al., *Classical Maryland* (Baltimore: Maryland Historical Society, 1993), p. 99.

10. Weidman, *Furniture in Maryland*, p. 94, no. 25.

11. Ibid., p. 161.

12. Stiles Tuttle Colwill, *Francis Guy, 1760–1820* (Baltimore: Maryland Historical Society, 1981), p. 85.

13. Ibid., p. 24.

14. William Voss Elder III, *Baltimore Painted Furniture, 1800–1840* (Baltimore: Baltimore Museum of Art, 1972), p. 11.

15. Colwill, p. 25.

16. Ibid.

17. Ibid.

18. Ibid.

19. Quoted in Elisabeth Donaghy Garrett, *At Home: The American Family, 1750–1870* (New York: Harry N. Abrams, 1990), p. 39.

20. Weidman, *Furniture in Maryland*, p. 144.

21. Garrett, p. 52.

22. Wendy A. Cooper, *Classical Taste in America* (New York: Abbeville Press, 1993), p. 123.

23. Weidman, *Furniture in Maryland*, p. 90.

24. Weidman, *Classical Maryland*, p. 100.

25. The authors thank F. Carey Howlett, conservator of furniture at Colonial Williamsburg Foundation, for the description of paint techniques employed on the card table.

26. The authors thank Julian D. Hudson, director of the Prestwould Foundation, for sharing information and providing photos of this extraordinary piece of furniture. The bills of sale for these tables and for other furniture ordered at this time are in the Manuscripts Department, Swem Library, College of William and Mary. These bills list twelve bronze chairs, a pair of pier tables, eight rush chairs, and twelve Greek rush chairs.

27. Weidman, *Classical Maryland*, p. 108.

28. The authors thank Gregory Weidman for the informative visit to the Maryland Historical Society and for information on the motifs colored verd antique on the Alexander Brown table.

29. Weidman, *Classical Maryland*, p. 101.

30. Ibid., p. 94.

31. Cooper, p. 145.

4. NEW YORK CITY

1. Mary Palmer Tyler, *Grandmother Tyler's Books; The Recollections of Mary Palmer Tyler (Mrs. Royall Tyler), 1775–1866*, ed. Frederick Tupper and Helen Tyler Brown (New York: Putnam, 1925), pp. 120–21.

2. *Commercial Information Relative to the Seale of New York* (Philadelphia: J. C. Kaysor & Co., 1823), p. 129.

3. Quoted in Berry B. Tracy, "For 'One of the Most Genteel Residences in the City,'" *Metropolitan Museum of Art Bulletin* 25, no. 8 (1967): 283.

4. *Carroll's New York City Directory* (New York: Carroll & Company, 1859), p. 8.

5. Daniel Longworth, ed., *American Almanack, New York Register and City Directory* (New York: Compiler, 1805), p. 111.

6. *New-York Gazette and General Advertiser*, February 22, 1797, quoted in Rita Susswein Gottesman, *The Arts and Crafts in New York, 1777–1799* (New York: New-York Historical Society, 1954), p. 124.

7. Longworth, p. 123.

8. Advertisements in Gottesman, listings in Longworth, trade cards, and signed examples; also Zilla Rider Lea, ed., *The Ornamented Chair* (Rutland, Vt.: Charles E. Tuttle, 1960).

9. The authors thank Peter Kenny for bringing this image to their attention.

10. Brock Jobe, ed., *Portsmouth Furniture: Masterworks from the New Hampshire Seacoast* (Hanover, N.H.: University Press of New England, 1995), pp. 362–63.

11. *Republican and Savannah Evening Ledger*, March 3 and March 1, 1810, quoted in Page Talbott, *Classical Savannah: Fine and Decorative Arts, 1800–1840*, exhibition catalog (Savannah: Telfair Museum of Art, 1995), p. 167, n. 57.

12. Nancy Goyne Evans, "American Painted Seating Furniture, Marketing the Product, 1750–1840," in Gerald W. R. Ward, ed., *Perspectives on American Furniture* (New York: Norton, 1988), p. 153.

13. Talbott, p. 160.

14. Nancy Goyne Evans, *American Windsor Chairs* (New York: Hudson Hills Press, 1996), p. 298.

15. Quoted in Marie G. Kimball, "The Original Furnishings of the White House: Part I," *The Magazine Antiques* 15, no. 5 (June 1929): p. 484.

16. Daniel Longworth, ed., *American Almanack, New-York Register and City Directory of New York* (Compiler, 1826), unpaged advertising supplement and *Wilson's Business Directory of New York City* (New York: John F. Trow, 1849), p. 119.

17. J. Milbert, *Picturesque Itinerary of the Hudson River and the Peripheral Parts of North America*, trans. and ed. Constance D. Sherman (1828–1829; reprint, Ridgewood, N.J., 1968), p. xxiv.

18. As quoted in Marshall D. Davidson, *Life in America* (Boston: Houghton Mifflin, 1974), p. 146.

19. William B. Adair, "Restoration and Conservation," in *The Regilded Age*, exhibition catalog (Washington, D.C.: Society of Gilders, 1991), p. 20.

20. Donald L. Fennimore, "Gilding Practices and Processes in Nineteenth-Century American Furniture," in *Gilded Wood: Conservation and History* (Madison, Conn.: Sound View Press, 1991), p. 148.

21. Quoted in Rita Susswein Gottesman, *The Arts and Crafts in New York, 1800–1804* (New York: New-York Historical Society, 1965), p. 148.

22. Robert D. Mussey Jr., "*Verte Antique* Decoration on American Furniture: History, Materials, Techniques, Technical Investigations." Paper delivered at the Williamsburg Conference, 1995, p. 20.

23. Fennimore, p. 143.

24. Quoted in Edward Rothstein, "When New York Was the New Place to Play," *New York Times*, July 2, 1995, Section H.

25. The authors thank Jodi Pollock, who shared her research on the Meeks family.

26. David A. Hanks, "Pottier & Stymus Mfg. Co.: Artistic Furniture and Decorations," *Art & Antiques*, September-October 1982, pp. 85, 88.

27. *Carroll's New York City Directory, Leading Mercantile Firms, in Every Commercial Pursuit* (New York: Carroll & Company, 1859), p. 114.

28. Dianne D. Hauserman, "Alexander Roux and His Plain and Artistic Furniture," *The Magazine Antiques*, February 1968, p. 210.

5. NEW ENGLAND

1. Nathaniel Hawthorne, *The House of the Seven Gables* (1851; reprint, New York: Penguin, 1986), pp. 32–33.

2. Compiled from Gerald W. R. Ward, *The Peirce-Nichols House, The John Tucker Daland House, The Assembly House, The Gardner-Pingree House* (Salem, Mass.: Essex Institute, 1976).

3. Marc Friedlander and L. F. Butterfield, eds., *Diary of Charles Francis Adams*, vol. 6 (Cambridge, Mass.: 1974), pp. 222–23.

4. H. Hudson Holly, *Modern Dwellings in Town and Country Adapted to American Wants and Climate* (New York, 1878), p. 194.

5. Quoted in Kenneth Joel Zogry, ed., *The Best the Country Affords: Vermont Furniture, 1765–1850* (Bennington, Vt.: Bennington Museum, 1995), p. 99.

6. Ibid., p. 100.

7. Phrases compiled from newspaper advertisements in Rita Susswein Gottesman, *The Arts and Crafts in New York, 1800–1804* (New York: New-York Historical Society, 1965), pp. 136–54.

8. Henry David Thoreau, *Walden and Other Writings*, ed. William Howarth (1854; reprint, New York: Modern Library, 1981), p. 59.

9. John W. Masury, *The American Grainer's Hand-Book* (New York: John W. Masury, 1872), p. 11.

10. H[ezekiah] Reynolds, *Directions for House and Ship Painting* (New Haven: Eli Hudson, 1812), p. 18.

11. Rufus Porter, *A Select Collection of Valuable and Curious Arts* (Concord, N.H.: Rufus Porter, 1825), p. 31.

12. Nathaniel Whittock, *Decorative Painters' and Glaziers' Guide* (London: Isaac Taylor Hinton, 1828), p. 28.

13. Edwin A. Churchill, *Simple Forms and Vivid Colors: An Exhibition of Maine Painted Furniture, 1800–1850* (Portland: Maine State Museum, 1983), p. 16.

14. Whittock, p. 16.

15. Zogry, *The Best the Country Affords*, p. 46.

16. The authors thank Stacy Hollander for sharing this information with us.

17. Kenneth Joel Zogry, "Urban Precedents for Vermont Furniture," *The Magazine Antiques*, May 1955, pp. 762–63.

18. The authors thank Stacy Hollander for pointing out another uniting feature of these chests: the straight molding at the bottom of each piece and the fact that all the different patterning is on the sides and front.

19. Thomas Sheraton, *The Cabinet Dictionary*, 1803; reprint, introduction by Wilford P. Cole and Charles F. Montgomery, vol. 2 (New York: Praeger, 1970), p. 259.

20. Francis J. Grund, *The Americans in Their Moral, Social, and Political Relations* (1837; reprint, New York: Augustus M. Keely, 1971), vol. 1, p. 136.

21. Jean Lipman, "The Rediscovery of Rufus Porter," *The Magazine Antiques* 119, no. 1 (January 1981): 206.

22. Photocopies of the articles are in the Archives of American Art and in the Library of the New York State Historical Association in Cooperstown. A condensed version appears in Porter, *Curious Arts*, pp. 27–29.

23. Nina Fletcher Little, Introduction to *Michele Felice Cornè, 1752–1845: Versatile Neapolitan Painter of Salem, Boston, and Newport*, exhibition catalog (Salem: Peabody Essex Museum, 1972), pp. x, xi.

24. George Davidson, waste book, 1793–1795, Boston. Manuscript in the collection of Old Sturbridge Village, Sturbridge, Massachusetts, February 18, 1793, and February 2, 1795.

25. Quoted in John Hardy Wright, *Vernacular Visions: Folk Art of Old Newbury*, exhibition catalog (Newburyport, Mass.: Historical Society of Old Newbury, 1994), p. 68.

26. Brock Jobe, ed., *Portsmouth Furniture: Masterworks from the New Hampshire Seacoast* (Hanover, N.H.: University Press of New England, 1993), p. 279.

27. Whittock, p. 67.

28. Sheraton, *Cabinet Dictionary*, vol. 2, p. 426.

29. Ibid., vol. 2, p. 427.

30. Ibid., vol. 2, pp. 425–26.

31. Donna Keith Baron, "Furniture Makers and Retailers in Worcester County, Massachusetts, Working to 1850," *The Magazine Antiques* 143, no. 5 (May 1993): 785.

32. Sheraton, *Cabinet Dictionary*, vol. 2, p. 188.

33. Whittock, pp. 188–89.

34. The authors thank the Museum of American Folk Art, New York, and Stacy Hollander for allowing us to go through the collection of the Historical Society of Early American Decoration, including the archival files of the late Esther Stevens Brazer.

35. Porter, *Curious Arts*, p. 44.

36. The authors thank Charlie Lynes for making the Hitchcock Museum accessible to them and for guiding them through the collection.

37. Reynolds, p. 6.

38. Ibid., pp. 15–18.

39. Ibid., p. 8.

6. THE MIDDLE ATLANTIC STATES

1. Quoted in Larry M. Neff, trans., "Jonas Heinrich Gudehus: Journey to America," in Albert F. Buffington, Don Yoder, Walter Klinefeltee, Larry M. Neff, Mary Hammond Sullivan, and Frederick S. Weiser, *Ebbes fer Alle-Ebber—Ebbes fer Dich: Something for Everyone—Something for You*, Essays in Memoriam, Albert Franklin Buffington, Publication of the Pennsylvania German Society (Breinigsville, Pa., 1980), vol. 14, pp. 217, 306.

2. Scott T. Swank, ed., *Arts of the Pennsylvania Germans* (New York: Norton, 1983), p. 5.

3. Beatrice B. Garvan and Charles F. Hummel, *The Pennsylvania Germans: A Celebration of Their Arts*, exhibition catalog (Philadelphia: Philadelphia Museum of Art, 1982), p. 39.

4. Benno M. Forman, "Germanic Influences in Pennsylvania Furniture," in Swank, p. 144.

5. Ibid.

6. Ibid.

7. Account book of John Peter Ranck, 1794 to 1814, Winterthur Museum, Gardens & Library.

8. Frederick S. Weiser and Mary Hammond Sullivan, "Decorated Furniture of the Schwaben Creek Valley," *Ebbes fer Alle-Ebber—Ebbes fer Dich: Something for Everyone—Something for You*, vol. 14, p. 333.

9. Ibid., p. 335.

10. Ibid., pp. 339–40.

11. Ibid., p. 335.

12. Forman, p. 131.

13. Henry M. Reed, *Decorated Furniture of the Mahantango Valley* (Lewisburg, Pa.: Center Gallery, 1987), p. 55.

14. Weiser and Sullivan, p. 355.

15. *Manufactured by Hand: The Soap Hollow School*, exhibition catalog (Loretto, Pa.: Southern Alleghenies Museum of Art, 1993), p. 14.

16. Ibid., p. 52.

17. Ibid., p. 6.

18. Ibid., p. 5.

19. Ernest L. Fritz and Charles Muller, "The Decorated Furniture of Jacob Knagy," *Antique Review*, April 1991, p. 31. The authors thank Daniel McCauley III for bringing to their attention furniture made by the Knagys.

20. The authors thank Daniel J. McCauley III for information on the Amish and their painted furniture.

21. Daniel and Kathryn McCauley, *Decorative Arts of the Amish of Lancaster County* (Intercourse, Pa.: Good Books, 1988), p. 15.

22. Richard M. Candee, "The Rediscovery of Milk-based Paints and the Myth of 'Brickdust and Buttermilk' Paints," *Old Time New England*, Winter 1968, p. 80.

23. Daniel J. McCauley III, "The Paintings of Henry and Elizabeth Lapp," *Folk Art Magazine*, Fall 1994, p. 54.

24. Ibid., p. 57.

25. Marie Purnell Musser, *Country Chairs of Central Pennsylvania* (Mifflinburg, Pa.: The Mifflinburg Telegraph, 1990), p. 22.

26. Allison P. Bennett, *The People's Choice: A History of Albany County in Art and Architecture* (Albany, N.Y.: Lane Press, 1981), p. 31.

27. Marie Antoine de Julio, "New York German Painted Chests," *The Magazine Antiques*, May 1985, p. 1159.

28. Marie Antoine de Julio, *German Folk Arts of New York State*, exhibition catalog (Albany, N.Y.: Albany Institute of History and Art, 1985), p. 11. This catalog includes an eighteenth-century engraving from Germany that is similar to the floral designs used on New York German chests. The engraving of an urn with flowers appeared inside the tailpiece of a book written by a German who worked in northern New York State in 1710. Published in Germany in 1717, this book describes the author's experiences in America.

29. Avis B. Heatherington, "The Ornamental Painter: Neglected but Not Forgotten, 1639–1860," *The Decorator* 36, no. 1 (1981): 21.

30. Jean Lipman and Tom Armstrong, eds., *American Folk Painters of Three Centuries* (New York: Hudson Hills Press, 1980), p. 130.

31. Nancy Goyne Evans, *American Windsor Chairs* (New York: Hudson Hills Press, 1996), p. 222.

32. Account Book of Allen Holcomb, Metropolitan Museum of Art, 47.31.

33. Deborah Lambeth, "Rufus Cole: A Mohawk Valley Decorator," *The Decorator* 35, no. 2 (1981): 4.

34. David A. Schorsch, "Living with a Collection of American Folk Art in the Midwest," *The Magazine Antiques* 138, no. 4 (October 1990): 782.

35. Evans, *Windsor Chairs*, p. 186.

36. Don C. Skemer, "David Alling's Chair Manufactory: Craft Industrialization in Newark, New Jersey, 1801–1854," *Winterthur Portfolio* 22, no. 1 (1987): 3.

37. Ibid., p. 6.

38. Ibid., p. 17.

39. Wendy Cooper, *Classical Taste in America* (New York: Abbeville Press, 1993), p. 226.

7 · THE SOUTH

1. "Tucked Away in Tennessee," *Colonial Homes*, June 1995, p. 51.

2. Klaus Wurst, *The Virginia Germans* (Charlottesville: University Press of Virginia, 1969), p. 96.

3. Henry Howe, *Historical Collections of Virginia* (Charleston, S.C.: W. R. Babcock, 1847), p. 468.

4. Ibid., p. 514.

5. J. Roderick Moore, "Wythe County Chests," *The Decorator*, Fall 1984, p. 12.

6. *Neat Pieces*, exhibition catalog (Atlanta: Atlanta Historical Society, 1983), p. 3.

7. Thomas H. Clayton, *Close to the Land: The Way We Lived in North Carolina, 1820–1870* (Chapel Hill: University of North Carolina Press, 1983), p. 25.

8. The authors thank J. Roderick Moore for providing additional information on this regional school. For more information on Wythe County, Virginia, chests see J. Roderick Moore, "Painted Chests from Wythe County, Virginia," *The Magazine Antiques* 126, no. 3 (September 1982): 516–21.

9. Donald Walters, "Johannes Spitler, Shenandoah County, Virginia, Furniture Decorator," *The Magazine Antiques* 108, no. 4 (October 1975): 731.

10. Quoted in William W. Griffin, "Nineteenth-Century Georgia and Its Plain Style Furniture," *The Magazine Antiques* 125, no. 3 (March 1984): 655.

11. All information on punched-tin food safes is from J. Roderick Moore, "Wythe County, Virginia, Punched Tin: Its Influence and Imitators," *The Magazine Antiques* 126, no. 3 (September 1984): 601–13.

12. *Neat Pieces*, p. 6.

13. Ibid., p. 93.

8 · THE WESTERN FRONTIER

1. Ralph Waldo Emerson, *Emerson in His Journals*, ed. Joel Porte (Cambridge, Mass.: Belknap Press, Harvard University Press, 1982), p. 92.

2. Alexis de Tocqueville, *Democracy in America*, ed. Phillips Bradley (1835; reprint, New York: Knopf, 1945), vol. 1, p. 292.

3. John M. Blum, Bruce Calton, Edmund S. Morgan, Arthur M. Schlesinger Jr., Kenneth M. Stumpp, C. Vann Woodward, *The National Experience* (New York: Harcourt, Brace and World, 1963), p. 195.

4. Charles R. Muller, *Made in Ohio: Furniture 1788–1888*, exhibition catalog (Columbus, Ohio: Columbus Museum of Art, 1984), p. 11.

5. Ibid., p. 25.

6. The authors thank Gale Frederick for the information concerning these chests. See also Muller, pp. 11, 12, 38.

7. Quoted in Jane Connell and Charles R. Muller, "Ohio Furniture, 1788–1888," *The Magazine Antiques* 125, no. 2 (February 1984): 467.

8. Ibid.

9. Quoted in Robert Bishop, *The American Chair: Three Centuries of Style* (New York: Bonanza Books, 1983), p. 432.

10. Marion J. Nelson, "The Material Culture and Folk Arts of the Norwegians in America," in *Perspectives on American Folk Art*, Ian M. G. Quimby and Scott T. Swank, eds. (New York: Norton, 1980), p. 81.

11. The authors thank Stacy Hollander for bringing this to their attention.

12. As quoted in Wendell Garrett, "Editorial," *The Magazine Antiques* 113, no. 4 (April 1978): 819.

13. W. H. Emory, *Notes of a Military Reconnaissance, from Fort Leavenworth in Missouri to San Diego, in California, Including Parts of the Arkansas, Del Norte, and Gile Rivers* (Washington, D.C., 1848), pp. 39–40.

14. Quoted in Reinhild Kauenhoven Janzen and John M. Janzen, *Mennonite Furniture: A Migrant Tradition, 1766–1910* (Intercourse, Pa.: Good Books, 1991), pp. 213, 214. Jacob Adrian's recipes were written consecutively on fifteen pages in a notebook, which he began in 1819 in West Prussia and which ended with his death in 1866 in South Russia. The recipes were transcribed by Helmut Ottenjann and translated by Hilda Voth.

15. Ibid., p. 214.

16. Mary Bywater Cross, *Treasures in the Trunk: Memories, Dreams, and Accomplishments of the Pioneer*

Women Who Traveled the Oregon Trail (Nashville, Tenn.: Rutledge Hill Press, 1993), p. 3.

17. Willa Cather, *O Pioneers!* (1913; reprint, New York: Vintage Books, 1992), p. 22.

18. Connie Morningstar, *Early Utah Furniture*, exhibition catalog (Logan: Utah State University Press, 1976).

19. Ibid.

20. Marilyn Conover Barker, *The Legacy of Mormon Furniture: The Mormon Material Culture, Undergirded by Faith, Commitment, and Craftsmanship* (Salt Lake City: Gibbs Smith, 1995), p. 14.

21. Ibid., p. 54.

APPENDIX A: PAINT

1. Nathaniel Whittock, *Decorative Painters' and Glaziers' Guide* (London: Isaac Taylor Hinton, 1828), p. 8.

2. Theodore Zuk Penn, "Decorative Finishes, 1750–1850: Materials, Prices and Craft," master's thesis, University of Delaware, 1965, pp. 71–74.

3. Ibid., pp. 73, 77, 79.

4. John Smith, *The Art of Painting in Oyl* (London: Daniel Browne, 1753), pp. 33–35.

5. Ibid., p. 77.

6. *Morning Chronicle*, Boston, April 19, 1803.

7. Rita Susswein Gottesman, *The Arts and Crafts in New York, 1800–1804* (New York: New-York Historical Society, 1965), p. 275.

8. Penn, p. 73.

9. Whittock, p. 241; Penn, pp. 72–74.

10. Whittock, p. 8.

11. Thomas Sheraton, *Cabinet Dictionary*, 1803, reprint, introduction by Wilford P. Cole and Charles F. Montgomery (New York: Praeger Publishers, 1970), vol. 2, pp. 248, 330, and 334, and vol. 1, pp. 245, 320, 330, 334; Richard Newman and Eugene Farrell, "House Paint Pigments: Composition and Use, 1600 to 1850," in Roger W. Moss, ed., *Paint in America: The Colors of Historic Buildings* (Washington, D.C.: Preservation Press, 1994), pp. 277–29; Richard M. Candee, *Housepaints in Colonial America: Their Materials, Manufacture, and Application* (New York: Chromatic Publishing Company, 1967), pp. 9–15; Richard M. Candee, "Preparing and Mixing Colors in 1812," *The Magazine Antiques* 118, no. 4 (April 1978): 849–53.

12. Compiled from research in the course of writing this book. The authors wish to thank Stephen Van Dyk, head librarian, Cooper-Hewitt National Design Museum, for making available many sources in the Rare Book Department. These books were the primary source upon which much of the book is based.

13. The authors thank Robert Mussey for the informative visit to the Boston studio and workshop of Robert Mussey Associates and for his ideas and suggestions with reference to the conservation and restoration of painted and gilded furniture surfaces. See also Susan Buck, "Shaker Painted Furniture: Provocative Insights into Shaker Paints and Painting Techniques," paper delivered at the Williamsburg Painted Wood Symposium, November 1994. The authors also thank Jack Lindsey for the opportunity to visit the Conservation Department of the Philadelphia Museum of Art. See also Gregory Landrey, "The Conservator as Curator: Combining Scientific Analysis and Traditional Connoisseurship," in Luke Beckerdite, ed., *American Furniture* (Hanover, N.H.: University Press of New England, 1993), pp. 147–59.

APPENDIX B: GILDING

1. Gilding was also applied to porcelain, glass, copper, iron, and paper.

2. Robert Desilver, *Philadelphia Directory and Stranger's Guide 1833*, p. 27.

3. Donald L. Fennimore, "Gilding Practices and Processes in Nineteenth-Century American Furniture," *Gilded Wood: Conservation and History* (Madison, Conn.: Sound View Press, 1991), p. 140.

4. The authors thank Deborah Bigelow, an art conservator, for providing assistance with information on gilding.

5. Robert D. Mussey Jr., ed., *The First American Furniture Finisher's Manual: A Reprint of "The Cabinet-Maker's Guide" of 1827* (New York: Dover Publications, 1987), pp. 66–67.

6. Ibid., pp. 68, 69.

7. Ibid., pp. 70–71.

8. Ibid., p. 72.

9. Rufus Porter, *A Select Collection of Valuable and Curious Arts* (Concord, N.H.: Rufus Porter, 1825), p. 13.

10. Mussey, p. 73.

SELECTED BIBLIOGRAPHY

Andrews, Carol Damon. "John Ritto Penniman (1782–1841), an Ingenious New England Artist." *The Magazine Antiques* 120, no. 1 (July 1981): 147–60.

Barker, Marilyn Conover. *The Legacy of Mormon Furniture: The Mormon Material Culture, Undergirded by Faith, Commitment, and Craftsmanship.* Salt Lake City: Gibbs Smith, 1995.

Baron, Donna Keith. "Furniture Makers and Retailers in Worcester County, Massachusetts, Working to 1850." *The Magazine Antiques* 143, no. 5 (May 1993): 784–94.

Barquist, David L. *American Tables and Looking Glasses in the Mabel Brady Garvan and Other Collections at Yale University.* New Haven: Yale University Press, 1992.

Beck, Jane C. *Always in Season: Folk Art and Traditional Culture in Vermont.* Montpelier: Vermont Council on the Arts, 1982.

Beeman, Richard R. *The Evolution of the Southern Backcountry.* Philadelphia: University of Pennsylvania Press, 1984.

Bigelow, Deborah, Elisabeth Cornu, Gregory J. Landrey, Cornelius van Horne, Catherine E. Hutchins, Patricia Anne Rice, eds. *Gilded Wood: Conservation and History.* Madison, Conn.: Sound View Press, 1991.

Bishop, Robert. *Centuries and Styles of the American Chair, 1640–1970.* New York: Dutton, 1972.

Bivins, John, and Alexander Forsyth. *The Regional Arts of the Early South.* Winston-Salem: University of North Carolina Press, 1991.

Bordes Johnson, Marilyn. *Baltimore Federal Furniture.* New York: Metropolitan Museum of Art, 1972.

Brazer, Esther Stevens. *Early American Decoration.* Springfield, Mass.: Pond-Ekberg, 1940.

Buckley, Charles. *The Decorative Arts of New Hampshire, 1752–1825.* Manchester, N.H.: Currier Gallery, 1964.

Candee, Richard M. *Housepaints in Colonial America: Their Materials, Manufacture, and Application.* New York: Chromatic Publishing Company, 1967.

———. "Preparing and Mixing Colors in 1812." *The Magazine Antiques* 118, no. 4 (April 1978): 849–53.

———. "The Rediscovery of Milk-based House Paints and the Myth of 'Brickdust and Buttermilk' Paints." *Old-Time New England* 58 (Winter 1968): 79–81.

Catalano, Kathleen M. "Cabinet-making in Philadelphia, 1820–1840: Transition from Craft to Industry." *Winterthur Portfolio* 13 (1979): 81–138.

Churchill, Edwin A. "Patterns in Paint: Maine Decorated Furniture, 1800–1850." *The Decorator* 38, no. 1 (Fall 1983): 4–13.

———. *Simple Forms and Vivid Colors: An Exhibition of Maine Painted Furniture, 1800–1850.* Exhibition catalog. Augusta: Maine State Museum, 1983.

Clayton, Thomas, H. *Close to the Land: The Way We Lived in North Carolina, 1820–1870.* Chapel Hill: University of North Carolina Press, 1983.

Clunie, Margaret Burke. *Furniture at the Essex Institute.* Salem, Mass.: Essex Institute, 1980.

Colwill, Stiles Tuttle. *Francis Guy, 1760–1820.* Baltimore: Maryland Historical Society, 1981.

Connell, E. Jane. "Ohio Furniture, 1788–1888." *The Magazine Antiques* 125, no. 3 (February 1984): 462–468.

Conradsen, David H. "The Stock-in-Trade of John Hancock & Company." In Luke Beckerdite, ed. *American Furniture,* 38–54. Hanover, N.H.: University Press of New England, 1993.

Cooper, Wendy A. *Classical Taste in America, 1800–1840.* New York: Abbeville Press, 1993.

Cross, Mary Bywater. *Treasures in the Trunk.* Nashville, Tenn.: Rutledge Hill Press, 1993.

Cullity, Brian. *Plain and Fancy: New England Painted Furniture.* Exhibition catalog. Sandwich, Mass.: Heritage Plantation of Sandwich, 1987.

Dabney, Virginius. *Virginia: The New Dominion.* Garden City, N.Y.: Doubleday, 1971.

Davidson, Marshall B., and Elizabeth Stillinger. *The American Wing at the Metropolitan Museum of Art.* New York: Alfred A. Knopf, 1985.

De Julio, Mary Antoine. *German Folk Arts of New York State.* Exhibition catalog. Albany, N.Y.: Albany Institute of Art, 1985.

———. "New York—German Painted Chests." *The Magazine Antiques* 127, no. 5 (May 1985): 1156–65.

———. "The Palatines and a Survey of Decoration on Mohawk and Schoharie Valley Chests." *The Decorator* 38, no. 1 (Fall 1983): 24–31.

Downing, Andrew Jackson. *The Architecture of Country Houses.* 1850.

Reprint, New York: Dover Publications, 1969.

Dubrow, Eileen, and Richard Dubrow. *American Furniture of the 19th Century, 1840–1880.* Exton, Pa.: Schiffer, 1983.

Ducoff-Barone, Deborah. "Philadelphia Furniture Makers, 1800–1815." *The Magazine Antiques* 119, no. 5 (May 1991): 982–95.

Elder, William Voss, III. *Baltimore Painted Furniture, 1800–1840.* Exhibition catalog. Baltimore: Baltimore Museum of Art, 1972.

———, and Jayne E. Stokes. *American Furniture, 1680–1880, from the Collection of the Baltimore Museum of Art.* Exhibition catalog. Baltimore: Baltimore Museum of Art, 1987.

Evans, Nancy Goyne. "American Painted Seating Furniture: Marketing the Product, 1750–1840." In Gerald W. R. Ward, ed., *Perspectives on American Furniture.* New York: Norton, 1988.

———. *American Windsor Chairs.* New York: Hudson Hills Press, 1996.

———. "Design Sources for Windsor Furniture, Part II: The Early Nineteenth Century." *The Magazine Antiques* 133, no. 5 (May 1988): 1128–43.

———. "Design Transmission in Vernacular Seating Furniture: The Influences of Philadelphia and Baltimore Styles on Chairmaking from the Chesapeake Bay to the 'West.'" In Luke Beckerdite, ed., *American Furniture,* 75–116. Hanover, N.H.: University Press of New England, 1993.

Fabian, Monroe H. *The Pennsylvania-German Decorated Chest.* New York: Universe Books, 1978.

Fales, Dean A., Jr. *American Painted Furniture, 1660–1880.* New York: Dutton, 1972.

———. *Essex County Furniture: Documented Treasures from Local Collections: 1660–1860.* Exhibition catalog. Salem, Mass.: Essex Institute, 1965.

Fennimore, Donald L. "American Neoclassical Furniture and Its European Antecedents." *American Art Journal* 13, no. 4 (Autumn 1981): 49–65.

———. "Egyptian Influence in Early Nineteenth-Century American Furniture." *The Magazine Antiques* 140 (May 1990): 1190–1201.

Flanigan, Michael J., ed. *American Furniture from the Kaufman Collection.* Washington, D.C.: National Gallery of Art, 1986.

Forman, Benno M. "Germanic Influences in Pennsylvania Furniture." In Catherine E. Hutchins, ed., *Arts of the Pennsylvania Germans.* New York: Norton, 1983.

Fritz, Ernest L., and Charles Muller. "The Decorated Furniture of Jacob Knagy." *Antique Review,* April 1991, pp. 29–32.

Garrett, Elisabeth Donaghy. *At Home: The American Family, 1750–1870.* New York: Harry N. Abrams, 1990.

Garrett, Wendell. *Classic America: The Federal Style and Beyond.* New York: Rizzoli, 1992.

Garvan, Beatrice B., and Henry Lapp. *A Craftsman's Handbook.* Philadelphia: Philadelphia Museum of Art, 1975.

———. *Federal Philadelphia, 1785–1825: The Athens of the Western World.* Philadelphia: Philadelphia Museum of Art, 1986.

———. *The Pennsylvania German Collection.* Philadelphia: Philadelphia Museum of Art, 1975.

Garvan, Beatrice B., and Charles F. Hummel. *The Pennsylvania Germans: A Celebration of Their Arts, 1683–1850.* Philadelphia: Philadelphia Museum of Art, 1982.

Garvan, James L. *Plain & Elegant, Rich & Common: Documented New Hampshire Furniture, 1750–1850.* Exhibition catalog. Concord: New Hampshire Historical Society, 1979.

Gottesman, Rita Susswein. *The Arts and Crafts in New York, 1777–1779.* New York: New-York Historical Society, 1951.

———. *The Arts and Crafts in New York, 1800–1804.* New York: New-York Historical Society, 1965.

Gray, Nina. "Leon Marcotte: Cabinetmaker and Interior Decorator." *American Furniture,* 1994, pp. 49–72.

Griffin, William W. "Nineteenth-Century Georgia and Its Plain Style Furniture." *The Magazine Antiques* 125, no. 3 (March 1984): 654–63.

Gudehus, Jonas Heinrich. "Journey to America." *Ebbes fer Alle–Ebber—Ebbes fer Dich: Something for Everyone—Something for You,* vol. 14. Trans. Larry M. Neff. Breinigsville: Pennsylvania Society, 1980.

Hageman, Jane Sikes. *Ohio Furniture Makers,* vols. 1 and 2. Jane Sikes Hageman, 1984.

Hall, Elton W. "New Bedford Furniture." *The Magazine Antiques* 113, no. 5 (May 1978): 1105–27.

Hanks, David A. "Pottier & Stymus Mfg. Co.: Artistic Furniture and Decorations." *Art & Antiques* 7, no. 5 (September-October 1982): 84–91.

Harlow, Henry J. "Decorated New England Furniture." *The Magazine Antiques,* 116, no. 4 (October 1979): 860–71.

———. "The Shop of Samuel Wing, Craftsman of Sandwich, Massachusetts." *The Magazine Antiques* 153, no. 3 (March 1968): 372–75.

Hastings, Lynne Dakin. *A Guidebook to Hampton National Historic Site.* Towson, Md.: Historic Hampton, 1986.

Hauserman, Dianne D. "Alexander Roux and His Plain and Artistic Furniture." *The Magazine Antiques* vol. 93, no. 2 (February 1968): 210–17.

Heatherington, Avis B. "The Ornamental Painter: Neglected but Not Forgotten, 1639–1860." *The Decorator* 36, no. 1 (Fall 1981): 10–33.

Hepplewhite, George. *The Cabinet-Maker and Upholsterer's Guide.* 1794. Reprint, New York: Dover Publications, 1969.

Hope, Thomas. *Regency Furniture and Interior Decoration: Classic Style Book of the Regency Period.* Reprint, New York: Dover Publications, 1971.

Howe, Henry. *Historical Collections of Virginia.* Charleston, S.C.: W. R. Babcock, 1847.

Howe, Katherine S., Alice Cooney Frelinghuysen, Catherine Hoover Voorsanger, et al. *Herter Brothers: Furniture and Interiors for a Gilded Age.* New York: Harry N. Abrams, 1994.

Howe, Katherine S., and David B. Warren. *The Gothic Revival Style in America, 1830–1870.* Exhibition catalog. Houston: Houston Museum of Fine Arts, 1976.

Hurst, Ronald L. "Prestwould Furnishings." *The Magazine Antiques* 147, no. 1 (January 1995): 162–67.

Janzen, Reinhild Kauenhoven, and John M. Janzen. *Mennonite Furniture: A Migrant Tradition, 1776–1910.* Intercourse, Pa.: Good Books, 1991.

Jobe, Brock, ed. *Portsmouth Furniture: Masterworks from the New Hampshire Seacoast.* Hanover, N.H.: University Press of New England, 1993.

Johnson, Marilyn. *Baltimore Federal Furniture.* New York: Metropolitan Museum of Art, 1972.

Kane, Patricia E. *300 Years of American Seating Furniture.* Boston: New York Graphic Society, 1976.

Kennedy, Roger G. *Greek Revival America.* New York: Stewart, Tabori and Chang, 1989.

Kenny, John Tarrant. *The Hitchcock Chair: The Story of a Connecticut Yankee.* New York: Clarkson N. Potter, 1971.

Keyser, Alan G., Larry M. Neff, and Frederick S. Weiser, eds. and trans. *The Accounts of Two Pennsylvania German Furniture Makers—Abraham Overholt, Bucks County, 1790–1833, and Peter Ranck, Lebanon County, 1794–1817.* Sources and Documents of the Pennsylvania Germans, vol. 3. Breinigsville, Pa., 1978.

Kimball, Marie G. "The Original Furnishings of the White House." *The Magazine Antiques.* Part I: 15, no. 5 (June 1929): 481–86; Part II: 16, no. 1 (July 1929): 33–37.

———. "Thomas Jefferson's French Furniture." *The Magazine Antiques* 15, no. 2 (February 1929): 123–129.

King, Thomas. *Neo-Classical Furniture Designs: A Reprint of Thomas King's "Modern Style of Cabinet Work Exemplified," 1829.* New York: Dover Publications, 1995.

Lahikainen, Dean. In *The American Spirit: Folk Art from the Collection, Peabody Essex Museum.* Exhibition catalog. Salem, Mass.: Peabody Essex Museum, 1994.

Lambeth, Deborah. "Rufus Cole: A Mohawk Valley Decorator." *The Decorator* 35, no. 2 (Spring 1981): 4–11.

Lea, Zilla Rider, ed. *The Ornamented Chair: Its Development in America (1700–1890).* Rutland, Vt.: Charles E. Tuttle Co., 1960.

Lichten, Francis. *Folk Art of Rural Pennsylvania.* New York: Scribner's, 1946.

Lindsey, Jack. "An Early Latrobe Furniture Commission." *The Magazine Antiques* 139, no. 1 (January 1991): 209–19.

Lipman, Jean. *Rufus Porter Rediscovered: Artist, Inventor, Journalist, 1792–1884.* New York: Clarkson N. Potter, 1980.

Little, Nina Fletcher. *American Decorative Wall Painting, 1700–1850.* New York: Dutton, 1972.

McCauley, Daniel, III, and Kathryn McCauley. *Decorative Arts of the Amish of Lancaster County.* Intercourse, Pa.: Good Books, 1988.

———. "The Paintings of Henry and Elizabeth Lapp." *Folk Art,* Fall 1994, pp. 53–61.

Marcus, George H., ed. *Philadelphia: Three Centuries of American Art.* Philadelphia: Philadelphia Museum of Art, 1976.

Montgomery, Charles F. *American Furniture: The Federal Period in the Henry Francis du Pont Winterthur Museum.* New York: Viking, 1966.

Moore, J. Roderick. "Painted Chests from Wythe County, Virginia." *The Magazine Antiques* 126, no. 3 (September 1982): 516–21.

———. "Wythe County, Virginia, Punched Tin: Its Influence and Imitators." *The Magazine Antiques* 126, no. 3 (September 1984): 601–13.

———. "Wythe County Chests." *The Decorator* 39 (Fall 1984): 12–19.

Morningstar, Connie. *Early Utah Furniture.* Logan: Utah State University Press, 1976.

Muller, Charles R. *Made in Ohio: Furniture, 1788–1888.* Exhibition catalog. Columbus, Ohio: Columbus Museum of Art, 1984.

Musser, Marie Purnell. *County Chairs of Central Pennsylvania.* Mifflinburg, Pa.: Mifflinburg Telegraph, 1990.

Mussey, Robert D., Jr., ed. *The First American Furniture Finisher's Manual: A*

Reprint of "The Cabinet-Maker's Guide" of 1827. New York: Dover Publications, 1987.

Neat Pieces: The Plain-Style Furniture of Nineteenth-Century Georgia. Exhibition catalog. Atlanta: Atlanta Historical Society, 1983.

Nelson, Marion J. "The Material Culture and Folk Arts of the Norwegians in America." In Ian M. G. Quimby and Scott T. Swank, eds., *Perspectives on American Folk Art.* New York: Norton, 1980.

Nineteenth-Century America: Furniture and Other Decorative Arts. Exhibition catalog. New York: Metropolitan Museum of Art, 1970.

Nylander, Jane C. "Henry Sargent's *Dinner Party* and *Tea Party.*" *The Magazine Antiques* 121, no. 5 (May 1982): 1172–83.

———. "New Hampshire Cabinetmakers and Allied Craftsmen, 1790–1850." *The Magazine Antiques* 94, no. 1 (July 1968): 78–87.

O'Neil, Isabel. *The Art of the Painted Finish for Furniture and Decoration.* New York: Morrow, 1971.

Owens, Hamilton. *Baltimore on the Chesapeake.* New York: Doubleday, Doran, 1941.

Page, John F. *The Decorative Folk Arts of New Hampshire: A Sesquicentennial Exhibition.* Concord: The New Hampshire Historical Society, 1973.

———. "Documented New Hampshire Furniture, 1750–1850." *The Magazine Antiques* 54, no. 1 (May 1979): 1004–15.

Passeri, Andrew, and Robert Trent. "Some Amazing Washington Chairs." *Maine Antique Digest,* May 1983, pp. 1C–3C.

Percier, Charles, and Pierre Fontaine. *Empire Stylebook of Interior Design: All 72 Plates from the "Recueil de Décorations Intérieures" with New English Text.*

Reprint, New York: Dover Publications, 1991.

Plain and Elegant, Rich and Common: Documented New Hampshire Furniture, 1750–1850. Exhibition catalog. Concord: New Hampshire Historical Society, 1979.

Plain and Fancy: New England Painted Furniture. Exhibition catalog. Sandwich, Mass.: Heritage Plantation of Sandwich, 1987.

Porter, Rufus. *A Select Collection of Valuable and Curious Arts.* Concord, N.H.: Rufus Porter, 1825.

Prime, Alfred Coxe. *The Arts and Crafts in Philadelphia, Maryland, and South Carolina, 1721–1785.* Topsfield, Mass.: Wayside Press, 1932.

Reed, Henry M. *Decorated Furniture of the Mahantango Valley.* Lewisburg, Pa.: Center Gallery, Bucknell University, 1987.

Reinhold, Meyer. *Classical Americana: The Greek and Roman Heritage in the United States.* Detroit: Wayne State University Press, 1984.

Rice, Norman. *New York Furniture before 1840 in the Collection of the Albany Institute of History and Art.* Albany, N.Y.: Albany Institute of History and Art, 1962.

Rodrigues Roque, Oswaldo. *American Furniture at Chipstone.* Madison: University of Wisconsin Press, 1984.

Roy, L. M. A. "Paint Grinding and Decorating." *The Magazine Antiques* 53, no. 1 (January 1948): 62–63.

Sander, Penny J., ed. *Elegant Embellishments: Furnishings from New England Houses, 1660–1860.* Lexington, Mass.: Museum of Our National Heritage, 1982.

Santore, Charles. *The Windsor Style in America: Volumes I and II: The Definitive Pictorial Study of the History and Regional Characteristics of the Most Popular Furniture Form of Eighteenth-Century America,*

1730–1840. Philadelphia: Running Press, 1992.

Schorsch, David A. "Living with Antiques: A Collection of American Folk Art in the Midwest." *The Magazine Antiques* 138, no. 4 (October 1990): 776–87.

Schwartz, Robert D. *The Stephen Girard Collection: A Selective Catalog.* Philadelphia: Girard College, 1980.

Sessions, Ralph, and Stacy C. Hollander. *The Art of Embellishment: Painted and Stenciled Masterworks from the Museum of American Folk Art.* Exhibition catalog. New York: Museum of American Folk Art, 1992.

Sheraton, Thomas. *The Cabinet-Maker and Upholsterer's Drawing-Book.* 1793. Reprint, New York: Dover Publications, 1972.

———. *The Cabinet Dictionary,* 1803. Reprint, introduction by Wilford P. Cole and Charles F. Montgomery. New York: Praeger, 1970.

Skemer, Don C. "David Alling's Chair Manufactory: Craft Industrialization in Newark, New Jersey, 1801–1854." *Winterthur Portfolio* 22, no. 1 (1987): 1–22.

Smith, George. *The Cabinet-Maker's and Upholsterer's Guide, Drawing-Book and Repository.* London: Jones & Co., 1826.

Smith, Philip, Chadwick Foster, and Nina Fletcher Little. *Michele Felice Cornè, 1752–1845: Versatile Neapolitan Painter of Salem, Boston, and Newport.* Exhibition catalog. Salem, Mass.: Peabody Essex Museum, 1972.

Smith, Robert C. "The Furniture of Anthony G. Quervelle, Part 1: The Pier Table." *The Magazine Antiques* 103, no. 5 (May 1973): 304–9.

Snyder, John J., Jr., ed. *Philadelphia Furniture and Its Makers.* New York: Universe Books, 1975.

Stalker, John, and George Parker. *A*

Treatise on Japaning [sic] *and Varnishing.* London, 1688.

Stanny, Carrie M. *Manufactured by Hand: The Soap Hollow School.* Exhibition catalog. Loretto, Pa.: Southern Alleghenies Museum of Art, 1993.

Stover, Donald Lewis. "Part One: The Furniture of Early Texas." In Cecilia Steinfeld and Donald Lewis Stover, *Early Texas Furniture and Decorative Arts.* Exhibition catalog. San Antonio: Trinity University Press, 1973.

Swan, Mabel M. "The Man Who Made Willard's Clock Faces: John Doggett of Roxbury." *The Magazine Antiques* 15, no. 3 (March 1929): 196–99.

Swank, Scott T., ed., *Arts of the Pennsylvania Germans.* New York: Norton, 1983.

Talbott, E. Page. "Allen and Brother, Philadelphia Furniture Makers." *The Magazine Antiques* 149, no. 5 (May 1996): 716–25.

———. *Classical Savannah, Fine and Decorative Arts, 1800–1840.* Exhibition catalog. Savannah, Ga.: Telfair Museum of Art, 1995.

———. "The Furniture Trade in Boston, 1810–1835." *The Magazine Antiques* 141, no. 5 (May 1992): 842–55.

———. "Seating Furniture in Boston, 1810–1835." *The Magazine Antiques* 139, no. 5 (May 1991): 956–69.

Taylor, Lonn. "Hispanic Cabinetmakers and the Anglo-American Aesthetic." *The Magazine Antiques* 124, no. 3 (September 1989): 554–67.

Taylor, Lonn, and Dessa Bokides. *New Mexican Furniture, 1600–1940: The Origins, Survival, and Revival of Furniture Making in the Hispanic Southwest.* Santa Fe: Museum of New Mexico Press, 1987.

Taylor, Lonn, and David B. Warren. *Texas Furniture: The Cabinetmakers and Their Work, 1840–1880.* Austin: University of Texas Press, 1975.

Teles, Rubens, and James Adams. *Folk Finishes: What They Are and How to Create Them.* New York: Viking, 1994.

Tracy, Berry B., and William H. Gerdts. *Classical America, 1815–1845.* Exhibition catalog. Newark, N.J.: Newark Museum Association, 1963.

"Tucked Away in Tennessee." *Colonial Homes,* June 1995, pp. 45–53.

Wagner, Pamela. *Hidden Heritage: Recent Discoveries in Georgia Decorative Art, 1733–1915.* Atlanta: High Museum of Art, 1990.

Walters, Donald. "Johannes Spitler, Shenandoah County, Virginia, Furniture Decorator." *The Magazine Antiques* 108, no. 4 (October 1975): 730–35.

Ward, Gerald W. R., and Karin E. Cullity. "The Furniture of Strawbery Banke Museum." *The Magazine Antiques* 152, no. 1 (July 1992): 94–103.

———. "The Wendell Family Furniture at Strawbery Banke Museum." *American Furniture.* Hanover, N.H.: University Press of New England, 1993.

Waring, Janet. *Early American Stencils on Walls and Furniture.* 1937. Reprint, New York: Dover Publications, 1968.

Warren, Elizabeth V. "Living with Antiques: The Collection of Helaine and Burton Fendelman." *The Magazine Antiques* 142, no. 4 (October 1992): 550–59.

Weidman, Gregory R., Jennifer F. Goldsborough, Robert L. Alexander, Stiles Tuttle Colwill, Mary Ellen Hayward, and Catherine A. Rogers. *Classical Maryland, 1815–1845.* Exhibition catalog. Baltimore: Maryland Historical Society, 1993.

———. *Furniture in Maryland, 1740–1940: The Collection of the Maryland Historical Society.* Baltimore: Maryland Historical Society, 1984.

Weigley, Russell F. *Philadelphia: A 300-Year History.* New York: Norton, 1982.

Weiser, Frederick S., and Mary Hammond Sullivan. "Decorated Furniture of the Schwaben Creek Valley." *Ebbes fer Alle-Ebber—Ebbes fer Dich: Something for Everyone—Something for You,* vol. 14. Breinigsville, Pa.: Pennsylvania German Society, 1980.

Whallon, Arthur. "Indiana Cabinetmakers and Allied Craftsmen, 1815–1860." *The Magazine Antiques* 98, no. 1 (July 1970): 118–28.

Whittock, Nathaniel. *Decorative Painters' and Glaziers' Guide.* London: Isaac Taylor Hinton, 1828.

Willard, John Ware. *Simon Willard and His Clocks.* Mamaroneck, N.Y.: Paul P. Appel, 1962.

Witmer, Margaret A. "Henry and Elizabeth Lapp: Amish Folk Artists." *Antique Collecting,* May 1979, pp. 22–27.

Wust, Klaus. *The Virginia Germans.* Charlottesville: University Press of Virginia, 1969.

Zea, Philip, and Robert C. Cheney. *Clockmaking in New England, 1725–1825: An Interpretation of the Old Sturbridge Village Collection.* Sturbridge, Mass.: Old Sturbridge Village, 1992.

Zogry, Kenneth Joel. *The Best the Country Affords: Vermont Furniture, 1765–1850.* Exhibition catalog. Bennington, Vt.: The Bennington Museum, 1995.

———. "Urban Precedents for Vermont Furniture." *The Magazine Antiques* vol. 147, no. 5 (May 1995): 762–71.

———. "Vermont Furniture in the Bennington Museum, 1765–1840." *The Magazine Antiques* 144, no. 2 (August 1993): 191–201.

INDEX